THE POLITICAL ECONOMY OF INTERNATIONAL MONEY

In Search of a New Order

edited by
Loukas Tsoukalis

GW00727956

The Royal Institute of International Affairs · London

SAGE Publications · London · Beverly Hills · New Delhi

SAGE Publications Ltd
28 Banner Street
London EC1Y 8QE

 SAGE Publications Inc
275 South Beverly Drive
Beverly Hills, California 90212

SAGE Publications India Pvt Ltd
C-236 Defence Colony
New Delhi 110 024

British Library Cataloguing in Publication Data

Tsoukalis, Loukas
   The political economy of international money.
   1. International finance
   I. Title
   332.4'5   HG3881
     ISBN 0-8039-9710-8
     ISBN 0-8039-9711-6 Pbk

Library of Congress Catalog Card Number 84-052389

Phototypeset by Sunrise Setting, Torquay
Printed in Great Britain
by J.W. Arrowsmith Ltd, Bristol

Contents

Notes on Contributors

Michel Aglietta: Professor of Economics at the University of Paris X-Nanterre, and scientific counsellor at the Centre d'Etudes Prospectives et d'Informations Internationales (CEPII). Author of many books and articles, including *A Theory of Capitalist Regulation* (1979).

Graham Bird: Senior Lecturer in Economics at the University of Surrey and Research Associate of the Overseas Development Institute in London. His publications include *The International Monetary System and the Less Developed Countries* (1978, 2nd edition 1982).

André de Lattre: Managing Director of the Institute of International Finance in Washington, DC. Professor of Economics at the Institut d'Etudes Politiques in Paris (1958–83). His previous appointments include: World Bank Special Representative for IDA negotiations (1983); Chairman of the Crédit National (1974–82); and Vice-Governor of the Banque de France (1966–74).

Tony Killick: Director of the Overseas Development Institute in London. Ford Foundation Visiting Professor at the University of Nairobi (1973–9). He has written extensively on the economic problems and policies of developing countries. His most recent publications are *The Quest for Economic Stabilisation* and *The IMF and Stabilisation* (1984).

David T. Llewellyn: Professor of Money and Banking and Head of the Economics Department at Loughborough University. He has served as an Economist at HM Treasury and the IMF, and has written extensively in the areas of domestic monetary policy and institutions, international finance and banking.

Tommaso Padoa-Schioppa: Deputy Director-General of the Banca d'Italia. Member of the Group of Thirty and of the Council and Executive Committee of the Centre for European Policy Studies in Brussels. Former Director-General for Economic and Financial Affairs at the EC Commission (1979–83). He began his career as an economist in the research department of the Banca d'Italia.

Susan Strange: Professor of International Relations at the London School of Economics. She was formerly Senior Research Fellow at the Royal Institute of International Affairs in London, and began her career working for *The Economist* and *The Observer*. Author of many publications on international political economy and international money.

Niels Thygesen: Professor of Economics at the University of Copenhagen, and Senior Research Fellow at the Centre for European Policy Studies in Brussels. His previous appointments include: Head of the Monetary Division in the OECD Economics Department and Adviser to Denmark's National Bank (1972–9). Author of many publications.

Loukas Tsoukalis: University Lecturer in International Relations and Fellow of St Antony's College, Oxford. Also Director of Economic Studies at the College of Europe in Bruges, Belgium. Formerly editor of the *Journal of Common Market Studies* (1980–4) and Research Fellow at the Royal Institute of International Affairs in London (1980–3). Author of various books and articles.

Manfred Wegner: Member of the Governing Board of the IFO-Institute for Economic Research in Munich. Former Deputy Director-General for Economic and Financial Affairs at the EC Commission, where he worked between 1964 and 1983. He had previously been engaged in economic research at the Universities of Heidelberg, Tübingen and Cambridge.

John Williamson: Senior Fellow at the Institute for International Economics in Washington, DC. Formerly Adviser, IMF (1972–4); Consultant HM Treasury (1968–70); Professor, PUC (Rio de Janeiro), MIT, Warwick, York. Author of numerous publications in the area of international economics.

Preface

This volume arose out of a research project on the international monetary system carried out at the Royal Institute of International Affairs in London and financed by the Social Science Research Council of the UK. Early drafts of many of the papers published in the volume were discussed by a study group consisting of academics, officials and bankers who met periodically at Chatham House.

The international monetary system has undergone a major transformation since the early 1970s. We invited some of the leading European experts to examine critically the main developments since the suspension of gold–dollar convertibility and the abandonment of fixed exchange rates, and also to consider possible reforms and the likely trends for the future. They dealt with a wide range of subjects, such as exchange rates and adjustment, international liquidity, commercial banks and the new currency standard, as well as the role of the official sector and the link between money and the real economy. This book is intended as a contribution to a growing debate about present international monetary arrangements and the search for a new order.

As editor of the volume and convenor of the Chatham House study group, I should like to express my sincere thanks to the Royal Institute of International Affairs for its hospitality and the support it has given me. I should also like to thank the SSRC for its generous help. Many of the contributors to this volume, including myself, owe much to the members of the Chatham House study group for their comments and advice. I am personally indebted to Susan Strange, William Wallace and John Williamson, who have contributed a great deal to the research project and the publication of this volume. I should also like to acknowledge the assistance of Thomas Thompson, my collaborator at Chatham House. Jean Pell and Ann De'Ath did a marvellous job in deciphering my Greek handwriting, and Pauline Wickham dealt with publication matters with much speed and efficiency. I am also grateful to Margaret Cornell for her admirable work in editing the book.

Loukas Tsoukalis

1
Interpretations of a Decade
Susan Strange

Looking back from the mid-1980s to the late 1960s and early 1970s, the contrast between general Western opinion on the international monetary system and the world economy then and now could hardly be greater. Recent years have been marked by strongly contending views about the world economy, about what is wrong with it and how it came to be in the state it is. There is also a good deal of uncertainty about whether any steps — and if so which ones — can be taken to improve it.

By contrast, little more than a decade ago, the literature devoted to theorizing about the system as a whole (as distinct from its component national economies) was very much slimmer. There were fewer divergent interpretations of recent developments, and more agreement about what could and should be done. Then, economic growth rates were still buoyant; trade was still growing and expectations were strong that living standards would be better next year than last. Despite some warning signals of a disintegrating international economic order, the majority view then prevailing among Western economists and politicians about the main changes that had taken place in the 1960s was relatively optimistic, not to say complacent. It seemed to many fairly clear that though the Bretton Woods system was not working in quite the way it had been planned, and although it had been substantially modified by various *ad hoc* measures of cooperation, it was nevertheless still capable of further reform and adaptation. New problems would be overcome in the way that the long agony of sterling's decline as an international currency had been endured and adjusted to. The ability of central banks to cooperate with swift efficiency when necessary had been reassuringly demonstrated. Agreement on a new man-made reserve asset, the IMF's Special Drawing Right, was widely thought to hold the promise of further gradual but steady progress toward a truly international currency and international management of the system. By about 1971, the need to get the dollar devalued was coming to be accepted by professional economists even outside the United States, and beyond that, most were hopefully anticipating a move towards floating exchange rates in the firm conviction that, for the major industrialized countries, this would solve the problems of domestic monetary management encountered under the fixed rate system.

But by the mid-1980s, little remained of the wide agreement about what had happened to the system. There was far less confidence and optimism about what lay ahead; and there was growing disagreement, and consequent uncertainty, about the appropriate solutions and reforms. In some quarters there was even a kind of defeatism, a nagging doubt as to whether the problems could ever be solved, and whether order could ever be restored. While some accepted the reassuring pronouncements of the central bankers and some international organizations, others remained sceptical and unconvinced. Important groups felt strongly that the deterioration had been at their expense. People in the big debtor countries believed that they had first been cheated and then callously punished for faults that lay more with the system than with them or even their governments. Unemployed workers in decaying industries in Europe and America who were facing a pretty hopeless future felt betrayed by a system that allowed the corporate managers and the bankers to shift their attention — and their money — profitably abroad while labour was left to rot. In the face of such discontents, it was hard to sustain the old faith in the evenhandedness, the neutrality as it were, of the international monetary and financial system.

It would seem useful in the circumstances to attempt some sort of plain person's guide to the full range of contending interpretations of the events of recent years, taking in the opinions of the extreme ideological right and of the extreme ideological left as well as the more conventional opinions in between.

Constructing such a guide would be an impossibly daunting task were it not that, as in other historical periods, the great majority of 'theories' that have been advanced are not theories at all. In the torrent of words that have been written about international economic developments in recent times, there is only a trickle which tells us not only *how* things happened but *why* they happened as they did and why A followed from B. One reason for this may lie in the ready availability of the wealth of statistical data which is such a characteristic of the post-1945 world. This has made it particularly easy for economists and commentators to sound authoritative. By going into considerable descriptive, statistical detail about how inflation accelerated and economic growth slowed down in the 1970s they can more easily evade the difficult questions of cause and effect.

Another characteristic of much contemporary economic writing is the widespread use of mechanical analogy as a substitute for rational explanation of economic processes. Terms like 'take-off', 'pump-priming', 'over-heating', 'gearing', 'deceleration' are so commonly used it is easy to overlook the inadequacy of analogy as explanation.

But though we may dismiss as unhelpful all the merely descriptive pseudo-theories, we should not restrict a review of interpretations to those that can be found in the strictly monetary literature. It is my contention that monetary mismanagement has been the underlying cause and protectionism the resulting consequence of economic disorder. If a much too limited place has been accorded in many broader interpretations of the past decade in the world economy to monetary factors and developments, then the historian should try to explain why and how this is so. Some attention — however brief — must be given to those alternative interpretations that tend to dismiss the monetary and financial aspects of world economic disorder as unimportant.

Broadly speaking, I find that these fall into two groups — the explanations that put the main stress and blame for disorder on the weaknesses in trade policies, and those which avoid putting the blame anywhere in particular by offering one or other form of determinist versions of recent economic history.

Part of the reason for this disregard of monetary explanations lies in the trend toward over-specialization in the study of economics. Trade and money, like investment and employment, have been progressively dealt with inside different theoretical boxes. Each has too often been treated as part of the data of the other and the connections between them have been consistently overlooked or discounted. Thus, when it comes to contemporary interpretations of the recent past, a split or schism appears between the two. And it is the opinions of the economists concerned with trade relations between states rather than those concerned with monetary relations that have predominated and have most influenced informed opinion — at least in the industrialized countries. Any review of the Western press at the time of the ministerial meeting of trade ministers in Geneva in November 1982, for instance, or at the Western economic Summits in 1983 or 1984 would show that protectionism was widely identified as the greatest danger to the world's future prosperity, not monetary mismanagement.[1]

Yet while the professional schism explains — at least in part — why there has been this broad division of opinion, it does not explain why the trade interpretation has been so predominant over the monetary one and why misunderstanding of the economic history of the world depression of the 1930s should be so widespread. Conventionally, inter-war unemployment and failing demand are ascribed to protectionism and beggar-thy-neighbour economic warfare between states. Yet this is not what most economic historians of that period actually said, either at the end of the inter-war period or subsequently.

Joseph Davis, writing a retrospective review of expert opinions forty years later, found that most economic historians were highly sceptical of the idea that tariffs were the culprit.[2] Schumpeter complained in 1939 that the importance of tariffs was commonly either ignored or exaggerated, and said 'protectionism as such played but a minor role in the cyclical process of the post-war epoch'.[3] John Williams, the respected Harvard economist, was well known for being highly critical of US tariff policy as put into effect by the Hawley-Smoot Tariff Act of 1930. In 1933 he said that US tariff policy 'had indeed been unsound in principle, extreme in degree and bad in effect'. But he added that, in his opinion, if US tariffs had stayed the same as they were in 1913, the post-war experience would have been little different. And Taussig, according to one of his assistants, remarked towards the end of his life that he was convinced that the effects of the US tariff — both good and evil — had been vastly exaggerated.

Arthur Lewis quite categorically wrote that 'It was the slump that caused the great burgeoning of trade quotas and trade restrictions in the 1930s'.[4] The big increase in the obstacles to trade came after 1929 when the international currency system had already broken down. He quoted the League of Nations report, which identified as a major problem the abnormal strain on the foreign exchange mechanism imposed by large short-term international movements of capital. 'The lower the state of confidence, the greater the need for a reserve.'[5] That reserve was missing and the resulting slump was due to the contraction of credit as well as to the fall in commodity prices. Lewis had declared that the decline in trade in manufactures was due neither to tariffs nor to the industrialization of new countries. 'The trade in manufactures was low only because industrialised countries were buying too little of primary products and paying so low a price for what they bought' (p. 155). Even so, he argued, trade in manufactures, despite the moaning and groaning, remained at a reasonable level throughout the period. Moreover, he added, 'the rate of imports [of Britain] was much greater under protection than after free trade was adopted: tariffs are less important determinants of international trade than the long-term factors'.

Another authoritative economic historian, William Ashworth, who was usually at pains to be descriptive and to avoid analytical statements, nevertheless made the same point, writing of 'the emergence of an acute international financial crisis which dealt blows at commercial institutions and business confidence'.[6] A contemporary report by a study group of the Royal Institute of International Affairs, published in 1933, was also quite plain and unambiguous on this point—that the key lay in monetary factors and that the falling-off of international lending had long preceded the increase in restrictions on trade:[7]

> While up to 1928 the volume of loans for abroad floated in New York was increasing, after that year American investors found it more attractive to purchase equity shares in New York and the volume of foreign loans fell off. The result was that foreign countries found that what they had come to look on as a normal source of borrowing was no longer available in the same way as it had been before.

The study group quoted figures from the final report of the Gold Delegation of the League of Nations which showed that capital issues floated in the United States for European and other foreign countries dropped sharply in the second half of 1928 — a year before the Wall Street crash — to less than half the total for the first half of that year.

The same report firmly put its finger on the key relationship between Germany and the United States. The two countries had reversed roles since the war, the United States becoming the world's biggest lender and Germany the biggest borrower. In two years it had borrowed over $2 billion from abroad, two-and-a-half times the amount payable in reparations.[8] So when in 1927 the Federal Reserve Bank decided to lower interest rates in order to avert recession in the US economy, this started a boom in Wall Street share prices, diverting funds from Europe and therefore, according to Robbins, 'was bound to be followed by a period of extensive depression'.[9] There were two reasons for this, only one of which he mentions. It was not simply because of the tendency of every bubble to burst (especially when share buying on Wall Street was founded on margin dealing[10]) but also because it put into reverse the circular flow of international funds on which international trade, investment and business confidence generally had relied. And though for a while the debtors could keep going by becoming more active and more agile in their movements from centre to centre and by resorting more and more to short-term borrowing, this process could not go on forever.[11]

As in our own more recent times, the existence of a large volume of highly nervous, mobile, short-term money put an abnormal strain on the foreign exchange system. As explained by Arthur Lewis, this pressed hardest on Britain because of the vulnerability of sterling as a reserve currency to monetary movements. This vulnerability had kept British short-term interest rates higher than those in New York throughout the 1920s — the British Bank Rate, he noted, was below 4 per cent for only two months between 1925 and 1929. But neither high interest rates nor the central bank cooperation developed between Ben Strong and Montagu Norman during the 1920s proved adequate. And, as Stephen Clarke noted in his classic study, *Central Bank Cooperation 1924–1931*, the resources of the bankers and the newly-founded Bank for International Settlements proved insufficient for crisis management.[12]

The puzzle remains why — despite the testimony of the historians — the trade-based interpretation of world economic depression should predominate so strongly over the financially-based interpretation. The reasons could be professional, historical or political — or a bit of all three. Professionally, it is much easier for teachers to explain and for students to understand the depressive effects of trade barriers than the more complex processes of credit shrinkage and monetary uncertainty. Historically, it must be remembered that a major foreign policy objective of the Roosevelt and Truman Administrations was to fashion a post-war world economy as wide open as possible to American commercial and financial domination.[13] To this end the belief that protectionism and discrimination must at all costs be avoided in the general interest as well as the national interest of the United States had to be confidently and repeatedly driven home.

Finally, there is a political explanation. Putting the main accent on protectionism serves to share the blame fairly equally among all concerned. The Europeans and the Japanese are as guilty — in some respects, more guilty — of this particular sin as the Americans. Even developing countries indulge in protectionism so it is not solely the rich who are at fault. Power over money and finance, however, is much more asymmetrically distributed among governments, the United States standing clear above all others. It would be hard enough for the Americans to accept such responsibility for the economic ills of other countries if there were more certainty and agreement about what ought to be done and more confidence in how, politically, to get it done. Lacking both, the hot seat is all the more uncomfortable and the monetary interpretation consequently all the more unpopular.

The technical version of determinism

One alternative to unpalatable monetary and financial interpretations of economic disorder is to put the emphasis on trade. Another is to find some reason why whatever happened was bound to happen. The determinist interpretations of current economic troubles go furthest in absolving any government or any class from blame or even responsibility. These are of two kinds.

While the political-determinist explanation excuses policy makers — in the United States specifically but in other countries as well — by saying that they could not do otherwise than they did because they had suffered a loss of power, the technical-determinist explanation suggests that the policy makers have been overwhelmed by the inexorable forces of economic history, against which no political system ever invented could prevail. The first assumes the loss of American power in the international political system, not to the Soviet Union so much as to Japan, Germany and the other members of the European Community, to OPEC and even to some developing countries. Beyond the United States' experience, it also refers to the loss by all states of the power to manage national economies in so closely knit and integrated a world market economy as we now have. The other — the technical–historical form of determinist thought — assumes the relative impotence of political organization in the face of economic, but more particularly rapid technological, change.

This rests on some empirical statistical work first done by a Dutch Marxist, van Gelderen, in 1913 and followed up in the 1920s by the Soviet economic historian, Nikolai Kondratiev. In analysing data on economic growth and on the relation of prices and wages, Kondratiev believed there was a discernible pattern of long waves of faster and slower expansion as well as shorter and less powerful trade cycles, and that this pattern had been fairly consistent since the early nineteenth century, with peaks in the 1850s and the 1900s and troughs in the 1820s, the 1870s and again in the 1920s. Though Kondratiev merely recorded the pattern and did not attempt to explain it, the very idea that the capitalist system had ups as well as downs and was not doomed, as Marx had proclaimed, to an inexorable decline as a consequence of its own internal contradictions, was heresy. So, Kondratiev ended up, according to Solzhenitsyn, in one of the millions of unmarked graves in Stalin's labour camps.

Since his time, economic and social historians have been coming forward with a variety of explanations of the Kondratiev long waves. The first was Schumpeter in 1939, who connected the first rising wave early in the nineteenth century with the introduction of steam engines in British manufacturing industry, the second with the spread of railways, the third with the technical revolutions in chemicals, electricity, and the internal combustion engine. In each, labour was absorbed in the growth industries faster than it was being shed in older agricultural and industrial occupations. In the downturns, the process was reversed and new industries could not absorb labour as fast as the old industries cut back. Modern exponents of the long waves interpretation of economic history thought they saw a fourth Kondratiev upswing in the 1950s led by the United States; at the end of the 1960s the crest of the last long wave was beginning to break, ushering in the long downturn of the 1970s. All the consumer durables and office machinery developed in the 1930s and marketed in the 1950s contributed to the last phase of expansion but it was not clear where the next technological advance would come from which would sustain the next upturn around the turn of the century.

One problem with this interpretation is that economic historians cannot entirely agree as to when or why the long swings up and down begin or end. Nor are they agreed on whether technical innovation acts as a starter of growth or whether conditions ripe for growth generate technical change. Is it demand or supply led?[14] They are consequently divided over how the downswings can be shortened and moderated or the upswings be extended and reinforced.

Some 20 years ago, Kuhn in the *Structure of Scientific Revolutions* suggested that a time-lag could be discerned between a scientific discovery or invention and its commercial exploitation, when it acted like a booster rocket accelerating the rate of economic growth.[15] The inventions, he suggested, came at the bottom of the troughs when the profitability of old technologies was becoming exhausted; the exploitations came on the upswing when investment resulted in mass production. But one trouble with applying these theories to the present times is that scientific and technological advance has become much more unremittingly constant and rather less cyclical. It is true that in some fields (pharmaceuticals, chemicals, for example), there are signs of diminishing returns setting in; but equally there are others (electronics, biogenetics) where scientific advance has not stopped over the last decade or more. Moreover, the extensive involvement of states, especially those with large defence establishments, in scientific research rather removes the implicit connection suggested by Kuhn between the exploitation of inventions and the state of the market.

An alternative and non-technical explanation came much later still, in the 1970s, from the American economist, Walt Rostow. In *The World Economy: History and Prospect* and other works,[16] Rostow has argued that the source of the long waves lay in the tendency of market economies led by the newest industrial sectors in any period first to over-invest in the production of primary products and then to under-invest. This produced a 'contrapuntal relation' between commodity prices and the industrial sectors which has continued into the post-war period.

But Rostow's rather individual interpretation has not been widely accepted. And indeed the popularity of the technical-determinist explanations of the recession for the most part has little to do with the cogency of rational argument. If there are weaknesses in the logic or yawning gaps in the empirical evidence, that is not so important as the seductive fact that such ideas absolve everyone from responsibility for the parlous state of the world. If past mistakes and errors of judgement are insignificant before these historical trends, then there is no point in recalling them, for they did not much matter. There is no point in the Europeans or the Japanese blaming the Americans, nor in the Latin Americans blaming the industrialized countries. Nor is there much point in people blaming their governments or their official bureaucracies. All the establishments around the world can heave comfortable sighs of relief and sleep with untroubled minds. So may corporate managers who can excuse themselves to the shareholders and to the redundant workers for the lamentable annual balance sheet by blaming it all — as they are all doing — on the state of the world economy. 'When things look up and business recovers', they can smugly report, 'the company will be able once again to offer jobs and dividends. We are doing our best. Please be patient.'

Meanwhile, the technologists and the scientific researchers can be consoled by the promise which long waves hold for the future. Blessed are those, it says, who can discover a new technology, conceive a new product for which there will be a mass market or design new processes that will be irresistible the moment the outlook brightens.

Even the changing nature of international politics favours this technical determinism. States are no longer seriously engaged in a competition over territory. It is not just that most frontiers have long been settled and that people have come to accept them for all their anomalies. They are also less important as factors determining the relative power of states in international relations. Where states can and must compete is over shares of the world markets, and markets not only of today but of tomorrow. The state which can design its own educational system, fund and run its own research centres and use its own procurement policies will be the one that stays ahead in the scientific race. A technical-determinist interpretation of recent world economic history gives an added incentive to governments, in alliance with scientists, to be first in catching the next long upswing. They will have an edge on others not only in economic growth but also in relative national power and influence.

Political determinism

The other form of determinism which seeks to offer an explanation of the mounting disorder and uncertainty for the future is more prevalent in the United States than elsewhere. It attributes the disorder to the loss of American authority in the management of the world's monetary and trade relations, and this loss in turn to a redistribution of power in the international political system among a wider circle of states. In this circle, West Germany and Japan figure especially large but it also includes on its fringes the Newly Industrializing Countries (NICs) like South Korea, Mexico, Brazil, Taiwan and the larger oil-producing states, notably Saudi Arabia. This view adduces as evidence such facts as their faster rates of economic growth, and increases in wages and GNP, in market shares and monetary reserves. It refers to some of the setbacks to US foreign policy, such as the retreat from Vietnam, the OPEC price rise, the fall of the Shah, the stalemate in the Arab-Israeli conflict, the uncontested Soviet invasion of Afghanistan — and sometimes to domestic political events like the Watergate scandal or to developments like the increase in Congressional intervention in foreign policy making.

But it rests on a rather narrow (and old-fashioned) understanding of power in world politics — an understanding which is totally blind to the idea of structural power (namely, power to shape and mould the structures of production, knowledge, security and credit within which others have no choice but to live if they are to participate in the world market economy). It takes power to be based on 'tangible resources that can be employed to affect the behaviour of others in desired directions'.[17] In this 'basic force model' the political analyst can see if outcomes correspond to the relative endowments of actors (states) with tangible and known capabilities. According to Keohane, it follows that power is the obverse of dependence and can be discerned in international monetary matters by the ability of a government to influence the behaviour of others relative to its own dependence on others' financial actions. Phrased thus, it could be interpreted as embracing structural power (for example, the power to raise interest rates worldwide). But in fact, Keohane attributes (p. 16) the so-called 'breakdown of Bretton Woods' in 1971 to the decline of American power from the high point attained towards the end of World War II: 'The decline of American power is a necessary condition for the collapse of the regime, since had the United States remained as dominant as it was in the late 1940s it could have forced its partners to revalue periodically while keeping gold at \$35 an ounce.' He argues that the United States in 1971 (and later) was therefore in a weak bargaining position and could no longer use its power to sustain the Bretton Woods system.

But this interpretation totally misunderstands the meaning of power and gravely misrepresents the reasons why the Bretton Woods system had become unsustainable. It was true that power to maintain order had been lost, but not to other states so much as to market forces liberated by the conscious decisions of the United States aided by Britain. And it had been lost because the United States had used its exorbitant privilege as the centre country of a gold-exchange system to run a perpetual balance of payments deficit and to finance a distant and expensive war in Vietnam by inflationary credit creation rather than by a transfer of resources from the civilians to the military by means of taxation.

Keohane wrote (p. 15, italics added):

Other countries held large quantities of dollars which the United States was required to redeem for gold at the fixed price of \$35 an ounce. *In order to preserve the regime the United States would have had to follow policies that would convince the holders of those dollars* (and after the change in the rules in 1968, the central banks holding dollars) *not to present them for redemption into gold*. This meant that United States macroeconomic policies would have been dependent on the financial decisions of foreign central banks.

But the 'fixed price' of gold had been fixed by the United States and could at any time have been refixed at a higher price. Moreover, it was the United States which made the decision which weakened the regime. It was the United States which chose not to follow policies sufficient to persuade the dollar-holders to be content *not* to ask for gold in exchange. And it was the United States which took the decision in August 1971 to bring about the system's collapse by suspending convertibility of dollars into gold, imposing an important surcharge and leaving it to the markets to determine exchange rates. Instead of attempting a negotiated realignment in the summer of 1971, Nixon and Connally used their power and that of the markets to bring about a forcible revaluation of the yen and the Deutschmark and a devaluation of the dollar.

Some while before Keohane wrote the above, however, the hegemonic interpretation of world monetary history had been popularized by others — notably by Charles Kindleberger and Robert Gilpin. Kindleberger had written an interesting and scholarly study of the inter-war depression which had concluded in its final chapter that the underlying explanation of why the world economy had fallen so deeply into depression in the 1930s and had taken so long to recover was that it had coincided with a kind of interregnum in hegemonic economic power.[18]

Comparing the position of the United States in the post-1945 period with that of Britain in the pre-1914 period, Gilpin thought the British experience showed the costs to the hegemon's own economy to have been far too heavy. Capital went abroad instead of to domestic industry. Military and other burdens were accepted beyond the capacity of the economy to sustain. The system therefore contained the seeds of its own destruction. The United States would be well advised to divest itself of the role before, like Britain, it too damaged its economy beyond repair. Gilpin was not interested and did not consider what consequences followed for the rest of the participants in the system.[19]

All these writers have had a great influence on American thinking throughout the past decade. More recently, an economist, Mancur Olson, has produced yet more supporting ammunition for the political-determinist view of trends in the world economy — and specifically for the alleged decline in the power of the United States. Olson already had a wide reputation in American political science as well as economics for his earlier book, *The Logic of Collective Goods* (1975), in which he developed an economic theory which accounted for the greater burdens which the United States was obliged to assume for military security and world economic development and the opportunities given to others to be 'free riders' enjoying the benefits without sharing the costs. In 1982, he produced a work of historical interpretation, *The Rise and Decline of Nations*, which (perhaps significantly) won immediate attention in American academic journals, but was less enthusiastically acclaimed elsewhere.[20] Olson's explanation for the rapid rise of Germany and Japan and for the decline of Britain in the postwar period rested on the proposition that the power of states in a world market economy depended on the speed with which new technologies were developed and adopted and the degrees of freedom allowed to new competitors to challenge established enterprises. Wars and foreign invasions, he argued, broke up the political, social and industrial coalitions of interests wishing to preserve the status quo and allowed the energy and enterprise of newcomers to accelerate investment, growth and the national dominance of foreign markets. According to this theory, the failure of the United States to maintain the dominant position it had had in the 1950s, therefore, was attributable to the comparative strength of change-resisting coalitions in American society and economy and their comparative weakness in the two most successful industrialized countries, Germany and Japan. Once again, the choices made and the decisions taken in US foreign economic policy were downplayed and depreciated as factors significantly contributing to the economic depression and disorders of the 1980s. The Washington bureaucracy and the politicians on Capitol Hill were not to blame because they had been betrayed by the loss of *élan* and adaptability, the progressive arthritis of American society.

The facts suggest a somewhat different story, however. In the mid-1970s the United States was able to recover faster than other countries from the post-oil-shock recession. And in all countries — Germany and Japan included — cartels and mergers have multiplied in recent hard times just as much as in the United States.[21] Facts, in short, suggest there is at least as much divergence in terms of adaptability between sectors as between states.[22]

Other variants of determinism

There are some other less general and more explicit forms of determinism which equally serve to absolve policy makers from blame. One similarly fatalistic idea particularly common with economists is that the troubles all started with the 'oil shock' and that this 'oil shock' was an 'exogenous factor' which somehow came from outside to knock the economic system for six.

R. C. Matthews, for instance, introducing a composite report by British economists on *Slower Growth in the Western World*, asserted that 'Most economists agree that the oil price rises of 1973–4 and 1979–80 had important adverse effects on real demand, both directly and by strengthening inflation, so leading to restrictive actions by governments. In so far as demand was responsible for the productivity slow-down, the oil price rise was thus an important constituent.'[23] Matthews refers several times to the view that the OPEC price rises could be regarded as exogenous shocks, and this view is shared by many fellow economists, especially in the United States where antipathy towards the Arabs is generally stronger than in Europe or Japan, and where the first oil shock produced a highly emotional wave of anger, resentment and hurt pride. In such emotional states, it is natural to look elsewhere for a scapegoat.

Beguiling as this is, it does not explain why the world economy proved so resilient at other times to other 'exogenous shocks' — the post-war adjustment in the 1940s, the Korean war in the 1950s. Why were policy makers then so much more ready to respond to a challenge? Why, in the 1970s, was it left to the banks and the private sector to adapt to change? From the oil producers' side the story was certainly somewhat different. In two ways, the structures of the world economy had worked against them. For over half a century and especially during the 1950s and 60s the structure of the world's oil industry had allowed the companies to keep profits up to finance new exploration, and other costs and oil prices down in order to expand sales. It was only when demand throughout the world did in fact expand very rapidly in the 1970s, even bringing the United States into the market as a net importer, that the oil-producing governments were at last able to use market forces as an ally in raising prices to the consumers. Having achieved that power through the Tehran Agreement of 1971, they then found that the extra dollars they had managed to wring out of the oil companies were being rather quickly depreciated as a result of US inflation and American domination of the international monetary system. Resort to floating rates looked like an indefinite licence to Washington to devalue the dollar, while the final slamming of the gold window in 1971 had already put the world on a paper dollar standard instead of a (nominal) gold-exchange standard.

This view of the oil price rises of 1973 not as an exogenous shock but as a rational response to an unstable and inequitable international monetary system is largely shared by most of the authoritative writers on the oil industry.[24] And John Blair's masterly book, *The Control of Oil*, added the ironic point that it was the United States itself which had done most to make the response so abrupt. Had it not pursued for so long the 'Drain America First' policy of keeping oil prices to the US oil producers and therefore output from US oilfields so high, the shift in the balance of power in world markets from consumers to producers would have been much more gradual.[25] Moreover, the United States had further set the stage for its own vulnerability first by giving a free hand to the oil companies in their political relations with the Middle East and secondly by allowing them to treat royalties to OPEC governments as a tax-allowable expense in the United States. Both these factors laid the companies wide open to pressure from the OPEC governments in 1971 and even more so in 1973. There is even a suggestion that the companies actually encouraged the OPEC price rise, if not the oil embargo on states like the Netherlands considered too friendly to Israel. Certainly, their profits in the mid-1970s were better than they had been when the oil price was lower. At the same time, as Mikdashi and others pointed out, the 'shock' administered by OPEC in 1973 soon lost its force as inflation gathered speed again and overtook and partly cancelled it out in real terms.

Other interpretations

At the risk of grossly oversimplifying all the differences, other interpretations of the 1980s could be divided, in political terms, into those which blame governments for making things worse than they need have been — in other words they think governments interfered too much; the market should have played a bigger role, the state a smaller one — and those which think that governments made things worse by not interfering enough, and by being not too active but too passive, in relation to the market economy. There is a more fundamental view still — that of neo-Marxists and radicals — which sees both the state and the economy — in other words, the capitalist system itself — as the ultimate source of the trouble. On the whole, since the aim is not to pin labels but to identify opinions and interpretations which overlook the monetary aspect of the problem and those which, on the contrary, ascribe a fairly central place to monetary policies and developments, it may be best to proceed by looking at each of these three approaches in turn.

All share, it might be noted in passing, a common tendency in the great majority of commentators to be wise after the event. As in the roaring 1920s so in the swinging 1960s, the warning voices who said *at the time* that times were too good to last were far outnumbered by those who later looked back and discovered the errors that made escaping the depression or learning to live through it harder than it need have been.

A major and obvious exception is, of course, Robert Triffin. His analysis of the international monetary system from the nineteenth century up to the 1980s repeatedly and unfalteringly focused on the creation of credit as the central issue. It was Triffin who, from 1958 onwards, steadfastly and patiently explained the weakness and vulnerability first of the gold-exchange system and then of the paper dollar standard and intermittently managed floating.[26] Against the rest of his profession, Triffin argued that floating was neither a panacea nor even a matter of central concern. Rather, it was the irresponsibility of the United States in first allowing the over-lavish creation of credit and then bringing about its drastic contraction at the end of the 1970s that lay at the root of other troubles. His decision to revert from American to Belgian citizenship reflected his concern for Europe's dependence on the United States, and for the consequent European vulnerability to the consequences of American policy decisions. Triffin was and always has been a fundamentalist among economists. No half-measures sufficed. He was convinced that the only ultimate solution lay in a world central bank and a truly international reserve asset. Like Rheinold Niebuhr's solution to the problem of war, this analysis of inflation and recession was too prophetic and idealistic to gain popular political support or to have much practical influence on the day-to-day discussions of monetary managers.

Pro-market opinion criticizes the state for interfering with markets for goods and services and with markets for factors of production — more especially with the labour market and money markets, with wages and with the money supply which affects price levels and income distribution throughout the system. Individual economists will differ as to which form of interference is the most damaging. Those concerned with international trade, and especially those connected directly or indirectly with the GATT, the IMF or the OECD, tend to be highly critical of national policies which obstruct or distort trade — with quota restrictions, subsidies, procurement policies, and state support for national industries both privately and publicly owned. They even attack regional policies which they say only make economic adjustment to change more difficult because they introduce rigidities into relative prices. The longer such state interference continues, it is argued, the harder it is for workers, farmers, managers and whole sectors of industry to accept change and for the national economy itself to compete in the world market.[27] The implication is clear that the world depression would have been less severe and recovery would have been quicker if all of these self-indulgent practices had been forsworn altogether at the beginning of the decade.

The element of truth in this, of course, is that protective measures do become harder to change as time goes on. But it does not necessarily follow that the longer they are maintained the greater the inefficiency imposed on the economy as a whole and the longer the recovery of demand is deferred. Where sectors of industry suffer acutely from cyclical variations in demand, for instance, the economy as a whole might be more damaged by throwing the whole workforce out of their jobs, thus increasing the fall in demand for other sectors, than it would be keeping them at work until the cycle turns. It will all depend on whether the forces of change are permanent or temporary. The point simply is that markets left to themselves can be wasteful and unstable as well as swift in reshuffling the resources that make up the pack of productive cards for an economic system. It may well be that there is a sort of critical threshold beyond which it is dangerous for a national economy to go in matters of protective cushioning for parts of the mechanism.

But the trouble is that no one knows where that threshold lies. Moreover, the constant emphasis of such argument on the need to compete with others overlooks the fact, already referred to, that the level of demand in the international system is not only affected by market restrictions but also by the rate of growth in global credit and thus the level of confidence in the future.

The error of the state in interfering over-indulgently with markets and trade is seen as complementary to the errors of over-indulgence committed in monetary policy. Broadly speaking, the monetarist economists see depression as the natural, deserved and to some extent inevitable consequence of the previous inflation. Like a hangover after an ill-advised alcoholic binge, it is no more than the victim's just deserts. Their theorizing consequently concentrates more on how the initial inflation was generated than on the processes by which, when 'correction' is applied, painful consequences for growth, employment, and trade necessarily follow.[28]

It blames the incompetence and feebleness of will of the state (or sometimes the 'unnatural' power of organized labour), not the economic system itself. And it does so because it makes the basic assumption of neo-classical theory going back to Walras, and even to Say, that the system has a natural tendency to equilibrium.[29] Hence, maybe, the tendency to express theoretical propositions and models in algebra because algebra is a means of communication based on the idea of balance between the right and left sides of the equation.

Much of this conventional 'liberal' theory, moreover, when it is not totally abstract and mathematical but tries to relate the equations and models to the real world, insists on treating national economic systems as if they were (a) totally isolated from the rest of the world, and (b) equally open to it. Each individual government can then be blamed — since it is never the system's fault — for the excesses of inflation or recession. Since market operators act on equal terms and with equal power — or so it is unconsciously assumed — the decision of the market must be fair and just and must not be interfered with. The element of ideology involved, especially in the United States, is of course largely unconscious. But it is nevertheless powerful and insidious — as demonstrated by the evangelism shown by some of its trainees and converts in other countries.

Not only national economies but also markets are treated as though they functioned in a sealed box, immune from all but 'exogenous shocks'. The reality (as any political economist is acutely aware) is that each market is at the mercy of others, and in turn its own demand, supply and price affect other markets. This is patently obvious even though it certainly complicates the task of description, let alone explanation. We saw all this with oil, but it is true of copper and aluminium; of shipping and insurance; of housing and timber; maize and beef — and would be so even if each in turn were not *inevitably* subject to the influence, if not the deliberate intervention, of the state.

Another major weakness in much monetary theorizing is the exclusion of all consideration of the nature of financial institutions and markets as generators of money. Much monetarist theory is thus unable — in fact, often does not even try — to explain the recurrence of financial instability in capitalist systems. Money is treated as just another commodity, with a supply that responds to demand, and not as something quite different from commodities. But this is misleading because the creation of money (especially in the form of credit) confers power as well as wealth on the creator. There is therefore a constant tension between the private creators and the public ones, between banks (and indeed, now, some non-banks) and the state.

This is well understood by economic historians and by a rare few who have spent a lifetime trying to teach students about the working of financial and banking systems. Most notable among these is Hyman Minsky.

Minsky's 'Financial Instability Hypothesis' is worth quoting for it is both succinct and to the point: 'A capitalist economy with sophisticated financial institutions is capable of a number of modes of behaviour and the mode that actually rules at any time depends upon institutional relations, the structure of financial linkages and the history of the economy.'[30]

By financial linkages, he refers to the relation of two sets of prices — prices of current output and prices of capital assets; the mark of a functioning capitalist system is that the price relationship between them should be such as to allow a balance between 'money today' and 'money tomorrow', between consumption and investment. With other self-styled 'post-Keynesians', Minsky stresses the importance of bringing time and uncertainty back into the analysis of people's decisions about borrowing and lending (and in what form) so as to direct attention to these two sets of prices. 'Prices of capital assets depend on current views of future profit (quasi-rent) flows and the current subjective view placed upon the insurance against uncertainty embodied in money or quick cash; these current views depend upon the expectations that are held about the longer run development of the economy.'[31] Taking Keynesian theory a step further, it is the flows of funds resulting from past financing decisions through financial institutions public and private that influence the linkage between the two sets of prices and therefore both inflation and depression. Minsky's argument, grossly oversimplified, is that by paying attention to the linkage and the intermediating institutions of the market and the influence of historical expectations on people's preferences and judgement, one can trace the route which would lead to financial crisis. The extent and nature of the crisis would then be moderated (or otherwise) by central bank behaviour, government deficits, gross profit flows and the balance of payments. His conclusion is that the way out 'lies through shifting policy from the encouragement of growth through investment to the achievement of full employment through consumption production'.

However, apart from the mention of the balance of payments, Minsky in common with many of his fellow-Keynesians still presents the argument largely in single-economy terms. The lay reader is not sure whether these plausible and realist-seeming arguments still hold when applied to an international economy in which funds flow in response to yet more variables — notably the price of oil, the size of the US deficit and the means currently chosen for financing it, interest rates and investment risks of various kinds including exchange rates and national debt profits.

In general, I think it fair to say that most other post-Keynesians were less inclined than Minsky to find the explanation *within the system* and were more inclined to put the blame on governments for applying the wrong deflationary policies, whether for political reasons to curb the power of organized labour or for economic reasons that recovery could be achieved by checking inflation and avoiding deficits on current accounts in the balance of payments. Michael Bruno, for example, blames the United States, the United Kingdom and Japan in particular for obstructing the necessary adjustment to 'supply shocks'. The observed productivity slowdown is thus directly linked to the choice of short-term and medium-term macroeconomic response strategy.[32] Many academic economists, beguiled with elegant theory, also paid far too little attention either to the institutional frameworks within which credit is created, or to the influence of past economic experience or the preferences of government in different countries.

Others are to be found straying further and further still into a sort of post-Galbraithian realm of socio-political analysis, paying much more attention both to Galbraith's point about the power of large corporations to administer prices (and thus to supplant or distort the market) and to the corresponding (but hardly countervailing) power of labour to hold real wages up and to delay the loss of jobs.[33] Yet, for all their shortcomings, it has clearly been the monetarist explanations which have received most attention in the economic literature, at least in English language journals. During the mid-1970s, events and popular perceptions of what was going on both told against the opposite Keynesian view that national economies were in a mess because governments lacked the courage and conviction to intervene enough. Meghnad Desai, writing mainly of the British experience, says that the tide both for policy and for theoretical interpretation was turned between 1974 when the House of Commons Select Committee on Public Expenditure heard only one monetarist advocate, David Laidler, and 1976 when Callaghan as a Labour Prime Minister addressing a Labour Party Conference pointed to high wages as the cause of rising unemployment, and allowed Denis Healey to override objections in the British Cabinet to the monetarist conditions demanded for an IMF loan. In those two years Friedman and Hayek got Nobel prizes and, according to Desai, 'the majority of younger economists were now willing to admit the relevance if not superiority of the monetarist framework in explaining the hyperinflation of 1974 and 1975'.[34]

Only the older Keynesians (Joan Robinson, Lord Kahn, Nicholas Kaldor and, in America, J. K. Galbraith) stuck to their guns. Although Desai in common with many economists believes (a) that sophisticated quantitative techniques can be used to test the comparative efficacy of monetarist policies and Keynesian demand-management policies and (b) that policy making will be swayed by their impartial findings from such tests, neither proposition is one which political economists or monetary historians can easily accept. However sophisticated the quantitative technique, there are too many variables in a real economy (some of a non-quantitative nature) to be able to tell for sure what would have happened in the alternative case. And there is also ample evidence that economic theories are like detergents on a supermarket shelf. Politicians decide on other grounds what ends they wish to achieve and will pick on the appropriate legitimating economic theory as a shopper picks off the shelf the detergent that suits the kind of washing or cleaning he or she wants to do.

In the mid-1970s, partly in consequence of volatile oil prices but partly also because of the resort to floating rates, the British were rediscovering the vicious circle of weak currency — dearer imports — added inflationary pressures — bigger wage demands — more inflation — weak currency etc. etc. The balance of political opinion shifted — as Jim Callaghan was shrewd enough to see — away from the Keynesian and toward the monetarist view, away from wages and incomes solutions to monetary stringency and spending cuts. The same experience and the same popular and political reaction came in the United States a little later in 1979. It had nothing whatever to do with Desai's 'objective scientific criteria for choosing between rival explanations of the same observable phenomena'. People even in the Labour Party or the Democratic Party became convinced that more government spending, starting from a base already high, would not remedy unemployment but would worsen inflation. The Phillips curve, which presupposed that governments had the freedom to choose between different combinations of the rate of change in wages and the rate of unemployment, had lost its magic and was subjected to increasingly critical attack.

But the majority of both monetarists and Keynesians were apt to look for explanation within a too narrowly national framework. This was why their explanations failed to account for the very different experiences in the mid-1970s of weak-currency countries like Britain and Italy and strong-currency countries like Germany or Switzerland, or between those like Japan which managed to adjust quickly to their oil deficit and those like the United States which found it difficult. In both camps, the interpretations offered by those who took a global view made a good deal more sense.

Among the Keynesians, there have been a number of development economists who took the same view, roughly speaking, about the 1970s and 1980s that Arthur Lewis took about the 1930s. World economic depression was exacerbated by the lack of purchasing power of the primary producing developing countries and especially those now dependent on imported oil. The lack was made good with credit from the banking system after the first oil price rise but became acute with the shrinkage of credit and the slowing of growth in the major market economies in the early 1980s. Most of these 'global Keynesians' are to be found in the World Bank and other international organizations and in academic circles concerned with the political economy of developing countries. Like the members of the Brandt Commission with whose findings many would agree, at least in part, the policy probably comes first — massive resource transfers to the developing countries of the South, preferably from a World Development Fund set up by collective international agreement. The explanatory theory follows.

Its strongest feature in my opinion is the implied criticism of redistributive countercyclical public policy when it is confined to small or even medium-sized national economies because of its inadequacy to the size of the problem. In the 1930s, when government spending constituted around 15 to 20 per cent at the very most of GNP, deficit financing could be undertaken without marked results on the interest rate structure. (Indeed, at the time the British government like others was busy forcibly substituting 3 per cent government stock for old 5 per cent War Loan.) And measures of income redistribution could be undertaken (food stamps in the United States, the National Industrial Recovery Act and other New Deal policies) that had a sharp and immediate effect on demand and consumption. Now, for a variety of reasons (defence, social welfare, medicine and education, support of ailing industries), an increase in government spending has unavoidable counterproductive effects, raising interest rates, reviving fears of inflation, all of which serve to undermine confidence and do little to revive investment; and because of unemployment and social security payments at fairly high levels (not to mention a thriving black economy), redistributive income policies do less to affect demand and business confidence than would a reduction in the rate of interest. The fearful paradox is that whereas the first — and to a less extent the second — oil price rise had initially deflationary effects because the OPEC surpluses went into real estate and bank deposits and it took time to translate the latter into OPEC demand on top of oil-deficit financing, the situation by the mid-1980s would allow oil surpluses to boost demand — but the surpluses had by then disappeared.

A similar objection can be made to much neo-mercantilist reaction to the world depression. This is better represented in the press, the media and in political discussion than it is in the academic literature.[35] Basically, the argument is somewhat fatalistic, like the long-wave determinists: there is little that can be done at this late stage, so it's a matter of *sauve qui peut* and *chacun pour soi*. In Britain, the Cambridge school so-called has advocated import controls and has found some support for the idea in industry and the Labour Party. It is also, I think implicit in Christian Stoffaes' bestselling book about French policy,[36] though that at least takes the point that international competition for markets for manufactures is now so far advanced that national companies if they are to survive cannot do so on the basis of the national economy alone. They therefore need state support and encouragement to be able to hold their market shares abroad and state control to stop them shifting too much production overseas too fast and too soon. Among monetarists too, the relative minority who have adopted a broader definition of money and have looked at the expansion of credit in the world market economy in the 1970s rather than at the monetary bases of national economies, seem to have made more plausible explanations and remedies for the depression. They might be aptly described as 'global monetarists'. One of the best-known and most effective proponents of this approach has been Professor Ronald McKinnon. Much of this argument, though, rests on a restricted view of WM^n based on national official reserves of gold, dollars and other foreign exchange and IMF drawing rights, which gives insufficient attention, in my view, to the flows of funds stressed by Minsky. In the international capital markets these have been larger than shifts in official reserves through Euromarket loans. Thus an argument which rests, as I understand it, on the supposition that when other central banks sell dollars to stop the weakening of their own currencies they will decrease their national money supply base because they will be buying francs, lira or pounds from the private sector, does not necessarily follow.

However, McKinnon is right in observing that there exists in the international monetary system a monetary cycle alongside the business cycle and that tensions in the two fields have a multiplying effect on each other; that US interest rates determine Euromarket rates and these govern the largest part of the international capital movements. All this is borne out by recent experience, as is the observation that 'the idea that floating exchange rates would give countries autonomy with respect to their monetary development has proved an illusion'.[37]

Some while ago, McKinnon argued forcibly for a coordination of US, West German and Japanese monetary policy in order to reduce the volatility and disruptive uncertainty in exchange rates and to stabilize between them, the global money supply and prices.[38] He has reiterated this proposal and it has been popular among economists. Unfortunately, the political realities of asymmetry between the vulnerability of Japanese and German financial markets to US policy and, conversely, the vulnerability of the United States to them mean that both would have to be prepared to accept a permanent loss of monetary autonomy while at present they can still hope one day to regain more of it. Politically, therefore, the proposal is naive and pays too little attention not only to the divergence of real national interests but also to the deeper differences still on what each perceives as the general interest of the world economy and the international community.

A more pessimistic but also more realistic appraisal was that of the late Milton Gilbert. Gilbert was an American economist who worked for ten years in the 1950s for the old OEEC, and then for 15 years as economic adviser to the Bank for International Settlements; a posthumously edited book about the evolution of the international monetary system from Bretton Woods to the mid-1970s ends as follows:[39]

> The problem for the monetary authorities in the 1980s and beyond will be how to maintain exchange stability in a fundamentally unstable environment. The march of events has often been described as being the result of impersonal and mysterious forces. But as I have seen it, the force and determination of political leadership, or lack of it, is a key element in the chemical compound of monetary affairs.

In Gilbert's view the blame for the inflation and by implication for the ensuing depression lay primarily with the United States, first for allowing such a huge deficit 'much beyond the system's reasonable need for liquidity' to develop, and then, when it did intervene in late 1978, for being inhibited about using temporary direct controls as a shock weapon to restore order and confidence. The United States has also, in Gilbert's view, been wrong to let the Group of Ten consultative mechanism fall into disuse, and he thought it should be revitalized.

Another and most recent practitioner's view — that of the former head of the IMF, Johannes Witteveen — also blames the United States essentially for overlooking the international aspect, and impact, of its monetary policy under Paul Volcker.[40] Keeping the monetary target within limits required such large changes in interest rates that it actually increased uncertainty and fostered rather than restrained the shift to short-term assets reflecting rational precautionary and speculative motives for increased liquidity preference. Witteveen pointed out that the increase between the end of 1978 and May 1982 of chequable deposits in the United States as a proportion of all deposits from 2 to 20 per cent was a major factor increasing the fragility of the system.

Marxist versions

The Marxist literature that directly addresses the question of why depression hit the world economy in the 1980s in the way and at the time it did is neither extensive nor well known outside leftwing bookshops and journals. But for serious students of international political economy or history, what there is of it should neither be under-rated nor overlooked — and not simply because of its powerful appeal to many victims of that depression. For although Wall Street and Greenwich Village (or the City and Hampstead, the Bourse and the Left Bank) seldom speak to each other — and have difficulty understanding one another's language when they do, the gulf dividing them on this issue is neither so wide nor so unbridgeable as ideology on each side would have them believe. When it comes to analysis, some of the more thoughtful and observant of the Marxists are not too far distant in their comments from some of the more thoughtful and observant of the financial conservatives.

If the present depression is different from others that came before it, it is chiefly because of some radical and rapid changes that have taken place in the last fifteen or twenty years in the world credit system and banking, and consequently in the structure of production. Yet many Marxists are inclined neither by training nor interest to delve into the intricacies of the Eurocurrency markets and the niceties of foreign exchange markets. Banking is seen as a sordid, despicable and antisocial activity; the politics of international monetary diplomacy and the technicalities of banking innovation and regulation seem distant from the welfare of the working class and therefore uninteresting. Taking in the monetary aspects of the world depression — which I believe to be central to the story — is thus by definition a minority pastime on the Left. It is only a few therefore that have perceived the main weakness of a modern global capitalist system to lie, not in the exploitation of labour nor the oppression of the working class, but in the inability of its leading governments to run a monetary system stable and viable enough to sustain a global production system.

There is a much more fundamental point about Western Marxism which has been admirably explained and documented by Perry Anderson. In his *Considerations on Western Marxism*, he traces the divorce of theory from praxis — the 'scission between socialist theory and working-class practice', which Marx always said was so important — to the disappointment arising from the failures of proletarian revolution in Europe after World War I, and the enforced sojourn thereafter of many Marxists in a political wilderness. The gulf opened up by the imperialist isolation of the Soviet state was institutionally widened and fixed by the bureaucratization of the USSR and by Soviet domination of the Comintern. The result, he says, was 'a seclusion of theorists in universities far from the life of the proletariat in their own countries and a contraction of theory from economics and politics into philosophy. This specialization was accompanied by an increasing difficulty of language whose technical barriers were a function of its distance from the masses.'[41]

This seclusion was accentuated in the United States by the bitter disillusion with the Soviet ally in the late 1940s, and the brutal alienation of the American Left in the McCarthy period and since. One might add that this long separation accounted both for the rejoicing — premature as it turned out — at the shortlived reunion of workers and intellectuals in Paris and elsewhere in 1968, and also for the continuing lack of interest on the part of the great majority of Marxist intellectuals in the profound and important changes that have taken place in industry, trade and, above all, finance. In Latin America, it is true, the 'scission' is far less apparent, and there has consequently been far more lively discussion of the relations between theory and praxis — particularly Marxist, structuralist and *dependencia* theory — and many more serious empirical studies in political economy than in any other part of the Third World. But the focus has generally been on the impact of international finance, production and trade on local political and social systems rather than on developments at the international level.[42] Meanwhile, in Europe most of the leading Marxist writers have concentrated on loftier philosophical themes and have shown little interest in contemporary economic developments.[43]

Little wonder, then, that the Left shares in good measure almost all the shortcomings of non-Marxist explanatory theorizing. It too is confused, contradictory and uncertain. It too has difficulty escaping from the mental straitjackets tailored by past experience. And the majority of those who do write about world depression — like their conservative or social-democratic counterparts — do not go far beyond descriptive accounts of a worsening situation and do not seriously attempt to offer a logically satisfactory explanation.

The Soviet literature, so far as I am aware, is even thinner. Although it is predictably critical of the United States for its exploitation of the role of the dollar, it shows curiously little interest in such key questions as why the recession of the 1970s was so shortlived and that of the 1980s so persistent. Not only is there little technical comprehension of such important debates as occurred over the use of Special Drawing Rights, the deregulation of banking or the limitation of the European Monetary System, but even the general analysis remains on a very general and superficial level. Possibly, ideology as well as ignorance inhibits explanation. For if all capitalist systems are inherently self-destructive it cannot be admitted that good government could have overcome difficulties that proved too much for bad government.

Only a relatively small group of writers, scattered by age as well as nationality, are the exceptions to this generalization. In them can be seen the two great strengths of the Marxist approach: a historical perspective which offers a longer and cooler view of changes in the world economy; and a systematic vision which transcends the differences in national economies and national experience. In neither respect, of course, are the Marxists alone. Many non-Marxists (Hirschman, Arthur Lewis, Paul Streeten, Michael Lipton, as well as Braudel and Perroux) also take a long view and look at the system broadly rather in narrowly national and international terms. But the nature of Marxist analysis does, I think, not just encourage both propensities, it actually demands them.

This is true even of a self-styled Marxist like Arghiri Emmanuel whom others repudiate as a heretical deviant.[44] Emmanuel's work has probably been translated into as many different languages as any other. His explanation of the unequal distribution of wealth in the world economy, and the unequal terms of North–South, rich–poor trade is truly systematic.[45] His analysis rests on the contradiction between the mobility of capital and credit, moving freely from country to country, and the immobility of labour, prevented by immigration laws from responding to differential wages in national economies. Trade, and income, thus become unequal and high wages are maintained in industrial countries while wages for exactly the same kind of work remain low in the developing countries. When goods are exchanged, the low-wage country is paid for its products at low prices, the high-wage country at high prices. By contrast, liberal economists usually take the limitation of migration for granted, as if it were an inherent rather than a politically-imposed characteristic of the system; nor do they inquire closely into the explanation of wage differentials.

The acclaim given to Immanuel Wallerstein's work in recent years rests on a similar ability to depict the totality of a world system where others see only a kaleidoscope of states. In *The Modern World System*, a study of European agriculture in the sixteenth century, and then in a book of collected articles, *The Capitalist World Economy*, Wallerstein raised the eyes of a new generation of American students from the post-1945 economic problems with which their 'current-affairs' textbooks had made them familiar to the more profound issues of social and economic change over long periods of time.[46] The same applies to the work of Johan Galtung,[47] who has followed Perroux's lead in discussing the world system in terms of core and periphery but probably describes himself as a structuralist rather than a Marxist. Neither Galtung nor Wallerstein, however, has been much concerned with the origins and analysis of the world depression of the 1980s or the monetary developments of the previous decade.

More directly relevant to such questions has been the work of an Egyptian Marxist, Samir Amin. His book, *Class and Nation, Historically and in the Current Crisis*, directs attention to the major difference between this depression and early ones, which is that it has coincided with very rapid internationalization of production through the preferential access to capital and technology enjoyed by the multinational corporation. The acceleration of change in the international division of labour whereby yesterday's producers of food and raw materials become today's producers of shoes, shirts, ships, cars and TV sets is largely attributable to the expansion of Euromarkets and the internationalization of banking. The results in one part of the world economy — structural unemployment, declining industries, uncertainty and failing confidence — are directly linked to the results in the other part — authoritarianism in government, expansion of the public sector, and nationalization of foreign enterprises, urban slums and low wages. Amin's argument links the relations of international capital (in the shape of banks and multinationals) with governments at home in the OECD countries, with their relations with Third World governments. Through the greater mobility of capital and technology they are able to compensate for the falling rate of profit at home by shifting operations to countries where more surplus value can be extracted from low-wage labour. Easy credit and fast growth rates allow the peripheral countries to pay the price for both the borrowed capital and technology and for the food which increasingly they find it necessary to import. Amin sees the capitalists engaged in transnational manufacturing, processing or services as confronted both by a militant working class at home and a hostile national bourgeoisie in the periphery. They cannot afford to fight both at the same time. So they avoid open conflict with the former by cooperating with governments in neo-corporatist incomes policies, and with the latter by sharing with them the proceeds of exploitation. They are indifferent to whether those in power in Third World states are democratic or repressive, militarist or civilian, one-party or pluralist, provided only that the regime is stable enough to maintain international financial and commercial confidence.[48]

Amin concludes that as long as these underlying conditions of the new international division of labour persist, the possibility of serious North–South negotiations does not exist. He does not see the apocalyptic collapse of the capitalist system, but rather its transformation through the break-up, during the long period of slow growth and change that he sees in prospect, both of alliances between states and of alliances of class interests within states and across state frontiers. Like many left-wing writers in Latin America including Cardoso and O'Donnell, Amin is familiar enough with the realities of Third World politics to recognize that not everything can be blamed on the world capitalist system. The inability of so many governments to solve the problem of rural poverty is a major factor ensuring their continued dependence, in one form or another, on the centres of financial, managerial and information power.

More generally speaking, however, there are two aspects of Marxist criticism which should be of interest to more conservative minds: its analysis of the inflationary policies pursued by the United States and others from the mid-1960s on; and the critical analysis by some Marxist writers of Keynesian interpretations and solutions.

On the first point, most Marxist writers agree with the monetarists (and with liberal historians like Kindleberger) that the stability of the system was fatally undermined once the United States, exercising what Jacques Rueff and General de Gaulle always called its exorbitant privileges under the gold-exchange standard, abused its responsibilities as banker to the world and allowed the financial markets to bring the system down in ruins. The resort to floating rates was another Dunkirk — hardly a victory but a defeat carried off without total disaster. The 'paper dollar standard' then adopted — the phrase is Triffin's — offered still more exorbitant privileges, and these were also abused as a weak dollar made up for the oil import bill on the US balance of payments and robbed the oil producers of much of the real value of the first price rise. The instability in the foreign exchange and other financial markets was reflected by the instability of commodity markets, exacerbating the impact of the oil price for many developing countries. The Third World and the workers at home were the victims, and both were able to perceive the inherent contradictions and weaknesses of the system.

This, with some Marxist embellishments, has been the theme elaborated for more popular consumption by Harry Magdoff and Paul Sweezy in issue after issue of the American left-wing *Monthly Review*. Their articles, collected together in *The Deepening Crisis of US Capitalism*, show a lively awareness of economic trends and an admirable refusal to be taken in by official apologies or by the academic benedictions so devastatingly lampooned by David Calleo in *The Imperious Economy*.[49] But Magdoff's pessimism does not even allow the possibility that the depression is cyclical and sooner or later will end. He sees it as structural and permanent, resulting from the inherent, strong, persistent and growing tendency (p. 179) for more surplus value to be produced than can find profitable investment outlets. Since he believes that no one in the United States who counts for anything has the faintest idea what to do about it, the only possibility is for socialists to continue to work for the overthrow of the whole system by revolution.

In common with many monetarists, Marxists see the inflation of 1965–70 as the necessary forerunner of subsequent deflation. But they add a twist to the conventional version. Besides stressing as that does the effects of government spending on defence, education, social security, etc. and the increased bargaining power of organized labour, some of them have added the increasing tendency of governments, whatever their political labels, to disguise, in effect, the falling rate of profit by arranging a variety of covert handouts to corporations; and not only support for what the British call 'lame ducks' but all kinds of subsidies, tax reliefs, and tax deferrals, some of them so complex that only former tax inspectors turned tax consultants can fully understand their significance.

Others are critical of neo-classical literature for grossly underestimating the role of capital accumulation. The collection of explanations of slower growth referred to earlier included a Marxist view by Andrew Glyn which makes this point:[50]

> Faced with the long-run relative constancy of the capital-output ratio in different countries, despite varying rates of growth of the capital–labour ratio, they (the liberal economists) have to postulate diverse rates of technical progress which allowed a faster or slower rate of accumulation. Marxists would view the causation as being primarily in the other direction: diverse rates of accumulation have brought with them different rates of productivity growth.

Glyn therefore addresses the question of capital accumulation suggesting (in common with many non-Marxists) that the seeds of depression were sown by the inflationary policies of the previous decade. The weakness of the argument lies in the obsolete assumption that investment is governed by past accumulation of capital through profit. The fact is that the modernization and internationalization of banking have effectively divorced both the creation of and access to capital (i.e. credit) from its accumulation. Glyn is stronger on his preferred ground — the consequences for the workers on the factory floor of management's response to the slowdown in productivity. While the 1930s brought in 'Fordism' (the label given to the relentless discipline of the assembly line), modern management has introduced the robot and the 'team-production' system — still better methods of enforcing obedience and extracting surplus value from the workers.

Another Marxist contribution likely to appeal to conservatives is the criticism of Keynesian explanations for the present crisis, and more particularly Keynesian prescriptions for recovery from it. A popular French Marxist, who has avoided the commoner concern with abstruse philosophical issues referred to earlier, is Suzanne de Brunhoff. Her book, *State, Capital and Economic Policy*,[51] shares with Hirschman the perception that capitalism does not function in a totally capitalist context but is shaped by earlier modes and ideas, including mercantilism.[52] Quoting Marx in support, she finds such ideas reappearing from time to time, effectively dividing the capitalist class. Her criticism of Keynesian theory and policy, correctly to my mind, judges the main purpose to have been psychological rather than purely economic or financial, for its aim was to dispel uncertainty about the future by using state policy to compensate for the perverse liquidity preferences of the capitalists. 'The link between the present and the future constituted mainly by credit was underwritten by the state which therefore changed the relationship between the certain and the uncertain' (p. 121).

But her conclusions have not advanced much beyond those of the 1930s: the only remedy is to destroy the bourgeois state and with it the capitalist infrastructure. Although she does attribute the crisis of over-production in the world economy to the evolution of the international monetary system and the mismanagement of credit, at the end she can only repeat the conclusions reached 40 years ago by Maurice Dobb and Michael Kalecki that the system leaves the capitalist class with the choice between renewed inflation, fascism and repression and unemployment.[53] Recently, she says, all three have been adopted with the consequent erosion of the capitalist consensus established after World War II. Fairly predictably, this is indeed the majority view among Marxists. Only here and there is the thought emerging that integration has gone so far now that the establishment of a 'pure' socialist state is no longer feasible.[54]

To my mind, a much more profound criticism of neo-Keynesian theories and solutions is to be found in the work of Ernest Mandel, a Belgian Trotskyist banned from the United States and author of *Late Capitalism* and *The Second Slump*. Mandel is equally sceptical of both the liberal/monetarist and socialist governments. Like other Marxists, he believes that increased capital inputs in production, by recruiting labour from the reserve army of the unemployed (women and *Gastarbeiter*), shrink that army in the long run while new opportunities for profitable productive investment become fewer, and governments are led to choose policies which postpone or mask the consequent decline in the rate of profit. 'The classical overproduction crisis was limited in depth and duration by deficit spending and a large-scale expansion of credit, but marked by a clearly declining efficacy of these anticrisis techniques to avert a repetition of the interwar depression.'[55]

Unlike many left-wing Europeans, however, Mandel does not think that pump-priming Keynesian solutions will work: 'A rise in household incomes really primes the cycle only if it is accompanied by a rise in the rate of profit *and a prospect of generalised expansion of the market*' (p. 177, italics added). But since the market is now global, and as bank lending declines, this third necessary condition frustrates the policy. Nor will liberal solutions work, because in depressions self-interest (for the worker, the enterprise, and the state) lead each into conflict, not cooperation, with others. Thus, it is a common illusion that national economic recovery can be achieved by export growth in such times. Equally, the 'strength through austerity' policies now propounded by Mitterrand in France, de la Madrid in Mexico and advocated by the late Enrico Berlinguer in Italy will be no more effective than were those of Stafford Cripps in the 1940s. Galbraithian ideas about neo-corporatist negotiation of incomes policies and 'sharing austerity' only lead in practice, says Mandel, to a reduction in the workers' real living standards. Nor is it true that if consumption is held down by such policies, investment will automatically rise. For, besides consumption and productive investment, there is a third hand dipping greedily into the GNP pot — the unproductive spending of governments and corporate bureaucracies whose pre-emptive power is far greater than either of the other two. The mixed economy therefore is 'a dangerous and disorienting myth', a 'trap for the working class'. Yet, despite the acuteness of his analysis, Mandel like many others clings to the illusion that workers, North and South, share a common interest and that the solidarity of the international proletariat must still be the goal.

Bob Rowthorn, an English Marxist whose work, like Stephen Hymer's, is read in business schools, agrees with Mandel on many points, specifically on the trend of state policies in the late 1960s and early and mid-1970s.[56] Rowthorn is rare among Marxists for understanding the role of bank credit:

> The key point is that it can increase total purchasing power in the economy. Banks are not merely the funnel through which people's savings are channelled. They can actually create new purchasing power by means of the overdraft system and in this way can provide investment finances in excess of what has been saved by capitalists or anyone else . . . Like the states, they can create new purchasing power (p. 101).

This perception leads to one basic disagreement with Mandel concerning the 'organic composition of capital' — a Marxist term referring to the amount of capital invested per worker in the production process. Mandel, believing it is the key variable in late capitalism and has risen, concludes that profits have not been squeezed. Rowthorn argues that, because of the increase in credit, the organic composition of capital has remained stable. Profits in recent times have therefore taken a lesser share of output because the profits per worker were falling, the state pre-empting some of the proceeds and the workers' share increasing through organization.

He also disagrees fundamentally with Mandel on the reason for the depression of the 1980s.[57] Mandel saw it as the inevitable consequence of the system — the conjuncture, as he put it, of a structural crisis of overproduction with other cyclical crises, including the reversal of our old friend the long wave, the growing militancy of the workers and the redistribution of purchasing power to the oil producers. In his view, the global production structure requires both the free flow of capital and its regulation by common rules which allow the 'law of value', which is the logic of capitalism, to arbitrate conflicts between states and resolve crises (cf. Gilbert and Witteveen above). The IMF therefore should not be seen as the malign tool of American imperialism but as the embodiment of this objective logic.

Rowthorn puts more emphasis on the political imperatives than the economic. His interpretation is that governments have exhausted the power of inflation to arrest the falling rate of profit; 'ever larger doses were needed' and eventually states were faced with just those hard choices that they had tried through inflation to avoid. The imposition of credit restrictions and the adoption of monetary targets caused the rate of profit to fall and this in turn led to a generalized world recession. The system itself was at risk because inflation rewarded the speculator and destroyed faith in the market by rewarding the strong at the expense of the weak. Like Samir Amin, Rowthorn also sees beyond the depression: 'During the next phase of capitalist development dynamism will shift from the present advanced capitalist countries toward the underdeveloped countries . . . and will represent a significant extension of the capitalist mode into hitherto unconquered areas.'[58]

Compared with either Mandel or Rowthorn, the Italian economist Riccardo Parboni has a much more acute awareness of the background of international monetary history and the place of currency roles and exchange rate manipulations in affecting the way in which different capitalist countries subjectively experienced the world depression.[59] His analysis of the dollar's role in the system leads to the observation that the United States was able to delay that experience until 1979, and to recover more quickly from the recession of the mid-1970s than its European partners. This is an important observation and is in sharp contrast to the perceptions of the American political determinists discussed earlier. While they see the United States sweating, like Atlas, to carry an intolerable burden, Parboni sees it in a position to exploit its relative invulnerability and the advantages of its domestic market to suffer later and less, and to recover sooner and faster, than other countries. Some comparative (US) figures on the utilization of surplus industrial capacity in the 1970s tell the same story[60] and the perception is shared by many Europeans. His conclusion, though, is much the same as Mandel's: capitalism in crisis loses its 'human face' and reverts to the 'wildcat capitalism', the 'unbridled cartelization' of earlier periods. Social democracy has failed to tame it and the workers of the Western industrialized world should regain their class consciousness, uniting with the socialist countries and the new masses of the Third World.

Parboni is typical of many European writers in seeking inspiration from the classical literature of political economy. The present crisis, he feels, has rehabilitated some of the ideas of Marx, Lenin and Schumpeter which had been prematurely declared obsolete. Marx saw crises in capitalist societies as redefining capitalist-worker relations. Lenin saw them as exacerbating conflict between capitalist states. Schumpeter saw them as strengthening oligopolies at the expense of small business. Parboni, anticipating disaster, draws on all three, rejecting Keynes's view that crises were merely an irrational aberration brought about by the perversity of the liquidity preferences of capitalists, and easily overcome by intelligent demand management.

The great weakness of Marxist interpretation of the current crisis is the same as the weakness of *Das Kapital*: the anticipation of a revolutionary response on the part of the workers. Marx proved mistaken in the expectation that the internal contradictions of capitalism would bring about the collapse of the system through revolution and its replacement by a socialist system in which money would no longer play a dominant part in human relations. In the 1980s the commonest weakness in Marxist interpretations is still the expectation that the collapsing capitalist world economy will bring together the workers of new and old industrialized countries in a common revolutionary cause. Amin and Rowthorn stand out as two writers who do not entertain such fond hopes and who see the internationalization of finance and banking as the Achilles' heel of the system, undermining political cooperation between governments and social classes and disrupting economic order.

Conclusion

Thus it seems that agreement on this key weakness is shared chiefly by those at opposite ends of a political spectrum: those who so object to the injustices of the capitalist system that they want to get rid of it altogether, and those who so highly value the freedom it promises from political tyranny and oppression that they seek to limit the state's involvement and thus its power to exploit it. Only those who are most keen to preserve it or to abolish it have eyes sharp enough to spot its weakest point — monetary mismanagement. Between them are to be found a few pragmatists, mostly senior officials like Gilbert or Witteveen or Schweitzer with long practical experience of the deterioration of order in the system. Only rarely are they academics.

The landscape of opinions surveyed in cursory fashion in the preceding pages therefore reveals a panorama dotted with individual names, rather than one strongly patterned with great blocs of defined schools of thought. Looking backwards, I am struck by the contributions to understanding of highly individual men — Minsky, Mandel, Triffin, Gilbert, Rowthorn — all of them essentially loners. None of them belonged to the great intellectual armies. The landscape of recent opinion therefore resembles not so much a continent divided into great plains and massive mountain ranges as it does an archipelago of volcanic peaks, randomly scattered about in a stormy and unsettled sea of ideas.

In sum, the last decade and more has been marked not by the triumph of coherent economic theories but by the general appearance of disarray. Considering the vast resources devoted in the Western world in the present century to the development of the study of economics, what is striking is that, instead of a rich harvest of convincing, well-documented explanations, we should find such poverty of theoretical interpretations of contemporary events.

This is surely a big change from the mid-century decades — the 1930s, 1940s and 1950s — when the great mass of expert opinion crowded into the middle ground, applauding the mixed economy and acknowledging the benefits of state intervention. Then, even Presidents of the United States could observe 'We are all Keynesians now', without anyone thinking it a remarkable statement. Though there were differences about ways and means of demand management, and about degrees of intervention and state support, large areas of agreement remained for this conventional congregation. It formed the intellectual base on which the centre parties of post-war France, Germany and Italy were built. This was where, in America, Democrats and new Republicans could agree and where, in Britain, Labour and Conservative could comfortably share the hybrid label of 'Butskellites'.

What happened in the 1970s, to judge by this cursory survey of contending interpretations of economic trends, was the totally unexpected impoverishment of this middle ground. It was not that the middle ground became exactly depopulated, for there were many in active politics or in academic economics who lingered there nostalgically. Like peasant farmers sentimentally attached to regions of declining marginal fertility, they were unwilling to leave, not knowing where else to go, and hoping in Micawber-fashion for something in the way of theoretical inspiration to turn up. It was just that it no longer yielded satisfactory rational explanations for the failures of government intervention and the malfunctioning of the system. It held little promise of permanent and effective solutions to pressing political problems.

There were two major reasons for this impoverishment, and neither is hard to find. One, obviously, was the accelerated internationalization of markets, and the incorporation, directly or indirectly, of ever larger parts of national economies into a world market system. In that system, because capital and technology moved easily across state borders, the assumptions that underlay the Keynesian middle ground about the power of government to order matters within the state no longer held good. Secondly and coincidentally, the same assumptions were being undermined by another major change. This was the overburdening of the bureaucratic machinery and the public sector budgets in most of the advanced economies. Mounting demands for social services and welfare systems — and in some cases for defence — often came on top of perceived needs for the state to find money both to support ailing old industries and to invest in advanced new ones. In such circumstances where state spending takes over half the national income, to ask governments to act as countervailing forces to correct the stubborn stickiness or the perverse pessimism of the market operators, is very different from making the same request when the proportion of public spending is down around 20 per cent. This is a point often reiterated by Milton Friedman and never adequately answered by the neo-Keynesians. As with other factors and situations, there comes a point where diminishing returns set in and when the old magic is no longer effective.

It is this intellectual impoverishment of the middle ground that I suspect is the most likely explanation for the resort by so many contemporary writers to different forms of determinism in their explanatory accounts of the events of the 1970s, and especially of developments in the monetary system. For determinism, whether economic, technical or political, is the social and political equivalent of existentialism for the individual. The existentialist writers of the 1950s and 1960s, following Sartre, held that individual choices and actions were shaped by the experiences imposed by the exogenous forces of society. Society, therefore, not the individual, was to blame for whatever consequences followed. The individual was exculpated and need feel no guilt if his or her acts were aberrant or destructive. In much the same way, the determinism that regards the choices made by governments as being conditioned and imposed by Kondratiev long waves, by technological change, or by the loss of some political predominance has the same superficial plausibility and leads to the same convenient conclusion that we need look no further for the source of our present ills.

By contrast, those who *do* look further and who are more familiar with the choices made by policy makers in the course of the last 20 years (or some would say in the last 40 years) find it hard to see anything inevitable or unavoidable about the present state of the monetary and financial system. Whether the attention to monetary history and to the political debates behind it comes from direct experience in government or banking or from academic study, it almost always leads to a common rejection, in my experience, of both the determinist fallacies and the exaggeration of trade policies as a cause of economic depression.

Such social determinism has a stultifying effect on the making of economic theory precisely because it always sees the causes of economic, and especially of monetary, problems as lying outside the realm of economics and therefore beyond the theorist's reach. Either it is technology or the Arabs, or else it is the labour unions or the media who have induced exaggerated expectations of non-stop increases in consumption. Whatever is to blame, economic theory can find no essentially economic answer because the root problem is not economic. That is true enough. But what is striking is the consequent failure even to try to look seriously for the explanation of the determining factor. Why was it that the United States could not or would not adjust to higher oil prices by non-inflationary means? Why was it that financing the Vietnam war could not be done by fiscal means? After all, the higher commodity prices during the Korean war had been met by the United States taking a lead in rationing consumption and controlling prices. And, although the examples are not too many, nevertheless there have been countries who fought wars without letting inflation rip.

Such social determinism is also consistent with (and indeed is only possible under) two conditions. One is that the element of choice in the management of money and finance (and especially of choice in the regulation of processes of credit creation and supervision over access to credit) is denied or else taken for granted. Whatever is, must be held to be inevitable. And the second condition is that the analysis of production, employment and trade must be divorced and treated in isolation from the management of money. Possibly because different international organizations are involved and international organizations do not easily communicate with one another, this intellectual separatism is easier to practise internationally than at the national level. But the separation then allows those who seek for explanations to look no further than the immediate financial circumstances of the firm or the state. Perhaps that is why both the monetarists, who take a rather moral attitude towards the management of money, and the Marxists, who assume a totally amoral attitude to money in the capitalist system, find it easier than most to avoid these two pitfalls. Both start from the contrary — and in my view, correct — assumption that the management of credit is necessarily highly political; that it is the way in which it is managed or mismanaged in a world market economy which makes or mars the world economy, and that it was political decisions regarding money and finance in the history of the world's monetary system in recent years which, more than anything else, determined the distribution across states and across classes of gains and losses, risks and opportunities.

Notes

1. See, for example, *The Economist*, 13 November 1982, which entitled an article, 'Import or Die — Protectionism would be the surest way to intensify world slumpflation'. Each of the 88 countries involved, it wrote, 'seems likely to believe that if it can improve its trade balance, it will shuffle off some of its joblessness. Since each country's improvement in trade balance is some other country's deterioration in it, this looks like a recipe for a mad Gatter's tea party, and an ill from which the world has suffered before. The London *Times*, the *Financial Times*, the *New York Times* and the *Wall Street Journal* all wrote similar dire warnings of the price of failure to stem the

rising tide of protectionism.

2. Joseph S. Davis, *The World Between the Wars 1919–39*, Baltimore, Johns Hopkins University Press, 1975.

3. J. Schumpeter, *Business Cycles*, 2 vols., New York and London, McGraw-Hill, 1939.

4. W. A. Lewis, *Economic Survey 1919–39*, London, Allen & Unwin, 1949, reprinted 1970, p. 165.

5. R. Nurkse (ed.), *International Currency Experience: Lessons of the Inter-War Period*, Princeton for the League of Nations, LN IIA, 4, 1944.

6. W. Ashworth, *A Short History of the International Economy Since 1850*, 3rd edition, London, Longman, 1975.

7. Royal Institute of International Affairs, *Monetary Policy and the Depression*, London, Allen & Unwin, 1933.

8. Quoted in J. A. Salter, *Recovery, the Second Effort*, 2nd edition, London, G. Bell & Sons Ltd., 1933, p. 101. For a larger study of this issue, see Irving Fisher, *Booms and Depressions*, London, Allen & Unwin, 1932; and *Debt-Deflation Theory of Great Depressions*, London, Allen & Unwin, 1933.

9. L. Robbins, *The Great Depression*, London, Macmillan, 1938.

10. For a full discussion of this factor, see M. Friedman and A. Schwartz, *A Monetary History of the United States 1867–1960*, Princeton, New Jersey, Princeton University Press, 1963.

11. The Bank for International Settlements mentioned the fact that at the beginning of 1931 short-term debt aggregated more than 50 billion Swiss francs or $2 billion, although this magnitude was not known at the time (Second *Annual Report*, 1932). $2 billion represented some 16 per cent of total world reserves. The comparable figure for Euroloans to non-oil developing countries in 1980 would be 50 per cent of world reserves.

12. S. V. O. Clarke, *Central Bank Cooperation 1924–31*, New York, Central Reserve Bank, 1967.

13. F. L. Block, *The Origins of International Economic Disorder*, Berkeley and London, University of California Press, 1977.

14. C. Freeman, J. Clark, L. Soete, *Unemployment and Technical Innovation*, Westport, Conn.: Greenward Press, 1982, especially Chap. 7 on 'Schumpeter's Theory of Business Cycles and Innovation'. See also A. Maddison, *Phases of Capitalist Development*, Oxford, Oxford University Press, 1982.

15. T. S. Kuhn, *The Structure of Scientific Revolutions*, Chicago, Chicago University Press, 1962.

16. W. Rostow, *The World Economy: History and Prospect*, Austin, Texas, University of Texas Press, 1976; *Getting From Here to There*, New York, McGraw-Hill, 1978; and *Why the Poor get Richer and the Rich Slow Down*, London, Macmillan, 1980.

17. James G. March, 'The Power of Power', in David Easton (ed.), *Varieties of Political Theory*, Englewood Cliffs, N.J., Prentice-Hall, 1966, Vol. 1, p. 54, quoted by Robert Keohane, 'Inflation and American Power', in R. Lombra and W. Witte (eds), *Political Economy of International and Domestic Monetary Relations*, Ames, Iowa State University Press, 1982. An earlier and better known work, using the same definition was Klaus Knorr, *The Power of Nations: the political economy of international relations*, New York, Basic Books, 1975.

18. C. P. Kindleberger, *The World in Depression*, London, Allen Lane, The Penguin Press, 1973.

19. R. Gilpin, *The U.S. and the Multinational Corporation*, New York, Basic

Books, 1975.

20. *International Studies Quarterly*, Winter 1983, for example, included lengthy reviews by C. Kindleberger and two other contributors. The full title was *The Rise and Decline of Nations: Economic Growth, Stagflation and Social Rigidities*, New Haven, Harvard University Press, 1982. The earlier book was *The Logic of Collective Action*, Cambridge, Mass.: Harvard University Press, 1975.

21. S. Strange and R. Tooze (eds). *The International Management of Surplus Capacity*, London, Allen & Unwin, 1981. See Editors' contributions.

22. Cf. F. Duchêne, *Industrial Adjustment Policies of Western Europe*, London, Macmillan, 1984.

23. R. C. Matthews (ed.), *Slower Growth in the Western World*, London, Heinemann, 1982.

24. Among them, Dankwart Rustow, Louis Turner, Zuhayr Mikdashi, Michael Tanzer and Edith Penrose. Of these writers Blair was and Rustow and Penrose are themselves American. Expert opinion is not differentiated by nationality.

25. John M. Blair, *The Control of Oil*, London, Macmillan, 1977.

26. R. Triffin, *The Evolution of the International Monetary System*, Princeton, New Jersey, Princeton University Press, 1964; *The Dollar Crisis*, New Haven, Yale University Press, 1960; *The World Money Maze*, New Haven, Yale University Press, 1966.

27. See, for example, the contributions of J. Tumlir and V. Curzon to Strange and Tooze, *The International Management of Surplus Capacity*, op. cit.

28. Milton Friedman, *Inflation and Unemployment: The New Dimension of Politics*, Nobel Lecture, 1977, published London, Institute of Fiscal Affairs, Paper No. 51, 1977. Cf. Martin Mayer, *The Fate of the Dollar*, New York, Times Books, 1980.

29. Though, as Minsky says, 'The very definition of equilibrium that is relevant for a capitalist economy with money differs from the definition used in standard Walrasian theory', Hyman Minsky, 'The Financial Instability Hypothesis', mimeo, 1981, p. 3, published as *Can 'it' happen again? Essays on instability and finance*, Armonk, New York, M. E. Sharpe, 1982.

30. Minsky, op. cit., 'Debt-deflation processes in today's international environment, *Banca Nazionale del Lavoro*, December, 1982.

31. *Can 'it' happen again?*, op. cit., p. 8.

32. J. P. Fitoussi, 'Politique monétaire passive ou politique economique?' *Observatoire français des Conjonctures Economiques*, Paris, June 1982.

33. Notably among some Scandinavian economists. See also Tibor Scitovsky, 'Market Power and Inflation', *Economica*, August 1978; and *The Just Economy* (1980).

34. Meghnad Desai, *Testing Monetarism*, New York, St Martin's Press, 1981.

35. A notable exception: Wolfgang Hager, 'Europe and Protection', *International Affairs*, Summer 1982.

36. C. Stoffaes, *Les Grandes Menaces Industrielles*, Paris, Calmann-Lévy, 1978.

37. R. McKinnon, 'Inflationary and deflationary world money', *American Economic Review*, June 1982, p. 23.

38. R. McKinnon, *A new bipartite monetary agreement or a limping dollar standard*, Princeton Essay in International Finance, 1974.

39. Milton Gilbert, with posthumous editing by Peter Oppenheimer and Michael Dealtry, *The Quest for World Monetary Order: the Gold-Dollar System and its Aftermath*, New York and Chichester, Wiley, 1980, p. 236.

40. Johannes Witteveen, interviewed in *The Banker*, November 1982.

41. Perry Anderson, *Considerations on Western Marxism*, London, NLB, 1976, pp. 92–3.

42. See, for example, the work of Fernando Henrique Cardoso and Guillermo O'Donnell in D. Collier (ed.), *The New Authoritarianism in Latin America*, Princeton, New Jersey, Princeton University Press, 1979. Also Cardoso and E. Faletto, *Dependency and Development in Latin America*, Berkeley, University of California Press, 1979, and O'Donnell, *Modernization and Bureaucratic-Authoritarianism: Studies in South American Politics*, Berkeley, University of California Press, 1973.

43. Among them, one could cite Louis Althusser, *Lenin and Philosophy*, London, NLB, 1971; and Nicos Poulantzas, *Political Power and Social Classes*, London, Verso, 1978 (originally published, London, NLB, Duckworth Press, 1973).

44. What, and who, is Marxist and who not is an insoluble question and the source of much fruitless debate. In my view 'Marxist' is a status — like 'liberated woman' — that can only be self-defined. In either case, you are one, if you think you are.

45. A. Emmanuel, *The Economics of Unequal Exchange: A Study of the Imperialism of Trade*, London and New York, Monthly Review Press, 1971 and *Le Profit et les Crises: une approche nouvelle des contradictions du capitalisme*, Paris, François Maspero, 1974.

46. See also T. Hopkins and I. Wallerstein (eds), *World Systems Analysis*, Beverly Hills, California, Sage Publications, 1982. Also I. Wallerstein, *The Capitalist World Economy*, Cambridge and London, Cambridge University Press, 1979; *The Modern World System*, London, Academic Press, 1974.

47. J. Galtung, *Social Imperialism and Sub-Imperialism: Continuities in the Structural Theory of Imperialism*, Oslo, University of Oslo, 1975. Cf. Andre Gunder Frank, *The Development of Under-Development*, Boston, Mass., Free Press, 1966.

48. The argument in more concentrated form can also be found in two interviews given by S. Amin, reported in *Politica Internazionale*, and published in S. Amin, *Class and Nation: Historically and in the Current Crisis*, New York, Monthly Review Press, 1980.

49. H. Magdoff and Paul Sweezy, *The Deepening Crisis of US Capitalism*, New York, Monthly Review Press, 1969. D. Calleo, *The Imperious Economy*, Cambridge, Mass.: Harvard University Press, 1982.

50. Andrew Glyn, 'The Productivity Slow-Down: A Marxist View' in R. C. O. Matthews, *Slower Growth in the Western World*, London, Heinemann, 1982, p. 149.

51. S. de Brunhoff, *La Crise de L'État*, Paris, Presses Universitaires de Grenoble, François Maspero, 1976; *State, Capital and Economic Policy*, London, Pluto Press, 1978. She has also written *Monnaie chez Marx* (translated from the French 1976), New York, Umzen Books Inc., 1976.

52. A. O. Hirschman, 'Rural Interpretations of Market Society: civilizing, destructive or feeble?', *Journal of Economic Literature*, December 1983.

53. Dobb was a Cambridge economist; Kalecki, whose work anticipated Keynes' General Theory, was a Pole who emigrated to Britain but returned to Poland in 1955. The same view was taken by Nicos Poulantzas, whose early death by suicide lost a potential leader in Marxist thought.

54. Perhaps more commonly hinted at now in Eastern Europe but see also such writers as Jacques Attali, 'L'acception des règles de l'économie mondiale est irréversible,' *La Parole et L'Outil*, Paris, 1977.

55. E. Mandel, *The Second Slump*, London, NLB, 1977, p. 180. Originally

published in German as *Ende der Krise oder Krise ohne Ende* — The End of the Crisis or Crisis without End. *Late Capitalism*, revised Edition, London, Verso, 1978.

56. R. Rowthorn, *Capitalism, Conflict and Inflation*, London, Lawrence and Wishart, 1980.

57. Both refer back to the same study, *British Capitalism: Workers and the Profit Squeeze*, by Andrew Glyn and Bob Sutcliffe, Harmondsworth, Middlesex, The Macmillan Press, 1972. The falling rate of profit was also documented by W. Nordhaus in A. Okun and Perry, *The Falling Share of Profits*, Washington DC, Brookings Paper No. 1, 1974.

58. Rowthorn, op. cit., p. 122. The quotation recalls Marx's prescient vision of 'the entanglement of all peoples in the net of the world market and with this the growth of the international character of the capitalist regime', *Capital*, Vol. I.

59. R. Parboni, *The Dollar and its Rivals: recession, inflation and international finance*, Etais Libri, Milano, 1980, tr. from Italian, *Finanza e crisis internazionale*, 1980.

60. Strange and Tooze, op. cit., p. 4.

2
The Theorists and the Real World
John Williamson*

International monetary economists like to pride themselves that theirs is a field characterized by a rather close relationship between theory and policy. They point to the origin of the monetary approach to the balance of payments in the IMF's lending programmes in Latin America, or the origins of the SDR in Triffin's diagnosis of the fragility of the gold-exchange standard, to illustrate the interdependence of theorists and officials. These close links were symbolized by the Bellagio Group, a joint group of academics and officials that met once or twice a year from 1964 to the mid-1970s to discuss the state of the international monetary system and the negotiations for its reform.[1] More recently Rudiger Dornbusch has written:[2]

> Unlike the pure theory of trade, open economy macroeconomics has become an applied and policy-oriented area of study. Models increasingly formulate the issues of the day — overshooting, real wage resistance, supply shocks, and virtuous and vicious circles. Moreover, as theories made their appearance, they soon had their painful encounters with empirical testing. Perhaps this is an optimistic picture of our field, but it does seem alive and kicking.

Compared to the levels of abstraction found in some other branches of economics, it is obviously true that international monetary economics has a close relationship with the real world — a feature that does not, incidentally, place the field particularly high in professional esteem, though most of its practitioners seem to exhibit a healthy indifference to this fact. But that still leaves open important questions. Has the academic community influenced the course of events? Have the theorists provided prompt and adequate intellectual guidance to those charged with policy formation? Has the agenda for academic research responded to the evolution of events?

* This chapter was completed in January 1983. A preliminary version was presented at seminars at Chatham House, City University and Princeton University. The author gratefully acknowledges comments made on those occasions, and in particular the helpful contribution of Jorge Braga de Macedo, Rudiger Dornbusch, Peter Kenen, Tadeusz Rybczynski and Susan Strange. The usual disclaimer applies.

Four subject areas are taken up in this chapter in the search for answers to those questions. The first is the reform negotiations. The second is the theory of floating exchange rates. The third is the monetary approach to the balance of payments. The fourth is the operation of the post-1973 international monetary 'system' (or 'non-system', as some believe semantic accuracy dictates it be called). Between them these cover the main subjects that international monetary economists studied in the 1970s.

The 'theorists' alluded to in the title of this chapter are, like the proverbial elephant, easier to identify than to define. They are those who write about international monetary economics in the professional economic journals, who attend conferences on the subject, and who teach it in universities. Most received a Ph.D. from a leading graduate school in the United States and, although they are scattered widely around the world, most retain close intellectual links with the United States. The officials and politicians who may or may not make use of academic developments in international monetary economics in the 'real world' are those in the key decision-making positions in the central banks and Finance Ministries of the non-communist countries, and also in the international organizations concerned with macroeconomic policy (the International Monetary Fund, the OECD, the European Community and the Bank for International Settlements). There are of course individuals who alternate between the academic and the 'real' worlds.

The reform negotiations

The probability that the Bretton Woods system would one day break down in a crisis of confidence had been accepted by most academic economists for years, ever since Triffin's writings in 1959. It is therefore not surprising that there was a measure of consensus about the nature of the reforms that should be sought when President Nixon suspended the gold convertibility of the dollar in August 1971. A good idea of mainstream thought at the time can be gleaned from Lawrence Krause's widely-acclaimed pamphlet *Sequel to Bretton Woods*,[3] published within a month of 15 August. His main proposals may be summarized as follows:

(i) Re-establishment of a system of pegged exchange rates, with par values expressed in terms of the SDR as numéraire, but a continuation of dollar intervention.

(ii) A wider band (margins of $2\frac{1}{2}$–3 per cent on either side of parity), and an inner band within which intervention would be prohibited.

(iii) Substitution of foreign exchange holdings (in excess of working balances) and gold in exchange for SDRs issued by the IMF. Former issuers of reserve currencies would have accepted an SDR liability to the IMF, and gold revaluation profits would have been devoted to development finance.

(iv) A positive IMF responsibility to prevent the emergence of exchange rate misalignments, consisting of an obligation to recommend exchange rate changes publicly and a requirement to authorize small par value changes whenever there was a presumption (evidenced either by spot exchange rates persistently on one side of parity or persistent intervention) that a country — including the United States — required adjustment.

Krause's proposals thus involved a combination of limited exchange rate flexibility, a quick move to adoption of the SDR as the principal reserve asset, and strengthened international management. Academics were not, of course, unanimous in their support of such a programme: there were also Friedmanian monetarists who wanted free floating and saw that as something of a panacea, nascent global monetarists who had just been converted to fixed exchange rates on the argument that flexibility aided adjustment only if there were money illusion, dollar standard advocates who didn't want to do anything much except allow countries to repeg to the dollar as they saw fit, not to mention the inevitable quota of gold bugs. But the consensus in favour of an internationally managed SDR standard with limited flexibility appeared to have broader support than it is customary to find among academics.

Comparison of Krause's proposals with the *Reform Report* agreed by the IMF's Executive Board in mid-1972 shows that the initial thrust of official thought ran parallel to the prevailing academic consensus. It is true that the official world never brought itself to the point of explicitly endorsing small par value changes, as opposed to formulas like 'prompter and therefore probably smaller' changes. But the *Report* advanced the mainstream analysis by recognizing that the essential objective of Krause's (iii) was the introduction of asset settlement, and it exhibited considerable ingenuity in devising alternative mechanisms that could secure that end while not requiring countries to give up the bulk of their gold and dollars for SDRs. Academics and officials were on the same wavelength.

However, compare Krause's proposals with the provisions of the Second Amendment to the IMF Articles agreed at Jamaica in January 1976 when the reform negotiations ended, and a completely different picture emerges. Instead of internationally supervised limited flexibility, there was the legalization of generalized floating — unlimited flexibility, with much intervention but only a figleaf of international surveillance. There was still lip-service to the objective of making the SDR the principal reserve asset, but there was no substantive action to promote that objective. The nearest approach to implementing one of Krause's proposals was the agreement to auction off one-sixth of the IMF's gold and devote the profits to a Trust Fund for the benefit of developing countries.

Why did the outcome differ so totally from the original intentions? Was the academic consensus fundamentally flawed? Were the negotiators suddenly convinced of the intellectual force of one of the rival schools? Or did they find themselves overcome by the force of events and incapable of giving effect to their intentions?

I have argued elsewhere[4] that the dominant factor influencing the course of events was the unwillingness to make commitments that would involve a sacrifice of monetary sovereignty. The United States had grown accustomed to the luxury of operating its monetary policy without an external constraint, and was reluctant to return to a situation conceived as one of 'the tail wagging the dog'. The Europeans had found the constraints on monetary sovereignty inherent in a dollar standard unacceptable, but floating was seen as providing a release from those constraints that did not require others to accept additional constraints (asset settlement for the United States, limitations on the freedom of reserve composition by the rest of the world). And so the world slipped to a 'non-system' which did not require anyone to accept *ex ante* any substantial curtailment of its freedom of action.

This diagnosis implies that, if national attachments to monetary sovereignty are either (a) rational or (b) irremovable, one would have to accept that the academic consensus was indeed flawed. The evidence that the devotion to monetary sovereignty is strongly *irrational* — that is, that countries can expect to benefit markedly by a mutual surrender of monetary sovereignty — is not to date conclusive, although I believe it to be true. And since most countries operated the Bretton Woods system and the gold standard (both of which constrained monetary sovereignty) reasonably contentedly for substantial periods, it is difficult to believe that the attachment is irremovable. Nevertheless, I find it difficult to deny that those favouring the consensus treated the question of sovereignty too lightly.

It is quite clear, on the other hand, that the failure to reform the system cannot be explained by mass intellectual conversion of the negotiators. The adoption of generalized floating in March 1973 was in fact commemorated by an explicit decision of the Committee of Twenty (C-20) that the float was not the reform, but that, on the contrary, the reformed system would be based on 'stable but adjustable par values'. Similarly, the *Outline of Reform* published by the C-20 at the end of its deliberations and the Second Amendment both genuflect toward the objective of making the SDR the principal reserve asset. These facts preclude interpreting the difference between intention and outcome as an intellectual triumph for one of the minority schools.

Nevertheless, it is possible to go too far in denying the influence of the academics on the course of events, at least in the case of the move to generalized floating. The majority of academics had been arguing — one might even say campaigning — for years for greater exchange rate flexibility. It is true that many of the statements in the late 1960s were cast in the form of advocacy of limited flexibility rather than of floating, but the arguments used in support of limited flexibility were a subset of those used to advocate floating, and the majority of academics left the impression that they were urging limited flexibility only because they judged floating to be 'politically impossible'. The attitudes of major policy makers to the issue of flexibility were clearly not as rigid in early 1973 as they had been in 1966. In some cases the policy makers changed — in particular, Paul Volcker became US Under Secretary for Monetary Affairs in 1969, and Sir Douglas Allen (Lord Croham) became Permanent Secretary to HM Treasury in 1968. In other cases, views changed over the years: Dr Emminger's conversion to flexibility is the outstanding example. One normally supposes that the evolution of views is influenced by the intellectual milieu in which people mature and move, and it strains credulity to suppose that in this particular case the views of the policy makers were fashioned solely by the course of events. As a group, the politicians and officials would clearly have preferred in 1973 to maintain a managed system incorporating the adjustable peg had that not presented difficulties, but their willingness to make sacrifices to that end had been undermined by the years of preceding discussion and the growing conviction that floating would not be a disaster. I therefore conclude that, while the development of capital mobility was the dominant factor compelling abandonment of the adjustable peg, the academics cannot disclaim all responsibility for the turn that events took in 1973.

The retreat from an SDR standard cannot be similarly attributed to a softening-up operation by the academic majority. Academic proponents of either a dollar or a multiple reserve currency system have been few and far between.

Given that both floating and the abandonment of the SDR standard represented the easy way out for those who did not care to make explicit commitments limiting their monetary sovereignty, some might ask why one should attribute responsibility to the academics for floating but not for the absence of an SDR standard. The answer is that if everyone had gone on doing what they previously did for fear of the unknown alternatives we would today not have floating rates, but we would have some form of reserve currency system.

Exchange rate analysis

When generalized floating was adopted in March 1973, the academics, and especially those with a US orientation, were in general suggesting (a) that floating rates would move rather smoothly; (b) that floating would insulate countries from shocks to demand or inflation in the rest of the world; and (c) that floating would enhance the ability of countries to use monetary policy in furtherance of conjunctural policy. All those expectations were quickly proved wrong, the first one dramatically so. The reason for this failure of academic insight was that the then prevalent theory of the determination of a floating exchange rate, the Mundell-Fleming model, was inadequate and in many respects misleading. This was remedied quite quickly by the development of the asset market approach, but the fact remains that the academic advocacy of floating was in large part based on a false prospectus.

Until the 1960s, the theory of floating exchange rates was essentially based on the assumption of capital immobility. It was of course recognized that short-term capital flows occur under floating, and indeed there was a lively debate as to whether such flows might not be destabilizing—a debate dominated by Friedman's contention that speculators could destabilize only if they were prepared to lose money. It was also no doubt recognized that long-term capital flows could occur with a floating rate, but such flows were regarded as exogenous. The essence of the theory of a floating rate was that the rate would adjust to clear the current account. This led directly to the theorem that floating would insulate an economy from shocks to foreign demand or inflation (or interest rates). Combined with the prevalent elasticity optimism of the period, it also implied that floating rates would move rather smoothly, whether the purpose were to offset differential inflation or to induce adjustment.

The writings of Robert Mundell and J. Marcus Fleming[5] in the early 1960s introduced capital mobility into the analysis in an essential way. The 'Mundell-Fleming model' assumed the *flow* theory of the capital account, in which a given interest rate differential is assumed to stimulate a given continuing capital flow. It also assumed, as did most models of that Keynesian-dominated period, that the price level was fixed (or at least pre-determined by some Phillips curve mechanism). This model also suggested that the exchange rate could be expected to move reasonably smoothly: even a change in the interest differential — the only case where the prediction would differ from that of the current balance model — would provoke an exchange rate change only to the extent necessary to change the current balance so as to transfer the change in the capital flow, which would be modest with high elasticities. The theorem that floating insulates a national economy from foreign shocks also survives in the Mundell-Fleming model so far as foreign shocks to prices and income are concerned, though not with respect to a shock to the foreign interest rate (since that changes the capital flow and thus the current balance). Finally, the Mundell-Fleming model concluded that floating would enhance the power of monetary policy to change income, even — indeed, especially — in the case of perfect capital mobility, where fiscal policy would become completely impotent. Given the assumption of price stability, the increase in income had to take the form of an increase in output: thus monetary policy was pictured as the prime, and efficient, tool of demand management policy under floating.

No doubt there were qualifications and reservations as to the adequacy of the Mundell-Fleming model and the accuracy of its predictions,[6] but there can be no question that the general thrust of economic analysis was guided by it. Economists did contrast the sudden lurches in exchange rates when parities were finally changed under the adjustable peg with the gradual adjustment to changing circumstances that floating would provide. They did deride the danger of undue volatility in a floating rate as a fantasy that would be realized only if there were a supply of stupid speculators intent on losing money. They did speak glowingly of the advantages of breaking the external constraint on monetary policy.

The reality proved, as we now know, very different. A professional response was not long in coming, in the form of the 'asset-market approach'. An early (1973) forerunner of this was Stanley Black's use of rational expectations, followed by a paper of Rudiger Dornbusch and the thesis of Pentti Kouri.[7] But the main impact on the profession came only with the Saltsjobaden (Stockholm) conference on 'Flexible Exchange Rates and Stabilization Policy' in August 1975.[8] The important papers there were those of Dornbusch, Frenkel, Kouri and Mussa, all of whom came to the subject strongly influenced by the Chicago intellectual tradition. But much of the subsequent vast outpouring of additional modelling, by (among the most prominent) Argy, Barro, Branson, Buiter, Calvo, Frenkel, Henderson, Isard, Kenen, Krugman, Obstfeld, Rodriguez, Sachs, and Salop, owed a great deal to the competitive Yale tradition of portfolio-balance modelling.

The asset-market approach is deliberately called an 'approach' or 'view', rather than a 'theory' or 'model', because of the absence of any single way of representing the behavioural relations regarded as central to the new line of thought. The basis of the asset-market view is the hypothesis that foreign exchange markets are dominated by the need to ensure that outstanding *stocks* of the several currencies are willingly held. This stands in contrast to both of the earlier models, where equilibrium in the exchange market was viewed as determined by the *flows* on current and capital accounts summing to zero. *Ex post* those flows must of course sum to zero (after adding in any intervention that may have occurred); the point is that potential stock adjustments are so large relative to current account flows as to justify disregarding the latter and concentrating on the conditions for stock equilibrium. Over time current account imbalances will redistribute wealth internationally, and in that way may change the conditions that determine stock equilibrium. If so, the expectation of *future* wealth redistribution will mean that an unanticipated current account imbalance will exert an *immediate* impact on the conditions that determine stock equilibrium. Nevertheless, the fundamental point is that one can and must model the exchange rate (along with other asset prices) as determined by the conditions for stock (asset-market) equilibrium.

The asset-market approach improves on the Mundell-Fleming model in three ways.

(i) It incorporates the stock theory of the capital account, which derives from portfolio theory, in place of the *ad hoc* flow theory of the 1950s.

(ii) It recognizes that asset holders know that relative international yields have two components, nominal interest rates and exchange rate changes, rather than always assuming the latter are expected to be zero.

(iii) It can accommodate the postulate that asset holders form expectations of exchange rate changes in a systematic way.

The simplest version of the asset-market approach is a 'monetary model', where the interaction between the demand and supply of money in each country determines the national price levels, and purchasing power parity (PPP) then determines the exchange rate so as to equate prices internationally. There are four main ways in which that simple framework has been extended in order to provide models capable of illuminating the real world (as opposed to misleading the simple-minded).[9]

First, it is possible to introduce imperfect mobility of goods, so that changes in competitiveness (and, in a non-small economy, the terms of trade) are possible. The trade balance depends on competitiveness, and the exchange rate depends on the interaction between goods and asset markets even with perfect capital mobility.

A second extension involves the assumption that expectations are 'rational' (i.e. forward-looking and essentially correct) rather than 'static' (i.e. assuming indefinite perpetuation of the present). The domestic interest rate must then be equal to the foreign interest rate plus the rate of depreciation. It is this type of model which shows that the exchange rate may overshoot in response to certain types of shock, notably to changes in monetary policy.

A third extension, motivated by portfolio theory, introduces imperfect substitutability of assets denominated in different currencies, which allows emergence of a risk premium and breaks the equality between rates of return on different currencies. This leads to exchange rates being influenced by current and prospective supplies of assets denominated in different currencies, and (typically) also by the distribution of world wealth, both of which provide additional channels through which current account imbalances may influence exchange rates.

A final dimension in which the models differ is with respect to the theory of inflation embodied. This may be the Keynesian assumption of price stability, or the simple quantity theory model of inflation, or the global monetarist hypothesis that prices are determined by arbitrage from abroad, or slightly more complex models such as a Phillips curve specification where the change in prices depends on excess demand and inflationary inertia, or a distributive conflict model where labour insists on a certain real wage.

The stylized facts of exchange rate volatility, continued cyclical synchronization, and constrained monetary freedom, which appear so paradoxical through the eyes of the Mundell-Fleming model, seem entirely natural when viewed in terms of the asset-market approach. It is worth elaborating on what the asset-market models imply for each of these topics, since that provides a convenient way of summarizing the main implications that have so far been drawn from the new theory.

The asset-market models certainly suggest that one should expect floating rates to exhibit much volatility (a better word than 'instability', which raises the red herring of rates shooting off to zero or infinity). The basic idea is that exchange rates are what they are because those are the levels that equate the risk-adjusted expected yields of holding the several currencies. Anything that changes those expected yields — any 'news' — must therefore be expected to have an impact on exchange rates. Moreover, certain changes in expectations may have a very large impact on rates. Suppose, to take the classic example, that there were a single once-for-all unexpected monetary expansion. This would induce a fall in the interest rate in that currency. In order to induce wealth-holders to hold the larger stock of that money despite the decline in the interest rate, it would be necessary that they be compensated by an expected future capital gain from *appreciation*. But to provide a base from which the rate could be expected to appreciate, it would first be necessary that it depreciate sufficiently far to create an expectation of a subsequent rebound; i.e. that it depreciate by *more* than needed to achieve the new equilibrium with proportionately higher prices following the monetary expansion. In other words, the rate must *overshoot*; even a once-for-all monetary expansion must be expected to induce a more-than-proportionate depreciation. A more rapid rate of monetary expansion expected to continue into the future would produce even more dramatic effects, since the domestic interest rate would be expected to decline semi-permanently, which could be offset only by an expected indefinite appreciation. In the limit, there is *no* exchange rate adjustment that can restore portfolio equilibrium under perfect capital mobility, when faced with a change in monetary policy that changes the expected permanent inflation differential without an equal change in the nominal interest differential. On the other hand, a monetary expansion that was expected to be reversed in the following period would produce no more than a hiccup in the exchange rate, because a marginal depreciation would suffice to create the expectation of a subsequent appreciation large enough to compensate for the temporary decline in the interest rate. Hence exchange rates depend very sensitively, not just on hard monetary news, but on the interpretation placed on the latest 'monetary' news. Nor is it just monetary news that is relevant. An unexpectedly favourable current account, in particular, may lead the market to revise its estimate of the equilibrium real exchange rate and its expectation of the extent to which claims to wealth will be transferred to residents, who presumably have a relatively high propensity to hold claims denominated in domestic currency. Both effects imply an ultimate appreciation of the national currency, and therefore the market will in anticipation induce an appreciation as soon as the 'news' breaks. And similarly with political news. Given that the world is a very unpredictable place with lots of news it is hardly surprising that floating rates are volatile rates.

Continued cyclical synchronization is a second stylized fact that is easily explained by the asset-market approach. Suppose that country A develops a boom. The traditional current balance model argued that this would cause its currency to depreciate to the extent needed to keep the current account in balance, and thus prevent the boom spilling over abroad. The Mundell-Fleming model implies that a domestic boom which encounters an accommodative monetary policy will be similarly confined to its country of origin, but that this is not true with a monetary policy dedicated to targeting the money supply rather than the interest rate. In the latter event, the boom will raise interest rates and attract a capital inflow, which will finance a current account deficit; that deficit is of course a surplus which stimulates income in the rest of the world. The asset-market approach suggests that the boom will be transmitted abroad even if monetary policy is accommodative (and *a fortiori* if it is not). The reason is that, since booms are temporary, an initial depreciation will create expectations of a rebound and thus attract a capital inflow even without a rise in interest rates. Indeed, the stylized fact that trade flows respond rapidly to changes in income but only slowly to changes in relative prices implies that a boom must induce a current deficit in the short run whatever happens to the exchange rate; the asset-market approach enables one to understand why a depreciation will enable that current deficit to be financed by a capital inflow. But note that, since a depreciation will induce a capital inflow only when it is expected to be temporary, one expects that floating will fail to provide the traditional insulation only in respect of *temporary* shocks. Since inflation is highly serially correlated, it is typically better viewed as a permanent shock, which explains why floating is still capable of effectively neutralizing differential inflation.

The reason that monetary policy failed to provide the effective lever over the level of output that the Mundell-Fleming model had promised it would, is that nominal wages are not fixed as the model assumes. Monetary expansion can indeed increase nominal income, but the trouble is that it may take the form of an increase in prices rather than output, since nominal wages are typically flexible (at least upward). The most important theorem so far established, by Sachs,[10] is that with perfect capital mobility and a fixed *real* wage the conclusions of the Mundell-Fleming model need to be reversed: that is, expansionary fiscal policy can increase output, but expansionary monetary policy cannot. To see why, consider first the case of monetary expansion. The traditional argument was that this would cause a depreciation and that would generate a current surplus which would expand output. But a real depreciation would also reduce the real wage, so if that is not possible the monetary expansion must be entirely absorbed by inflation. Fiscal expansion, in contrast, causes an appreciation which increases the price of output relative to that of imports and thereby permits the same real wage in terms of consumer goods to be reconciled with a lower real wage in terms of output, and therefore more output. The cost is, of course, a bigger current account payments deficit. After the strict assumptions on which that result is based (no lags in wage adjustment, perfect capital mobility, and so on) are relaxed, my impression is that the general theorem says that fiscal expansion with a floating rate can increase output, at the cost of an increased current account deficit but without necessarily inducing much extra inflation; while monetary expansion can increase output at the expense of additional inflation, but without much cost in terms of the balance of payments. To the best of my knowledge, however, this theorem has not yet been rigorously formulated and established, although several strands of the literature, such as that on vicious and virtuous circles, point in that direction.

Mention of vicious and virtuous circles reminds one that a distinctively European literature, which reflected the widespread European concern that floating rates subvert rational economic management, emerged in the years following the move to floating. The origins of the idea that currency depreciation feeds through to domestic inflation, which subsequently causes further depreciation and hence inflation in a cumulative process, can be traced back to the inter-war period, as represented most particularly by the writings of Nurkse.[11] The idea was resurrected, first by journalists and officials, in the year after abandonment of the adjustable peg. It was given an element of academic respectability by Basevi and de Grauwe, but attacked from the other side of the Atlantic — most outspokenly by the US delegation to the OECD, and most subtly by John Bilson, who summoned the arts of contemporary model-building to argue that a vicious circle is an optical illusion reflecting the fact that monetary expansion depreciates the exchange rate before it inflates the price level.[12] The subject remained in acute need of amplification as the decade ended.

The development of the asset-market approach enables one to understand much better why generalized floating functioned as it did, even though empirical models of exchange rates have been notoriously unsuccessful to date.[13] But have the new theories influenced policy? They have certainly been invoked in policy arguments: Artus and Crockett's 1978 *Princeton Essay* on surveillance and Artus and Young's 1979 'Renewal of the Debate' on fixed versus flexible exchange rates both contain brief references to overshooting and allied ideas, and the 1979 Rio conference on the crawling peg contained papers by Black and others which brought the new theories to bear on the choice of an exchange-rate regime.[14] Nevertheless, the role of the new theories was marginal; neither the asset-market view nor the vicious circle hypothesis seems to have played a central role in motivating the adoption or form of the European Monetary System (EMS), or the intervention that brought to an end the exaggerated appreciation of the Swiss franc and depreciation of the dollar in late 1978. Those operations were more instinctive responses to crises than policy acts conditioned by a coherent body of theory. It is only in the 1980s, with Niehans' inquest into the 1980 sterling overvaluation and the recent Group of Thirty (G-30) papers by Mussa and Levich, that one begins to sense that the asset-market view is at last taking centre stage in policy discussions.[15]

The monetary approach

While the developers of the asset-market view may be able to escape the charge that they are the academic scribblers of a few years back to whom the practical men (and women) of today are in bondage, the monetarists of the 1960s can no longer take similar comfort in their unimportance. However much they may protest that governments have failed to implement their advice properly, the fact is that some government somewhere has recently been doing its best to implement almost any variant of monetarist advice that one can think of. Money supply targets, monetary base targets, wages free-for-alls, 'cleanly' floating exchange rates, strong exchange rates . . . name the advice, and a country that has adopted it springs readily to mind.

As the above remarks imply, monetarism is not a monolithic school. The main division is between the 'closed economy monetarists' who follow Milton Friedman in urging a constant growth rate of the money supply (or monetary base) and a freely floating exchange rate, and the 'open economy monetarists' who follow Robert Mundell in urging fixed exchange rates and non-sterilization of payments imbalances. Although it is the former group that has had the major impact on policy, except in the Southern Cone of South America, our interest here is primarily in the international monetarists, for it is they whose theoretical contributions dominated international monetary economics in the first half of the 1970s.

In that period, vast numbers of papers were written on some variation on the theme of how in a small open economy with a fixed exchange rate monetary policy is unable to influence anything except the level of reserves. Other papers dealt with the issue of 'what the monetary approach really is'. The definitive work was the collection of papers edited by Frenkel and Johnson and published in 1976. The following year the IMF produced a volume with an identical title containing papers written by its staff members over the years, which bore the interpretation of staking the Fund's claim to have been the pioneer in introducing the monetary approach.[16]

It is certainly true that the first 'monetary approach' papers arose from the involvement of the IMF in designing payments adjustment programmes in Latin America in the 1950s. It seems that both Robert Triffin, who spent the war years dispensing monetary advice to Latin American governments on behalf of the United States, and J. J. Polak, then Deputy Director of the Fund's Research Department, had brought a recollection of pre-war Benelux monetary analysis to bear on the Fund's early work. Triffin's analysis in the 1950s already showed awareness of the importance of the concept of 'internal credit monetization', or what we would now call domestic credit expansion,[17] while Polak's 1957 paper provided the first formal 'monetary approach' model and established the basic conclusions of the monetary approach, especially the theorem that at the margin domestic credit creation all ultimately leaks out abroad with a fixed exchange rate.[18] The Polak model became the standard basis for the operations of IMF country missions, though sometimes it seems to have been applied eclectically as one of several elements, while at other times its application may have been mechanistic and combined with the dubious (and dangerous) quantity theory assumption that all endogenous changes in nominal income involve changes in prices rather than output.

For a long time the Fund's approach was little known or regarded outside the Fund itself, and Robert Mundell displayed no awareness of its work in the papers he wrote in the 1960s which established Chicago as the intellectual home of international monetarism. In his hands and those of Harry Johnson, the monetary approach became not just a technical tool for bringing order to the external accounts of ill-administered countries, but a weapon for doing battle with a dominant Keynesian ideology. Devaluation was treated as merely a technique to reduce the real value of the money supply, while its Keynesian role as an instrument of expenditure switching was derided as dependent on money illusion. The elasticities analysis was dismissed as erroneous, rather than qualified as something whose *ceteris paribus* assumptions had to be carefully weighed when the analysis was used. Great play was made with the result that changes in real income, prices and interest rates have exactly the opposite implications for the balance of payments from those predicted by 'orthodox' theory:[19] increased real income and prices both increase the demand for money and therefore tend to create a balance of payments surplus, while a higher interest rate decreases money demand and therefore tends to generate a deficit. It is ironic that Harry Johnson, whose Ely lecture of 1970 had so brilliantly dissected the polemics practised by Keynes and Friedman in the Keynesian-monetarist controversy, should have adopted similar tactics in proselytizing for the monetary approach to the balance of payments.[20]

The main outlines of the monetary approach were already clear by 1970, but there were three significant developments in the early 1970s. The first involved the use of the theory to explain the outburst of global inflation. The basic story was that the US resort to monetary expansion to finance the budget deficit resulting from the

Vietnam war had spilled abroad through a payments deficit, which led to an expansion in world reserves because of the reserve currency role of the dollar. Those reserve increases led to monetary expansion, which fuelled a worldwide inflation that under fixed exchange rates was transmitted by arbitrage even to countries that might in the short run succeed in sterilizing their own reserve inflows.[21] The thesis that there is a dependable relationship between the quantity of global reserves and the level of world prices has been termed the 'international quantity theory'. It received much emphasis in the discussions on how the IMF should determine the level of SDR creation, with Johnson using it to argue that all SDR creation was inherently inflationary and would simply serve to increase world prices rather than real reserves in the long run.[22] The argument certainly received attention in policy-making circles in the IMF, but it was never accepted as correct. Subsequent empirical investigations have suggested that even under pegged exchange rates the link from reserves to money supplies is too loose to validate the international quantity theory.[23]

A second development crystallized at the Wingspread I conference in 1972. Papers by Argy and Kouri, and McKinnon, argued that, if more than one country attempted to sterilize reserve changes, the system would become unstable.[24] This conclusion is in fact a corollary of Mundell's theorem that under fixed exchange rates there is a unique equilibrium distribution of money in the world economy.[25] From this it follows that, if two (or more) countries both have money supply targets, they cannot both achieve them permanently (except of course if by happy coincidence they were consistent with the unique equilibrium distribution of money). But the attempts of both to achieve their targets will cause a continuing reserve shift from the country with a money supply that is high relative to equilibrium to the country with a target that is low (relative to equilibrium): the system is unstable. Under perfect capital mobility the system would break down instantaneously, and one country or other would have either to abandon its money supply target or to impose capital controls or to change its exchange rate (with the onus of action falling on the reserve-losing country unless the latter were a reserve centre). With imperfect capital mobility the breakdown would not be immediate, but the same options for policy choice would ultimately emerge.

McKinnon in particular has drawn policy implications from this analysis in a series of subsequent papers.[26] The basic recommendation is that countries pegging their mutual exchange rates should agree on consistent[27] rates of expansion of domestic credit, and should avoid sterilizing their reserve changes. This is clearly in the same family of ideas as the traditional IMF prescription that deficit countries should limit their rate of domestic credit expansion to a level consistent with a satisfactory payments outcome. The idea was conspicuous by its absence from the agenda of the C-20, and it has subsequently continued to be ignored at the global level. But some trace of this idea does seem to have permeated the thinking of the designers of the European Monetary System, inasmuch as a modification of monetary policy is supposed to be one of the prime candidates for action when a country hits the divergence indicator.

The third major development in the monetary approach was the emergence of what Marina Whitman christened 'global monetarism'.[28] This was associated primarily with the names of Robert Mundell and Arthur Laffer. It argues that the world economy has become so integrated that one should not treat national economies as a series of distinct though interdependent units, as is traditional, but as mere geographical subdivisions whose destinies are determined by the evolution of the system as a whole. Global monetarists make three central assumptions about the nature of the world (by which they mean the OECD augmented, for a brief spell in the late 1970s, by the Southern Cone): that arbitrage in goods is perfect, that assets denominated in different currencies are perfect substitutes, and that output is essentially fixed at full employment. From these assumptions — none of which in my judgment stands up to empirical examination — they derive their policy conclusions about the pointlessness of flexible exchange rates, the superiority of monetary union and the need for monetary discipline. Some though not all of the signatories of the All Saints' Day manifesto favouring creation of an inflation-proofed European parallel currency seem to have been inspired by this vision.[29] Most of the advocates of reinstatement of a gold standard, who pushed for appointment of the Gold Commission in the United States, seem to belong to the school.

But it is not at all clear how many of those economists who have characteristically conducted their analysis within the framework of the monetary approach would be prepared to subscribe to the global monetarist assumptions as useful approximations to reality (as opposed to convenient simplifications to incorporate in models designed to explore questions to which they are not central). Certainly there are recent signs that some leading monetarists are conscious of the need for more general models than those produced by sticking with the global monetarist assumptions. One thinks in particular of the development of moves to integrate the monetary and traditional approaches. There are two fundamentally different ways in which this can be done. One, which can be based on the assumption of capital immobility or the flow theory of the capital account, argues that income, interest rates and the balance of payments are determined simultaneously, *given* a predetermined money supply, but that the money supply adjusts over time depending on the payments outcome (with non-sterilization).[30] In IS/LM/BP terms, the short-run outcome is determined by the IS/LM intersection, but as long as that short-run equilibrium does not lie on BP there are payments flows which shift LM (and perhaps IS as well). Such models have orthodox Keynesian properties in the short run, and orthodox monetary properties in the long run. They resolve the famous contradiction between the predictions of monetary and orthodox models by pointing out that income, prices and interest rates are endogenous variables, whose variations may be associated with a change in the balance of payments in either direction, depending on the source of the variation.[31]

The second way of integrating the two approaches, first developed by Kouri and Porter in 1974, treats the monetary approach as the one that is valid in the short run, and the orthodox approach as relevant in a longer time frame.[32] Based on the stock theory of the capital account, they argue that the financial markets equilibrate day by day, in which time-frame income and prices — and therefore the current account — can be taken as pre-determined. Hence the payments balance is the part of the increase in demand for money that is not satisfied either by domestic credit expansion or by a current account surplus, where the latter is determined by conventional Keynesian variables.

The task that now confronts the theorists seems to be that of choosing between, or integrating, the two integrations that have been offered. A central question must be: which markets adjust more rapidly, goods markets or financial markets? And since the answer is surely the financial markets, there seems no doubt but that the Porter-Kouri version must find a place in any grand synthesis. With suitable modification, where payments flows drive the evolution of wealth rather than of the money supply *per se*, there seems no reason why the other approach should not also contribute to the grand synthesis. But the purpose of this chapter is that of reviewing past theoretical developments and their impact on events, not that of foreshadowing future theory, so the matter may be left here.

It is in any event now clear that orthodox and monetary approaches are correctly viewed as representing complementary aspects of reality rather than as mutually antagonistic. It is no doubt far too soon to expect this to have any impact on policy debates, and indeed the range of policy advice on offer shows no obvious sign of narrowing. In particular, I am not aware that the theoretical reconciliation has mellowed the advice to choose a 'strong currency option' that has been dispensed by international monetarists. And that advice has most certainly been influential. Belgium allowed itself to become grossly overvalued in the 'snake'; Mrs Thatcher's Britain passively watched the destruction of a substantial part of its manufacturing capacity; Argentina stuck with a decelerating pre-announced crawl despite the failure of its inflation rate to follow the programmed deceleration, until a new crisis exploded; and Chile terminated its crawl before its inflation and in consequence developed a massive current account deficit which in due course proved unsustainable. (Not all countries have made such disastrous errors: both Germany and Switzerland tempered their restrictive monetary policies when this was necessary to head off a critical degree of overvaluation.) There were economists who urged such policies: with the benefit of hindsight we can surely not doubt that they gave bad advice.

The functioning of the non-system

As the Jamaica meeting of the IMF's Interim Committee which agreed the Second Amendment was being planned, Peter Kenen invited a number of academics to contribute short assessments of the outcome to a special Princeton *Essay*. Eight of these invited papers appeared as *Reflections on Jamaica* early in 1976.[33] While several of the contributors drew satisfaction from some of the specific decisions, and Kindleberger welcomed the abandonment of grand designs, several regarded the rejection of the aims of the 1960s as a betrayal. One author, quickly joined by other economists, termed the arrangements to be legalized a 'non-system'. Haberler's sub-sequent quip that those calling it a non-system were those whose reform plans had been rejected *was* rather funny, for it contained an element of truth — but surely not the *whole* truth.

It is clear enough that the world functions at present without a monetary constitution: there are no international rules governing the choice of exchange rate regime, of a peg, or of margins; there are no substantive international restrictions or pressures on intervention policy, or on monetary-fiscal policy; and there are no limits on the choice of reserve assets, or on reserve switching. In that sense there can be no doubt that present arrangements constitute a 'non-system'. But of course on that test one would also have to speak of a 'price non-system', whereas perhaps the most basic test of an economist is his ability to understand how — and when, and to what extent — prices permit the efficient decentralization of decision-making. And so the question has kept cropping up in the literature: can the markets reconcile that which is not deliberately coordinated? Do the foreign exchange and capital markets resolve what Benjamin Cohen has termed the 'consistency objective'?[34] Or is there still a need for some mechanism to coordinate the actions of the various countries (and also of effectively extra-territorial actors like the Eurobanks) so as to ensure that the sum of the policies pursued adds up to a whole consistent with real global constraints?

Although I believe this to be the central issue and it has indeed cropped up in many forms — in the debates about locomotives and convoys, in the discussion of whether there is still a need to control international liquidity, on the future of gold, on the need to regulate the Euromarkets, on the case for a substitution account or evaluation of the emergent multiple reserve-currency system — it has not customarily been identified as the central issue. Apart from some of my own writing, the most explicit treatment would seem to have been that of Corden, who argued quite explicitly that there was no need for explicit coordination because capital flows and exchange rates could adjust to allow all countries to achieve their own 'internal and external balance' objectives whatever other countries were doing.[35] I have challenged some of Corden's arguments, but I believe I am representative of the profession in believing that neither of us has yet provided the definitive analysis of the question.

The lack of substantive academic analysis has not, however, prevented debate at the official level. The developing countries have tended to favour the restoration of a more structured system, and to that end the Group of 24 has commissioned a number of studies.[36] The OECD also advocated coordination, specifically in the form of the 'locomotive' and 'convoy' proposals for coordinated economic expansion. Opposition to such ideas has been led by conservative governments: at one stage Germany was the arch-conservative on these matters, but this role was usurped first by Mrs Thatcher's Britain and subsequently by President Reagan's United States. The Group of Thirty and the IMF have both tended to pursue a rather *ad hoc* line, calling for specific institutional reforms (such as a substitution account) or 'firm surveillance', within the context of existing arrangements. The debate has so far taken place without much of an intellectual framework.

On specific questions, academic contributions have been more substantial. There is, for example, a major literature now on the functioning of the Euromarkets, ranging from Swoboda's masterly taxonomy on multipliers to Herring and Marston's econometric estimates.[37] This provides a background for the debate over whether there is a need to regulate the Euromarkets with a view to both/either (a) controlling the growth of liquidity, and/or (b) reducing the danger of a collapse of the international banking system. The academics have not, however, played a particularly active part in the policy debate itself, which has been carried on more in the confines of the Bank for International Settlements and the Group of Thirty.

One topic on which the academics did appear to have achieved a measure of consensus, and in the process to have influenced policy, is the control of international liquidity. (The term 'international liquidity' is in this context used as a synonym for official reserves, rather than in the sense of private-sector liquid assets or credit availability that people usually have in mind when discussing regulation of the Euromarkets.) Haberler took the lead in arguing that this was not an important objective in the current international environment at the 1976 conference convened in memory of J. Marcus Fleming.[38] The basic argument is that the combination of high capital mobility and floating exchange rates makes the quantity of reserves demand-determined. Control over the supply of reserves, as widely advocated in the 1960s and sought by the C-20, would not be feasible in the world that came into being after 1973. And even if feasible, it would not achieve any serious objective: as long as countries can order their state enterprises to borrow more in the Euromarket, or their central banks to buy more dollars in the exchange markets, the ease of liability financing will prevent control of the stocks of assets from exerting any powerful leverage over policy. No limit on global reserves can hope to coordinate national economic policies: the international quantity theory is not just dead but buried. The argument that the total level of reserves was demand-determined, so that the absence of any evidence of a global liquidity shortage could be disregarded, was invoked by the IMF staff in developing a rationale for resuming SDR allocation in 1979. One may conjecture that that was not the policy implication that Haberler had in mind when he developed his argument!

Another area where a substantial academic literature has emerged is that of choosing an exchange rate policy in a world of generalized floating. Not much has been added to the old 1950s' question of whether to float or to peg. The Rio conference drew together analysis on the 1960s' question of by how much and when to change one's peg if one has a peg. A completely new literature developed in the 1970s on the question of *to what* a country should peg in a world of generalized floating. The first to recognize that this was an interesting problem amenable to economic analysis was Stanley Black in 1975.[39] The basic policy recommendation to emerge for most countries is the desirability of pegging to a basket. I do not know to what extent one might attribute the growing popularity of basket pegging to the rationale developed in the theoretical literature, but presumably it was a contributory influence.

There are also topics on which there was rather little serious literature. One is gold, which has generally been regarded not so much as a 'barbarous relic', more as a boring relic. Even the efforts of Brodsky and Sampson to stir up indignation at the 'reverse link' that the rich countries indulged in were met with polite yawns.[40] Another was the proposal to create a substitution account: the spectacular *ad hoccery* of the scheme finally cooked up by the IMF provoked no academic denunciations such as would surely have been forthcoming in the 1960s (despite which the IMF's members rejected the scheme). A third is the evolution of a multiple reserve currency system, which passed almost unnoticed until 1981.[41]

Concluding remarks

International monetary economics did not lose touch with reality in the 1970s. Emerging problems continued to motivate the theorists to build new models able to provide understanding and advice, and there is reason to suppose that at times the counsels of the theorists had at least some influence on the course of events. But the relationship may have become less close in the 1970s than it had been in the 1960s: for example, the Bellagio Group ceased to meet. If this reflected a dissatisfaction with the quality of the advice dispensed, our survey has suggested that this might not be without foundation: there was a failure to recognize the significance of the question of monetary sovereignty to the design of an international monetary system, floating was sold on a false prospectus, bad policy advice was given by those who took literally counterfactual assumptions incorporated in the monetary approach, and there is still no authoritative body of analysis of whether the markets are succeeding in reconciling the uncoordinated. Perhaps it is some comfort to the theorists that they cannot be accused of the *ad hoccery* to which the practical men regularly succumb whenever the influence of their favourite academic scribbler of a few years back wanes. Or perhaps it suggests that we still have something to learn in the matter of using economists to good effect.

Notes

1. For an account of the Bellagio Group, see the paper by R. Triffin in J. S. Dreyer (ed.), *Breadth and Depth in Economics: Fritz Machlup — The Man and His Ideas*, Lexington, Mass., D. C. Heath, 1978.

2. R. Dornbusch, *Open Economy Macroeconomics*, New York, Basic Books, 1980, p. 5.

3. L. B. Krause, *Sequel to Bretton Woods*, Washington DC, The Brookings Institution, 1971.

4. J. Williamson, 'The Failure of World Monetary Reform: A Reappraisal' in R. N. Cooper *et al.* (eds), *The International Monetary System under Flexible Exchange Rates: Global, Regional, and National*, Cambridge, Mass., Ballinger, 1982.

5. R. A. Mundell, *International Economics*, London, Macmillan, 1968, chap. 18, and J. M. Fleming, 'Domestic Financial Policies under Fixed and Floating Exchange Rates', *IMF Staff Papers*, November 1962.

6. For example, some worries about the possible volatility of floating rates began to emerge when the J-curve was incorporated into dynamic models of the foreign-exchange market following A. J. C. Britton, 'The Dynamic Stability of the Foreign Exchange Market', *Economic Journal*, March 1970. The literature provided several counter-examples showing the possibility of profitable destabilizing speculation. John Helliwell found that floating rates did not insulate Canada according to the RDX2 model.

7. S. W. Black, *International Money Markets and Flexible Exchange Rates*, Princeton Study in International Finance No. 32, 1973; R. Dornbusch, 'Capital Mobility and Portfolio Equilibrium' in E. M. Claassen and P. Salin (eds), *Recent Issues in International Monetary Economics*, Amsterdam, North-Holland, 1976; and P. J. K. Kouri, 'Essays in the Theory of Flexible Exchange Rates', unpublished Ph.D. dissertation, MIT, 1975.

8. J. Herin, A. Lindbeck, J. Myhrman (eds), *Flexible Exchange Rates and Stabilization Policy*, Boulder, Col., Westview Press, 1977.

9. The following discussion is based on R. Dornbusch, 'Equilibrium and Disequilibrium Exchange Rages', mimeo., 1982.

10. J. Sachs, 'Wages, Flexible Exchange Rates, and Macroeconomic Policy',

Quarterly Journal of Economics, June 1980.

11. R. Nurkse in *International Currency Experience: Lessons of the Interwar Period*, Princeton for the League of Nations, LN11A, 1944.

12. G. Basevi and P. de Grauwe, 'Vicious and Virtuous Circles: A Theoretical Analysis and a Policy for Managing Exchange Rates', *European Economic Review*, 1977; J. Bilson, 'The Vicious Circle Hypothesis', *IMF Staff Papers*, March 1979.

13. R. Meese and K. Rogoff, *Empirical Exchange Rate Models of the Seventies: Are Any Fit to Survive?*, International Finance Discussion Paper No. 184, Federal Reserve Board, June 1981.

14. J. R. Artus and A. D. Crockett, *Floating Exchange Rates and the Need for Surveillance*, Princeton Essay in International Finance No. 127, 1978; J. R. Artus and J. H. Young, 'Fixed and Flexible Exchange Rates: A Renewal of the Debate', *IMF Staff Papers*, December 1979; J. Williamson (ed.), *Exchange Rate Rules: The Theory, Performance and Prospects of the Crawling Peg*, London, Macmillan, 1981.

15. J. Niehans, 'The Appreciation of Sterling: Causes, Effects, Policies', Center Symposia Series No. CS-11, Center for Research in Government Policy, University of Rochester, New York, 1981; M. Mussa, *The Role of Official Intervention*, New York, Group of Thirty Occasional Paper No. 6, 1981; R. M. Levich, *Overshooting in the Foreign Exchange Market*, New York, Group of Thirty, Occasional Paper No. 5, 1981.

16. J. A. Frenkel and H. G. Johnson (eds), *The Monetary Approach to the Balance of Payments*, London, Allen & Unwin, 1976; H. R. Heller and R. R. Rhomberg (eds), *The Monetary Approach to the Balance of Payments*, Washington DC, IMF, 1977.

17. R. Triffin, *Europe and the Money Muddle*, New Haven, Yale University Press, 1957, p. 50.

18. J. J. Polak, 'Monetary Analysis of Income Formation', *IMF Staff Papers*, November 1957.

19. 'Orthodox' theory is the combination of foreign trade multiplier and elasticities analyses as synthesized in the work of J. E. Meade, *The Theory of International Economic Policy: Vol. I, The Balance of Payments*, London, Oxford University Press, 1951.

20. The point is made by J. F. Helliwell, 'The Balance of Payments: A Survey of Harry Johnson's Contributions', *Canadian Journal of Economics*, November 1978.

21. H. G. Johnson, *Inflation and the Monetarist Controversy*, Amsterdam, North-Holland, 1972; A. K. Swoboda, 'Gold, Dollars, Eurodollars and the World Money Stock Under Fixed Exchange Rates', *American Economic Review*, September 1978.

22. IMF, *International Reserves — Needs and Availability*, Washington DC, IMF, 1970.

23. J. M. Parkin, 'International Liquidity and World Inflation in the 1960s', mimeo, March 1975; H. R. Heller, 'International Reserves and World-Wide Inflation', *IMF Staff Papers*, March 1976, claimed to have found evidence favouring the hypothesis, but it was very weak indeed.

24. R. Z. Aliber (ed.), *National Monetary Policies and the International Financial System*, Chicago, University of Chicago Press, 1974.

25. Frenkel and Johnson, op. cit., chap. 4.

26. R. I. McKinnon, 'On Securing a Common Monetary Policy in Europe', Banca Nazionale del Lavoro *Quarterly Review*, March 1973; 'Dollar Stabilization and American Monetary Policy', *American Economic Review*, May 1980.

27. The basic principle is that trend growth in money demand should be satisfied by domestic credit expansion, which should therefore be equal to the common agreed

rate of inflation plus the estimated growth rate of supply capacity of the economy multiplied by the income elasticity of the demand for money.

28. M. v.N. Whitman, 'Global Monetarism and the Monetary Approach to the Balance of Payments', *Brookings Papers on Economic Activity*, No. 3, 1975.

29. Theo Peeters *et al.*, 'The All Saints' Day Manifesto for European Monetary Union', *The Economist*, 1 November 1975, reprinted in M. Fratianni and T. Peeters (eds), *One Money For Europe*, London, Macmillan, 1978.

30. J. A. Frenkel, T. Gylfason, and J. F. Helliwell, 'A Synthesis of Monetary and Keynesian Approaches to Short-run Balance-of-Payments Theory', *Economic Journal*, September 1980. I take this occasion to point out that I anticipated (if regrettably obliquely) their synthesis in my review of Mundell's *Monetary Theory*, published in *Economica*, August 1982.

31. This point and much of the preceding argument is developed in greater detail in J. Williamson, *The Open Economy and the World Economy: A Textbook in International Economics*, New York, Basic Books, 1983, chap. 9.4.

32. P. J. K. Kouri and M. G. Porter, 'International Capital Flows and Portfolio Equilibrium', *Journal of Political Economy*, May/June 1974.

33. E. M. Bernstein *et al.*, *Reflections on Jamaica*, Princeton Essay in International Finance No. 115, 1976.

34. B. J. Cohen, *Organizing the World's Money*, New York, Basic Books, 1977.

35. W. M. Corden, 'Expansion of the World Economy and the Duties of Surplus Countries', *The World Economy*, January 1978, on which I commented in the October 1978 issue; and *The Logic of the International Monetary Non-System*, Discussion Paper No. 4, Centre for Economic Policy Research, Australian National University, Canberra, March 1981.

36. See S. Dell and R. Lawrence, *The Balance of Payments Adjustment Process*; J. Williamson, *International Monetary Reform: A Survey of the Options*; G. K. Helleiner, *The Impact of the Exchange Rate System on the Developing Countries*, all Reports to the Group of 24.

37. A. K. Swoboda, *Credit Creation in the Euromarket: Alternative Theories and Implications for Control*, Group of 30, 1980; R. J. Herring and R. C. Marston, *National Monetary Policies and International Financial Markets*, Amsterdam, North-Holland, 1977.

38. R. A. Mundell and J. J. Polak (eds), *The New International Monetary System*, New York, Columbia University Press, 1977.

39. S. W. Black, *Exchange Policies for Less Developed Countries in a World of Floating Rates*, Princeton Essay in International Finance No. 119, 1976. The literature is surveyed in J. Williamson, 'A Survey of the Literature on the Optimal Peg', *Journal of Development Economics*, August 1982.

40. D. A. Brodsky and G. D. Sampson, 'Gold SDRs and Development', in S. Al-Shaikhly (ed.), *Development Financing: A Framework for International Financial Cooperation*, London, Frances Pinter, 1982.

41. C. F. Bergsten, 'The Evolution and Management of the Multiple Reserve Currency System', mimeo, 1981; R. V. Roosa *et al.*, *Reserve Currencies in Transition*, New York, Group of Thirty, 1982.

3
Floating, Uncertainty and the Real Sector
André de Lattre*

Has floating increased uncertainty for the real sector? What exactly is floating today? What do we mean by the 'real sector'? If we agree that this concept covers mainly what are known in national accounts as 'non-financial agents' and that, as regards matters of exchange rates and exchange markets, business firms are the main actors, we can focus the discussion by asking how these firms have reacted to the new environment.

Other chapters of this book deal with essential aspects of these questions as they analyse national policy experiences or assess the destabilizing influence of the *de facto* move to a multi-currency system which has accompanied floating. This particular chapter will try to define the frontiers of floating, and to analyse what the attitude of business firms has been. It will therefore be divided into two parts. After a brief review of the main factors which led, some ten years ago, to the generalization of floating rates, we shall turn to the present content and limits of floating, taking account of the substantial elements of fixed rates which still exist. The second part of our remarks will deal with the reactions of business enterprises and their adaptation to this unstable world.

* In an area where little evidence exists, I wish to acknowledge my debt to those whose findings have been widely used and reported in this chapter — particularly the works of the British North American Committee, the Laboratoire d'Analyse et de Recherche Economique of the University of Bordeaux and the various Working Parties of the Group of Thirty. Other international organizations have also made factual inquiries. As far as can be known, the findings do not differ from the above-mentioned. I am also greatly indebted to Mrs Marie-Pierre Mol-Vedrenne, Assistant Professor in the Institut d'Etudes Politiques in Paris, who has taken a leading role in the preparation of this chapter by gathering evidence and helping me in the writing of the text.

The measure of floating

From Bretton Woods to floating rates (1945–73)

The purpose of this book is not of course to present a summary of the past forty years of monetary history. Nevertheless it seems useful to recall the chain of events which has led to floating and how, without having been really prepared for the change, business firms have been confronted with the problems — new at least in their magnitude — of this new regime.

There was not, in March 1973, a decision to move to floating rates in order to experiment with a new theory which was expected to permit a better functioning of the international monetary system and to provide more freedom in domestic monetary policies. The move to floating was made because there was no other alternative.

During the early post-war years, there were practically no exchange markets and little international banking activity; in many European countries, exchange markets were not reopened until 1950. European countries were linked with each other and with developing countries through bilateral payments agreements operated by Central Banks or Exchange Offices; the part of their balance of payments deficit which was not covered by foreign aid was settled by the use of their gold and dollar reserves (gold being somehow 'convertible into dollars'), and the management of these reserves was also assured by central banks. These bilateral agreements were progressively replaced by multilateral agreements, then subsequently merged into the European Payments Union (EPU), one of whose objectives was to economize on gold and convertible currency reserves.

At the same time, international organizations, and particularly the International Monetary Fund, were conducting important theoretical studies, which clearly demonstrated the shortcomings and the dangers of bilateralism. This naturally led, in 1958, to the end of the European Payments Union and to the general return to convertibility, within the framework of a regime of fixed exchange rates which was considered, if not the only possible one, at least the best that could be devised. But it was not clearly seen at the time that, under a fixed rate regime, central bank reserves would quickly be completely insufficient to cope with waves of speculation on a much wider scale than in the past.

These speculative capital movements were highly attractive for operators, because, as has often been explained, the expected change in value of a currency under a fixed rate regime is a one-way move. A devaluation which is expected on a certain date will indeed occur on that date, or it will not, but the currency will not be revalued. Operators are not always sure of winning, but they are sure of not losing. Moreover, until the middle of the 1960s, there were very few revaluations (the Deutschmark revaluation of March 1961 was exceptional). Pressures were usually put on currencies that were expected to devalue, and it was only at the end of the decade that the burden was more equally shared among weak and strong currencies. By then, the size of the movements was unprecedented. The original IMF rules, such as those pertaining to convertibility at fixed exchange rates and to the maintenance of cross rates, had been established only for current payments. Indeed, shortly before the return to convertibility in 1958, some proposals included a variable exchange rate for capital movements; and even today, after the amendments of the Fund's rules, capital movements are still considered under Article VI of the Fund as a special category. A member country is not expected to draw from the Fund the resources needed to meet exchange losses due to capital movements, and the Fund itself may prevent it from doing so.

The volume of current payments increased dramatically, for trade as well as for invisible transactions. Consequently, the importance of capital movements 'hidden' in current payments, especially through 'leads and lags', rapidly became unmanageably large in relation to central bank reserves. Finally, genuine capital movements, such as direct investments (particularly US investments in Europe), portfolio investments and bank loans, increased very rapidly.

Crises became frequent, concerning in the first instance the weak currencies (the Deutschmark in 1950, sterling in 1949, the French franc in 1948–9, 1952–3, 1956–7). The situation was reversed but not improved when the United States moved from a positive to a negative balance of payments. Technically, the correction of the US deficit was made more difficult by the fact that the United States was not prepared to devalue the dollar in terms of gold, as defined in the IMF agreement and that, to achieve the same objective, it would have had to ask its partners to revalue their own currencies under the rule of 'N–1'. But the technical aspect was not essential. The heart of the problem was that, in the mid-1960s, neither the United States nor its partners were yet ready to accept a reduction in the value of the dollar, even though such a fall would have been fully justified for at least two reasons: the fact that the dollar values of most European currencies had been fixed at what many thought to be too low a level at the time of the sterling devaluation in September 1949; and the sharp increase in US inflation, due mainly to the Vietnam war and to rapidly rising social security programmes. To restore the balance in its external accounts, the United States would have had to run very large trade surpluses, much bigger than those that it normally recorded with Europe, a development which European industry was not prepared to accept.

All these factors contributed to making the fixed rate system even less adaptable and its breakdown even more likely. Moreover, in order to increase the pressure on deficit countries to put their house in order, it was rightly thought appropriate to refuse such facilities as widening the margins of fluctuation, although the suggestion was discussed in academic circles.

At the same time, the large interbank Eurocurrency market (at that time mainly Eurodollars) was developing. Its flexibility was evidently convenient for lenders and even more so for borrowers, especially sovereign states, which could obtain important resources free of any conditionality. The failure of efforts to reorganize the international monetary system was another cause of the seemingly irreversible move towards floating. Nevertheless, one must not forget that on two occasions, in 1964 and 1973, these efforts had almost been successful.

In 1964, the first report of the Group of Ten proposed two important innovations. Multilateral surveillance of balances of payments and exchange rates was to be accompanied by the creation of an international payment mechanism, associating gold and national currencies. The 'Collective Reserve Unit' (CRU), which would have served simultaneously as a unit of account, a standard of value and a means of payment, would have been the sole and ultimate means of settling balance of payments surpluses and deficits, and it would probably have been easy, at that time, to keep control of the development of the Eurocurrencies which were still of fairly limited size, by submitting them to national reserve requirements.

In the event, the IMF Special Drawing Rights were not able to play this role. They are primarily created by means of negotiation, a process which was further complicated by the proposal to allocate some of the new rights to the developing countries, a suggestion which is still put forward by many supporters. So it was quite natural that they were created in small amounts, all the more so since the explosion of the Eurocurrency market made it clearly unnecessary to increase international liquidity by creating new SDRs. Moreover, this asset (the stabilizing nature of which could have been attractive, as it inevitably varies less than any of its components) today accounts for only some 5 per cent of world reserves, while its use in private deposits is progressively becoming more important.[1]

Again, in September 1973, there seemed to be a serious chance of achieving a rational organization of international payments. Although the dollar had begun to fluctuate in February–March 1973, it still seemed possible and appropriate to reduce its depreciation and limit its use as a world vehicular currency. Unfortunately the then relatively advanced studies on a 'Multi-currency Intervention System', and on the use of the SDR as a means of settlement in private transactions, were soon abandoned. A week after the Nairobi meeting of the IMF, which should have given the start to this reform, the Yom Kippur war sparked off the first oil shock. The European countries, which had deplored the weakness of the dollar and the increasing level of their claims on the United States, were soon again to be on the 'debtor' side—the creditor then being OPEC —and would no longer complain about a dollar surplus.

The dollar became fully autonomous. It was to fluctuate freely, affecting also the values of assets and liabilities on the Eurocurrency market, in connection with the evolution of US interest rates after the dramatic change in US monetary policy in October 1979 and with the results of the fight against inflation.

This situation explains at least in part why since 1974 the value of the dollar has moved from 380 to 180 yen, then back to some 240 yen, and from 5.5 French francs to less than FF4, and then to more than FF8.

For business firms the problem was not new in principle. They had already had to cope in the past with the weakness of certain currencies by substantial and expensive forward coverage. But the problem now took on another dimension because fluctuations became much wider, affecting many currencies and occurring both upwards and downwards.

The geographical dimensions of floating

At present a substantial proportion of world payments is not conducted under floating. The proportion was much larger some years ago, because of the existence of so-called 'monetary areas' operating more or less on the principle of fixed rates. The most important of those still in operation is, of course, the European Monetary System.

A quick look at the IMF's *International Financial Statistics* helps to distinguish various foreign exchange regimes among the world's 146 currencies.[2]

(i) One group of currencies have their exchange rates pegged to one other currency. As of 31 March 1984:
  – 33 currencies (46 in 1976) were pegged to the US dollar. Most are in Latin America, but some are in the Middle East, such as Egypt, Syria, Oman and Yemen.
  – 13 currencies (the same as in 1976) are pegged to the French franc, constituting what has been known since World War II as the 'franc zone', a fact not unrelated to the existence of two multinational central banks.
  – 5 currencies (8 in 1976) are pegged to another currency. These are mostly exceptional situations, such as Bhutan linked to the Indian rupee, Equatorial Guinea to the Spanish peseta, and Swaziland to the South African rand. The only one remaining linked to sterling is Gambia.
  – A much more important group of currencies, among which are Saudi Arabia, Bahrain, Qatar, the United Arab Emirates and also Indonesia, are more loosely linked to one currency (mostly the US dollar). They do not maintain a fixed exchange rate with it, but operate within a relatively wide margin of flexibility (± 7.25 per cent). They have in fact maintained a fairly narrow relation with the dollar.
  – In the category of flexibility within narrow limits are, of course, the currencies grouped in the European Monetary System.
(ii) A second category includes regimes where the exchange rate is established in relation to a composite unit, such as the SDR or another composite currency. This group includes 39 countries (25 in 1976), mostly in Africa, and such countries as Austria, Burma and the People's Republic of China.
(iii) 6 countries (3 in 1976) modify their exchange rate at regular intervals in connection with a certain set of indicators, such as price indexes, etc.
(iv) Some countries operate with a relatively large measure of flexibility but by managed floating, so as to avoid excessive fluctuation. In 1984 they were 24, including New Zealand, India, Pakistan and Sri Lanka, and Spain, Turkey and Yugoslavia.
(v) Lastly, only 8 countries were registered as operating under what the IMF calls 'independent floating'. But this group includes those which, in addition to the countries in the European Monetary

System, are the most important in the world: namely, the United
States and Canada, Japan, the United Kingdom and Australia.

This list inspires a few comments:

(a) The present exchange rate situation is substantially different
from that of 1976. Independent floating has spread rapidly among
developing countries. More generally, the changes which have
occurred since 1976 were motivated by the desire to limit the
perverse effects of exchange rate fluctuations, which react
differently on domestic earnings, depending on the exchange
regime. It is no surprise that during the period 1976–82 the IMF
recorded 55 changes in the developing countries' exchange
regimes, while, for the same reason, the number of countries
pegging their currency to only one foreign currency, most
frequently the dollar, fell substantially, to be generally replaced by
the use of a basket of currencies or the SDR.

Such a decrease is particularly visible in the case of developing
countries. Professor Kenen[3] has shown that 85.8 per cent of those
developing countries which are members of the IMF, accounting
for 83.6 per cent of the group's imports, had their currency pegged
to a single currency in 1974. In 1979, countries with their currency
pegged to a single currency were only 55.6 per cent of the total
number, and accounted for no more than 28.9 per cent of the
group's imports. The reasons for such an impressive change are
clear enough. Pegging to a single currency implies that an
exchange variation between that currency and another will cause
various changes in the import and export prices. If an oil-
importing country has its currency pegged to the dollar and the
price of its oil imports is denominated in dollars, a rise or fall in the
dollar value will have no effect on the price of oil in the national
currency, but there will be variations in the domestic currency
prices of other imports. This factor is too important for many
developing countries to follow the dollar in the sometimes abrupt
evolutions it has registered since 1974, first downwards, then
upwards since 1981.

A notable exception has been the maintenance of a relatively
large number of developing countries' link with the French franc.
This is partly explained by historical and institutional factors, as
well as by the still relatively large proportion of their external trade
which is conducted with France. But the existence of the
European Monetary System also plays a role because it markedly

enlarges the area of pegged exchange rates to which they have access through the French franc.

(b) Another point must be made. Though a number of countries define their currencies' values in terms of the SDR, their currencies are nevertheless freely floating, since they do not commit themselves to maintain a fixed relationship with the SDR, even within a margin of fluctuation. They must in fact be added to the list of the few big countries registered as 'independent floaters', such as the United States, the United Kingdom, Canada and Japan, thus giving a wider and more accurate picture of the world of floating.

(c) Finally, only EMS members operate in what can be termed an area of relative exchange stability. They represent an important component of the international monetary system, with $15 billion of reserves (i.e. 35 per cent of total world currency reserves), 13,000 tons of gold (46 per cent of the world total), and 28 per cent of the IMF's quotas. As we have seen, the franc zone enlarges their international basis, but this addition is not very important, since the franc zone's money supply is equivalent to only 3 per cent of that of France, and 0.7 per cent of the European Community's money supply. As the EC is still the largest exporting area in the world, and since nearly 50 per cent of the member countries' foreign trade is done inside the EMS area, its importance must not be underestimated.

One of the merits of the EMS, which was not so clearly seen when it started, is that it has been able to function fairly smoothly in spite of the wide structural differences among the member countries, the frequent incompatibility of their economic policies, and the more technical difficulty of the very structure of the System: namely, the obligation to maintain a fixed maximum margin of variation among the members' currencies, while the System itself is operating in a world of wide fluctuations. In addition to its high rate of inflation or its diverging economic policy, a currency in the System can be put under heavy pressure, leading to costly foreign exchange intervention, and possibly to an exchange rate adjustment, for reasons which are exterior to the System. For instance, if, for reasons due to the domestic American or the international situation, the dollar is weak against the Deutschmark, the weakest currency in the System must rise to maintain the agreed margin with the Deutschmark, even if at that moment all the indicators would point to a lowering of its value. Such pressures led to the French franc being obliged to leave the snake in 1973 and again in 1975, and similar pressures on the weakest currency occurred again on various occasions in more recent times.

How clean is floating?

Another factor to keep in mind in assessing the consequences of floating is, of course, that there has never been anything like 'clean floating' during the past ten years. Whereas central banks are no longer bound to intervene to respect fixed margins and have supposedly regained increased freedom in their domestic monetary policies, in practice exchange rates have remained constantly managed.

Certain studies (see particularly Professor McKinnon's papers[4]) express the view that monetary policies in some countries, if they are conducted in a really autonomous way, inevitably lead to imbalances in the world financial system. McKinnon uses the example of Japan from 1976 to 1978. Between December 1976 and May 1978, the Bank of Japan tried to curtail the yen's strong and rapid appreciation vis-à-vis the US dollar, with a consequent increase in its dollar reserves by 81 per cent from $13.8 billion to $25.1 billion. McKinnon explains the failure of this policy by the much faster rate of growth in the monetary base in the United States than in Japan (13 per cent between May 1977 and May 1978, as against 10.2 per cent in Japan). In Japan, the expansive monetary effect of these increased dollar holdings was compensated by a decrease in domestic refinancing of the commercial banks, a move which was helped by the relatively stagnant demand for credit. But in the United States, these dollar holdings mainly took the form of US Treasury bills, and therefore did not have an automatically restrictive effect on the US money supply.[5] As Robert Roosa told Jacques Rueff already in the early 1960s, an increase in dollar holdings by foreign central banks has no automatic effect on the monetary supply in the United States. It is only by a decision on the part of the American monetary authorities that the money supply will ultimately be affected, namely, whether they choose to compensate this increase in foreign dollar holdings by open market operations, or not.

It should be noted that the IMF has considered it its duty to continue to exercise surveillance over member countries' exchange rate policies, and has improved and developed its procedures to this effect. Whereas Article I of the Fund's Statutes makes it obligatory for member countries at all times to cooperate with the Fund and with other members to maintain orderly exchange rates, the new amended Article IV reinforces their commitment towards the orderly functioning of the international monetary system. In particular, a decision by the IMF's Board, clarifying the principles of the Fund's 'Surveillance over Exchange Rate Policies' states that 'a member should intervene in the exchange market if necessary to counter disorderly conditions which may be characterized, inter alia, by disruptive short-term movements in the exchange value of its currency'.

The repeated acknowledgement by the Fund of this much needed surveillance to ensure sound and harmonious international monetary relations clearly demonstrates the system's inability to regulate itself in a satisfactory way. Accordingly, member countries have pursued global exchange rate policies, and not simple foreign exchange interventions. To take the example of France, these policies have included such actions as exchange controls, foreign borrowing — particularly by the nationalized industries — and interest rates policy.

But central banks cannot hope to do much more than smooth exchange markets' fluctuations, as is shown by quite a few studies. For instance, in an article assessing the efficiency of central banks' interventions, V. Argy[6] relates them to the following three main objectives: contributing to an efficient resource allocation when exchange markets do not dispose of sufficient information to achieve this allocation by themselves; contributing over time to the efficient redistribution of the changes in purchasing power, to avoid abrupt repercussions; and contributing to overall economic stability. Argy sees this policy as relatively insufficient over the long run in Germany, Japan and the United Kingdom, though with some significant successes in the short term.

Recent experience also shows that, in many cases, the extreme exchange rate instability is related to abrupt variations in domestic monetary or budgetary policies. In such circumstances, market interventions have not been able to counter the adverse effects which can, in the short run, accompany such policies and hasten their acceptance by the markets, once they have been well received.

Lastly, it seems that commercial banks appraise with some severity the influence of central banks' interventions. As shown by the Group of Thirty inquiry,[7] a majority of the British, Swiss and German banks interrogated did not approve of the way central banks had intervened; some of them even thought that these interventions had increased, rather than decreased, exchange rate instability.[8]

Floating, instability and uncertainty

No one would deny that instability has been greater since floating. Let us try to see by how much, using mainly the evidence gathered in four studies: namely, studies by Professor Kenen and Geoffrey Bell of Schröder's for the Group of Thirty, the report by a working party of the Group of Thirty, and a study by the British North American Committee.[9] The findings are as follows:

(a) Exchange rate instability has increased strongly. Professor Kenen's average index of nominal exchange rate fluctuations for 36 countries increased threefold between 1970–2 and 1974–6, from 0.696 to 2.17.

For the years 1978 to 1980, a look at the monthly percentage exchange rate variations shows that more than 6 per cent of these variations were larger than 100 per cent. And of course these variations have been particularly erratic since the dramatic changes in US monetary policy after October 1979. Lastly, daily variations of 3 per cent to 5 per cent have become frequent. Even if these variations ultimately taper off, they remain a serious problem for business firms which must make commitments and decisions for relatively short periods.

(b) Kenen's index for the volatility of real exchange rates calculated on wholesale prices nearly doubled between 1970–2 and 1974–6, from 1.355 to 2.535.

(c) While the theory of purchasing power parity suggests that real rate volatility should be less than that of nominal rates, Kenen's findings point to the opposite in most cases.

(d) The difference tends to narrow between exchange rate volatility in the developed and in the developing countries. Developing countries' real exchange rates remain more unstable than those of developed countries, but the increase in their volatility has been smaller during the last fifteen years than that in the developed countries, which used in the past to enjoy more stable exchange rates.

(e) 'Overshooting' has been a frequent phenomenon in the exchange markets, and is now a characteristic of floating. This phenomenon, which is due mainly to the operators' insufficient — or sometimes excessive — information, was not unknown under fixed rates; but floating has aggravated its magnitude.

The Group of Thirty's report gives interesting indications on this subject. It singles out the following, among other factors which show the deep changes in the markets' functioning in recent years:

(a) An increase in the number of operators, many of whom now deal in small amounts, with little knowledge of the facts, and are therefore inclined to follow any recent trend, thus magnifying the 'bandwagon' effect.

(b) Correlatively, a certain decrease in the 'market's depth', with a decreasing proportion of large-scale operators who could play a stabilizing role.

(c) The fact that, with the development of Asian markets such as Tokyo, Hong Kong or Singapore, which, because of the time difference, are open when Western markets are closed, world markets now operate 'around the clock', thus facilitating the transmission of excessive reactions and increasing 'resounding' phenomena.

(d) At the same time, there is a concentration on spot markets, as market instability makes it more difficult for operators to find counterparts in forward contracts, especially of over one year.

In turn, 'overshooting' has contributed to instability through the influence of exchange rate variations on the balance of payments, particularly the trade balance. Kenen shows how long it takes for import and export volumes to adjust to changes in exchange rates, with all the consequent risks of 'overshooting' or 'undershooting', the adjustment being made all the more difficult as these variations become excessive and irrational. Enterprises' business expectations are the first victim of these excessive cycles.

(e) Substantial changes have occurred in the ranking of currencies by growing instability. For instance, between 1964–6 and 1974–6, Italy moved from the 7th to the 32nd rank, Sweden from 28th to 9th, and the United Kingdom from 9th to 30th.

(f) Interest rate variations have played a major role, particularly, of course, US interest rates.

As a consequence of these wide and largely unpredictable interest rate variations, floating has led to dramatic discrepancies in returns on financial assets. Calculations made for the Group of Thirty by Schröder in New York on the possible yield from the placement in various currencies and for various maturities of a sum of $100 invested from 1973 to 1980 in three-month renewable certificates of deposits, show the considerable divergence of the results. The yield of the best placement (the operator having supposedly chosen at each renewal the best currency and the best interest rate) was forty times larger than the worst one (1612.5 against 42). There was a similar gap between placement which would have been made every three months in the currency bringing in the following quarter the highest gain compared to the dollar and the one bringing the smallest gain (1127.2 against 50.4). These are financial placements, which only the big firms' treasurers are familiar with. But they vividly illustrate the influence on economic calculations of these wide and abrupt fluctuations.

This instability also has its effect on the general framework of a national economy. For instance, the dollar's steep rise in 1981–2 profoundly affected France's import costs, without French economic policy having anything to do with it. From 1981 to 1982, France's oil import bill increased abruptly, while the nominal price of oil remained stable or even went down slightly. Conversely, on various occasions and particularly during 1975 and 1980, many French enterprises were confronted with serious difficulties, leading in some cases to bankruptcy and closure, due simply to the abrupt and unexpected fall in the value of the dollar.

An attempt has also been made to assess the increased costs for an economy of the higher charges for forward cover. These include, to some extent, transfers from business firms to the banks (the latter benefit from the increased activity on exchange markets, as shown by the rapid development of banks' foreign services in recent years). There has also been redistribution between the banking system and the central banks (the Group of Thirty report indicates that banks make larger profits when central banks intervene in 'leaning against the wind'), between the private sector and the public sector when the central banks' profits are, as is generally the case, transferred to the state as taxes on profits or dividends, and finally between the national collectivity and the outside world, when exchange gains and losses are not evenly spread between domestic and foreign operators.

It seems obvious, then, that instability has increased *during* floating. But one must ask whether it has increased *because of* floating and what is the direct link — if any — between the two concepts.

One channel, which is partly indirect, is, as we said earlier, the influence of interest rate fluctuations. As has often been demonstrated, interest rates exert an influence on exchange rates particularly when, if a currency is rising somewhat for other reasons (favourable balance of payments, political concerns affecting other currencies), the monetary authorities of that country take some time in lowering their domestic interest rates by means of an appropriate monetary policy. Many have thought that this was the case with the Deutschmark in 1981.

As already mentioned, a second set of interpretations is linked to the whole question of changes in the world money supply. The strong and abrupt increases in world money supply in 1971–2 (when in many countries M1 was seen to grow by some 30 per cent a year) and in 1978–9 (at the time of American 'benign neglect') had a direct influence on the sharp price increases linked to the two successive oil shocks.

But, of course, the main link is the effect on the balance of payments because of the long time it takes to register the changes in export and import volumes which should normally result from exchange rate variations. In recent years no automatic adjustment mechanism has functioned; in particular, relative price increases have played no part in the direction of a return to equilibrium. Indeed, relative price changes can be felt only after a certain interval.

In the IMF's World Trade Model, the sum of import and export demand elasticities is inferior to one for more than one and a half years for nine out of the fourteen industrialized countries considered,[10] while, during this period, exchange rate variation has the well-known perverse effects of the 'J' curve.

In the short term, some factors appear more important than relative price variations, for instance, innovation and creativity, delivery delays, and after-sale services. High-quality exports do not suffer too much from the national currency's appreciation. More generally, one can agree with Professor McKinnon that, insofar as floating has increased uncertainty, trade has become less concerned with price and cost differentials and more with non-quantifiable factors.

Two other theoretical explanations also link the increase in instability to floating. One is the view of Professor Nordhaus,[11] who sees the exchange market as an 'auction market', with volatility as precisely the essence of such a market. The other is the asset-market theory, which takes exchange rates as the price of a financial asset and draws attention to the influence of expectations on the behaviour of this price. Short-term exchange rate instability is then explained primarily by the instability of expectations. But since, in turn, expectations are all the more unstable when general economic conditions are themselves unstable, we again come up with a cause which is only very loosely — if at all — linked to floating.

The real sector's reaction to floating

We now know a little more about floating, its magnitude and its links with instability and uncertainty. How did it affect the business sector? How did enterprises react? Exchange rate volatility increases uncertainty as regards their competitiveness, the export-demand for their products, the value of their balance sheets (for those which have branches or affiliates abroad), their import-induced production costs and the results of their foreign investment policy. We can therefore consider in turn the impact of floating on their pricing policy, and on their financial situation and direct investments.

Enterprises' pricing policy

Floating can lead to changes in firms' pricing policy for two reasons: it implies increased costs resulting from the need for increased cover and firms can increase their competitiveness by modifying their prices in accordance with exchange rate variations.

(i) *Exchange risks and prices.* The foreign exchange position of a firm in a given currency is equal to the balance of its assets and liabilities denominated in that currency. The position of an exporting firm reflects its global transactions with foreign countries. If it operates worldwide, its exchange position includes, in addition to transactions inside the group, the 'exposed' part of its assets and liabilities that it holds abroad. Hedging techniques are then more easily available for a firm with branches and subsidiaries abroad, as we shall see later when we turn to the subject of the maintenance of asset value. Enterprises can minimize exchange risks in various ways, such as the choice of the invoicing currency, the transferring of the exchange risk to a subsidiary or branch abroad, the use of compensation ('netting'), or guarantees of the contracts themselves.

To avoid exchange risks, firms can invoice in their national currency or in a strong foreign currency. Invoicing in the national currency is of course simpler. Nevertheless, no general trend appears in the various studies and questionnaires undertaken. There seems to be a wide diversity among countries, and indeed among enterprises in the same country or in the same sector. The main reason may be that firms are not free to choose national currency invoices, for instance, since they have to comply with the conventions and conditions prevailing on the market at the particular time. In France, for example, foreign currency invoicing has developed since floating, as many firms choose to invoice in strong currencies wherever possible. Firms can alleviate the burden for their clients of invoicing in the national currency by introducing in the contract, as seems to be frequently the case, a clause whereby the two parties more or less share the exchange risk entailed by the invoicing.

Management of exchange risk can also be left to branches or subsidiaries abroad. This may imply a gain in terms of costs if the interest rate that the subsidiary will have to pay is less than the one the parent company would have borne. In this field, too, no general rule has emerged. The inquiry conducted in France in 1977 by the Laboratoire d'Analyse et de Recherche Economique (LARE) of the University of Bordeaux shows that the practice of leaving this responsibility to subsidiaries is rather exceptional (it is not followed by American and Canadian firms, for example), whereas the study, already quoted, of the British North American Committee (BNAC) reveals a strong tendency on the part of British firms to delegate to, or to share exchange risks with, their subsidiaries and branches.

The use of 'netting', i.e. reciprocal foreign currency payment, among subsidiaries and branches, and between them and the parent company, is only possible when foreign exchange flows are available, are sufficiently diversified and, of course, are flowing in opposite directions. It presupposes a centralized management which will aim at coordinating the foreign currencies chosen for invoicing and the maturities. The 1977 LARE inquiry showed that in France such a practice remains exceptional, being used by only 13 per cent of the enterprises interrogated. The BNAC inquiry showed an identical result for a sample of US, Canadian and British firms (15 per cent of the firms declared they were using it as fully as possible). Lastly, the contracts may include indexation — subject, of course, to market conditions. But the BNAC study records no clear move in this direction.

Generally speaking, it is difficult today for firms to avoid running an exchange risk, and the inquiries have shown that they are very conscious of this risk, and ready and willing to minimize it. When the risk does materialize, the techniques available to them are well known. They include, among others, 'spot' cover, 'forward' cover, and foreign currency borrowing to cover the transaction by the parent company or its subsidiary.

However, the facts are rather different from what the theories would imply, both as regards the theory of 'efficient markets' —

according to which enterprises cannot expect to 'beat' the market in the long run, gains and losses being bound ultimately to level off — and as regards those theories which recommend total coverage. The reason is that all cover techniques imply a direct real cost which should be weighed against the exchange risk, which at that time is still only potential. They also imply an indirect cost, with the need to develop services to deal with these problems.

The reality lies somewhere between the two; most firms do take exchange risk into consideration but they seem to evaluate it carefully against the cost of coverage. If they do not cover themselves, they may or may not lose. If they do cover themselves, they anyway incur the substantial cost of coverage.

As operating costs have increased with floating, one might have expected a parallel increase in prices. Surprisingly, the Group of Thirty study, already quoted, shows that enterprises have generally not increased their prices to compensate for increased expenditures on exchange risk management and cover. Nevertheless, one should not attach too much weight to this, since the inquiry has shown that forward cover developed substantially after floating, and since the cost of forward cover has quite a few times been mentioned as a normal operating cost. Once again, the 'missing link' between the cost of forward cover and price variation is, of course, the weight of competition and general market conditions.

Forward cover management has been made substantially easier for enterprises by the development of interbank markets, 'futures' markets and 'currency swaps'.

(a) Interbank markets have proved to be a very efficient way of spreading the risks. When a company wants to protect itself against an exchange risk, it will sell forward the expected proceeds of its activity. While, as explained earlier, it could get the same protection by contracting a balancing obligation itself (i.e. borrowing in the same currency), it will generally ask its bank to sell forward the anticipated proceeds of its exports. The bank, being generally unwilling to incur an exchange risk, will sell spot the same amount of the said currency after having borrowed it, the effect — a net borrowing in the currency — being the same. The Eurocurrency markets provide a wide network from which the banks can borrow and where they invest the amounts needed for their clients' covering operations.

It is difficult to pass judgement on the role of the interbank market. There is no doubt that, had it not existed, business firms and the banking system would have faced greater difficulties in weathering the consequences of floating. At the same time, the size and the absence of controls of the market itself have been a significant factor in the instability of currencies.

(b) The second and more recent instrument is the development of that part of the financial futures market which deals with foreign currencies. The origins of financial futures are well known. Operators had intervened for many years in commodities such as grains, coffee, cocoa or minerals to provide some hedge for firms dealing in these commodities. The introduction of floating exchange rates in the early 1970s, and later the increased volatility in interest rates in a period of inflation and turmoil in the international money markets, created opportunities for gains and profits in interest rate arbitrage. The International Money Market (IMM) was created by the Chicago Mercantile Exchange 'to facilitate foreign trade and investment by providing a mechanism to insure the risks of international traders arising from fluctuation in the prices of various currencies. The IMM was designed to complement existing active spot and forward contracting markets in world trade centers'.[12]

The Chicago IMM expanded from less than 200,000 currency contracts in 1977 to 6 million contracts in 1981, 12 million in 1983, and some 14 billion on an annual basis for the first five months of 1984. In spite of this swift expansion, however, the numbers remain much smaller than those bearing on interest rates. For the US futures markets considered as a whole, currency futures increased from 3.8 million contracts in 1980 to 11.4 million in 1983 and 15.8 million on an annual basis during the first five months of 1984, while financial futures increased from 10.2 million contracts in 1980 to 40.2 million in 1983 and to 45.2 million on an annual basis in the first five months of 1984.

The New York Futures Exchange, which opened trading in contracts in Deutschmarks, Swiss francs, Canadian dollars, UK pounds and yen in August 1980, plays a less important role, while the London International Financial Futures Exchange (LIFFE), which opened in September 1982, reached the figure of 1.5 million contracts in 1983, of which, however, only 7 per cent were currency contracts.

How futures markets will evolve depends on the volatility of interest rates and exchange rates, on the pace of deregulation in finance, on the more aggressive use of financial instruments and techniques by market participants, and on the more flexible approach of regulators to financial activities that has developed in recent years. Large institutional investors are also entering these markets at a rapid pace and non-financial corporations are using the futures market as their cash and portfolio management techniques become more sophisticated.

The opening of the new futures markets in Singapore and Sydney, in conjunction with the expectation of a more open Japanese capital market, will no doubt affect the growth of the financial futures market in the Asian region. The Singapore Monetary Exchange (SIMEX), opened in June 1984, will have important implications for the futures market. With Chicago, London and Singapore, futures will now be trading around the clock around the world. Hedgers and speculators will be able to manage overnight risks better and to take advantage of overnight price movements. The mutual offset system between Chicago and Singapore will allow market participants in Chicago to establish a position during Chicago trading hours and to liquidate it in Singapore. The same could occur between Singapore and the London LIFFE.

There is a big difference between forward markets and futures markets. Forward contracts are tailor-made to meet specific client needs and require a partner ready to go along with the particulars (date, amount, etc.) of each transaction. Contracts traded in the futures market are all identical; no operator knows who the counter-party is in the operation, since all traders deal with the futures exchange clearing corporation which acts as buyer to each seller and seller to each buyer.

(c) A third hedging vehicle is currency options. This mechanism gives the holder the right to buy or sell a given amount of currency at a prearranged price. The buyer or seller pays a price to exercise this right, known as the option premium. Unlike the case of forward contracts, where a buyer is committed to fulfilling the terms of the contract regardless of circumstances, in the case of options the buyer has the right but not the obligation to exercise the contract.

(ii) *Price variations and competitiveness.* Another aspect of a firm's pricing policy in a world of floating currencies is its capacity to modify prices in relation to exchange rate variations in order to increase its competitive position and to speed the return to equilibrium in the national balance of payments.

In the case of an appreciation in the national currency, the return to equilibrium is encouraged by prices in the national currency remaining unchanged and the prices in the foreign currency rising as a result of the exchange rate realignment. When the national currency depreciates and export prices denominated in that currency do not change, national competitiveness will increase and the level of receipts can remain unchanged. This result is also obtained when export prices denominated in a foreign currency are decreased by the equivalent of the depreciation of the national currency.

Nevertheless, the answers given to the various inquiries seem to show that enterprises do not behave as expected. Microeconomic studies in such a field are doubtless imperfect, but it seems that the few macroeconomic observations which were possible point in the same direction.

The most frequent characteristic of the firms' attitude, as described by the inquiries we have already quoted, is inertia. In most cases, firms did not make the price changes that would have given them the benefit of the exchange rate modification. According to BNAC's findings, variability in exchange rates has increased the frequency of price changes, but for less than half the firms. Similarly, the number of fixed price contracts has not been substantially modified. More than half the firms answering the BNAC inquiry, in the United States, Canada, and the United Kingdom, said they did not change their attitude towards such contracts after floating was generalized.

The LARE study of French firms leads to the same conclusions.[13] In answer to the 1977 inquiry, between 80 and 90 per cent of firms said they did not modify their attitude. The question was: 'When the exchange rate between the French franc and the currency of the country where you export varies significantly, what attitude do you usually adopt as regards the export prices of your products (a) in the case of a fall in the French franc, and (b) in the case of a rise in the French franc?'

The answers showed: (a) when exports were denominated in French francs, 79 per cent did not change their prices and only 21 per cent raised them, in the case of a fall in the franc; 83 per cent did not change their prices and only 17 per cent lowered them, in the case of a rise in the franc. (b) When exports were denominated in a foreign currency, 96.5 per cent did not modify their prices and only 3.5 per cent lowered them in the case of a fall in the franc; 90 per cent left their prices unchanged and only 10 per cent increased them in the case of a rise in the franc.

Curiously, the inertia was less strong when the French franc was used for invoicing. One would have expected the contrary, particularly since, at the same time, 85 per cent of the firms acknowledged that price was an essential element of their competitiveness, and 70 per cent that competition was stronger abroad than at home.

The new LARE inquiry conducted in 1982 appears to show that the inertia persists. M. Bourguinat notes[14] that there seems to be a direct link between the use made by French firms of the possible currencies for invoicing (in fact, more being denominated in national currency and less in foreign currency) and the sort of export premium which results from the fall in the value of the French franc. As regards contracts invoiced in foreign currency, 83.3 per cent of exporters do not modify their prices after a fall in the value of the French franc, being in fact interested in receiving an improved margin without any explicit action on their part. In the case of invoicing in francs, the foreign currency value of the exports decreases if there is no change in the franc price. Sixty-three per cent of the French exporters who invoice in francs maintain their prices, and those who increase them do it only very slightly.

Two kinds of explanation can be given for this passive behaviour: (a) market and (b) cost. (a) Some exporters obviously maintain their prices when they operate on a 'sellers' market where their product is well identified and in demand (high-quality goods, etc.). This is another aspect of the famous 'specialization' index. Secondly, prices are set by the markets and it is very difficult to depart from them. Thirdly, a trigger effect is also frequent, as downward adjustments are much less frequent than upward ones. (b) Cost is also an explanation. In 1977, 20 per cent of the French enterprises said that they did increase their prices in the case of a downward movement of the French franc, thus losing a possible competitive advantage. Such behaviour can be explained by the increased cost of the import content of their export products.

BNAC also notes that in such industries as automobiles or home appliances, firms had never sought to exploit the gain in competitiveness which was available when a fall in the national currency made imports of such products more expensive. In such highly concentrated sectors, where enterprises enjoy a significant freedom of price fixing, they have found it more profitable to align their prices with those of their foreign competitors.

This sort of behaviour, of course, destroys the classical adjustment mechanisms, and in the long run will lead to an increase in domestic inflation. Nevertheless, it has often been noted that when a currency is devalued and the export prices in foreign currency are not modified, an indirect positive effect can sometimes be felt, since the improvement in the profit margins of the exports may in the long run lead to a development of exports and an increase in trade results.

The same problem can be studied in macroeconomic terms at the national level. Econometric models can be used to test the effectiveness of exchange variation on the trade balance. Nevertheless, the results given for France by three widely used models ('METRIC', 'DMS' and the Bank of France model) do not lead to clearcut conclusions. The results of the three models are indeed quite contradictory. 'METRIC', for instance, shows an almost complete absorption of the competitive advantage in about a year, whereas the Bank of France model indicates that, after a year, three-quarters of the advantage is still felt; 'DMS' shows results in between these two extremes. Indeed, the international transmission of inflation during the period under review seems to indicate that the trigger effect has been fairly general.

The financial situation of firms

This can be appraised globally through balance sheets, and more particularly through firms' foreign investment and foreign borrowing policy.

For multinational firms, the exposure to risk occurs not only through receipts and debts in foreign currency related to trade transactions; the whole of the balance sheet can be regarded as exposed. In addition to the transaction accounting position, there is a 'translation exposure'; to establish a consolidated balance sheet the various items of the balance sheets (of the subsidiaries) must be 'translated' into the parent company's currency. The management of such a risk is an exercise in balance-sheet structure forecasting.

Four principal methods can be used:

(a) The 'current rate' method translates all the items of the balance sheet at the consolidation date. Fixed assets and short-term assets are treated in the same way.
(b) The 'liquid assets and liabilities' method converts assets and liabilities of less than one year at the current rate, and those of more than one year at their historical rate.
(c) The 'monetary/non-monetary assets' method distinguishes monetary assets such as cash, clients, suppliers and debts of any length, from non-monetary assets. The first are converted at the current rates and the second at their historical rates.
(d) The 'historical (temporelle)' method is close to the 'monetary/non-monetary' method but applies a different treatment to inventories and deals also in a particular way with forward contracts, depending on whether or not they are linked to a trade

transaction. This was the method used by the American regulation known as 'FASB.8'.

This regulation must be mentioned here, since another side-effect of floating for multinational companies has been the need to report in their accounts, together with actual exchange rate gains and losses, the potential gains and losses arising from the calculation in the parent company's currency not only of their foreign currency assets and liabilities, but also of their non-monetary assets and of the monetary or non-monetary assets of their foreign branches or subsidiaries. It is the problem well known to specialists as 'FASB.8' from the denomination of a Federal Accounting Standards Board decision first issued in 1975, under which US companies must include in their consolidated accounts their potential exchange gains and losses.

In its original form, this decision raised two problems. First, by requiring the evaluation of non-monetary assets at their historic value and that of monetary assets at the current exchange rates, it introduced a much criticized distortion. Second, the requirement that potential gains and losses should be reported in the accounts of the parent company introduced into these accounts fluctuations of an origin not easily explained, and so possibly influenced the financial markets' and shareholders' judgement unfavourably.

Two important modifications were therefore introduced in 1980. First, non-monetary assets were to be computed just like monetary assets, at the current exchange rate. Second, losses were no longer to appear in the 'profit and loss' accounts of the parent company but were to be reported in the balance sheet on a separate line, these potential losses being subsequently offset by later gains, or, if they persisted for too long, being written off. Although these two substantial changes have been criticized (it is difficult in accounting matters to please everybody), they have finally been adopted.

But, whatever the accounting solution, the important thing is that covering transactions which the multinational companies undertake to meet the potential losses appearing under FASB.8 had the consequence of increasing exchange transactions, influencing forward markets and probably increasing general instability. A working party assembled in 1978 by the New York Federal Reserve Bank and the US Treasury found that this increase had not been particularly strong; but its importance cannot be overlooked.

Multinational firms can also keep their subsidiaries' liquid assets to a minimum by accelerating their repatriation in the form of dividends, interest or royalties or by settling accounts between the parent company and its subsidiary or between subsidiaries located in weak-currency and strong-currency countries.

As regards 'receivables', multinational companies can, more easily than others, shorten the payment facilities granted to their subsidiaries' clients. But, in fact, these powerful companies do not seem to resort very much to this practice. The BNAC inquiry shows that 59 per cent of the firms stated that exchange rate volatility did not lead them to alter their payment conditions; if one adds the firms for which this alteration is either limited or insignificant, the percentage reaches 83 per cent.

When the local interest rate is low, 'receivables' can be discounted. Liquid exposed assets can then be transformed into non-exposed assets by investing them in such non-liquid assets as properties and buildings. Alternatively, the risks can be minimized by increasing the exposed liabilities through borrowings in local currency. Such methods are, of course, easier for the big firms. But only up to a certain point.

The flexibility of non-financial enterprises to adjust their assets in consideration of exchange risks is not unlimited. The volume of their fixed assets, such as their factories, is given; even their short-term assets usually correspond to precise needs, generally to a given stage of their technology, and shifts among them cannot be great. Exchange risk adjustment will then be made mainly through debts.

This is particularly true for long-term covers. Eighty-five per cent of the firms answering the BNAC inquiry said that they used foreign-currency-denominated debts in combination with other strategies, to cover long-term risks. Marina Whitman has also noted, in a study on General Motors,[15] that this company correctly sought to minimize the exchange risk linked to its direct investments abroad by balancing assets in a given currency by liabilities in that currency.

Exchange risk and borrowing abroad are also linked in an entirely different kind of operation which has developed considerably in the last ten years and which has nothing to do with multinational firms' offsetting operations. Many entities, which do not export and cannot expect foreign currency receipts to balance their indebtedness, have nevertheless felt the need to turn to heavy foreign borrowings for such reasons as cash-flow shortage, tariff rigidities, or too narrow a domestic financial market. This has particularly been the case with very large investment programmes, such as nuclear or telecommunication projects in France. Of course, interest rate differentials also played a role, particularly in France, where domestic rates were high.

The Group of Thirty study shows that cost is recognized as the determining factor in the choice of the currency for borrowing. This concept of cost is a wide one, covering both interest rate and exchange rate. Nevertheless, since exchange variations have been significantly larger than interest rate differentials, one might expect that many firms having suffered the realization of exchange risks, will now turn towards more national currency borrowings. American companies say they have curbed their foreign borrowing, particularly in the long term, which is, of course, linked with the period of dollar weakness from 1978 to 1981, while, in the strong-currency countries, companies said they were more ready to borrow abroad, both short and long term.

Another aspect of enterprises' financial situation is their policy regarding investment abroad. In spite of legitimate fears, it seems that direct investments abroad have not decreased, and may even have increased, since floating. Exchange rate expectations are only one of the determining factors — and not the most powerful one — of the decision to invest. As national economies become gradually more open, interdependent or integrated, firms must invest abroad to confirm their presence in world markets and to adapt their structure to foreign competition. Accordingly, financial terms and conditions offered abroad, tax regimes, and general cost conditions appear as more important than exchange rate variation. For instance, France, which until 1974 took in more foreign investment than it invested abroad, reversed its position in 1976.

The Group of Thirty inquiry confirms this result for non-French firms. While considering floating as a new element of risk and uncertainty, these firms said that it had had no restrictive effect on their investments. The BNAC study also confirms this. Fifty-six per cent of the enterprises interrogated considered as nil or insignificant the changes in their foreign investment behaviour, the percentage reaching 66 per cent in Canada and 77 per cent in Great Britain. Only 4 per cent of the firms contemplate a possible cut in the level of their investments because of floating. In all other cases, the exchange risk is taken into consideration, but accepted. The evolution of the US direct investment position also confirms these answers. Direct investments abroad have continued to increase since floating from $101 billion in 1973 to $168 billion in 1978.[16]

All this evidence shows that investors have been able to avoid or to face exchange risks. This is all the more interesting since there is no forward market for the long term, which is the area of investments. One explanation is that firms believe in purchasing power parity. If, in the medium or long run, purchasing powers are in parity, the risk linked to long-term investment can be carried. If an American enterprise invests in a country whose currency is depreciating, this normally corresponds, according to the purchasing power parity theory, to an increase in the cash flows obtained in that country, which compensates for the depreciation. It is not even necessary for the theory to be true, so long as investors believe it is. Another factor is important. Since many firms are exposed in several countries, it may happen that the relationship between the various exchange rates provides some natural reduction or spreading of the risk.

Nevertheless, let us see how the enterprises which seek to cover their long-term risks operate. Various techniques can insure such cover in spite of exchange control regulations. They are known as parallel loans, swap arrangements, and simulated dollar loans. They are activated by two treasurers having parallel needs.

'*Parallel loans*', which were first used in the United Kingdom to avoid the cost of 'the dollar premium',[17] are two loans in two different currencies between different branches of two firms for the same maturity. The spot rate will be used for the conversion and the local interest rate will be used in each loan. As the future evolution of interest rates is uncertain, parallel loans generally include a revision clause. The maturity of such loans is usually five to ten years.[18]

Straight 'currency swaps'. In this case currencies are not lent but sold, and at the same time a repurchase commitment is entered into for an agreed date. The characteristics and objective of this technique are similar to those of parallel loans, but the operation is simpler, since it implies only one transaction. Such financing can be arranged for a period up to ten years. What the contracting partners essentially agree upon is to service each other's borrowing. Thus, if the interest rate is 10 per cent in the United States and 14 per cent in the United Kingdom, the British firms will pay the US partners 14 per cent (sterling cost) while the US firms will pay the British firms 10 per cent (dollar cost). That way, both firms pay debt service in their home currency base. The repurchase is normally made at the initial exchange rate, since any exchange variation would normally have been reflected in the differential in interest rates already paid during the loan. Nevertheless, a revision clause bearing on interest and exchange rates is usually included.[19] The total of long-term swaps in the US, UK, German, Dutch and Canadian currencies has grown from $1 billion in 1977 to some $15 billion in 1984. The World Bank/ IBM deal, in particular, opened the swap market to large transactions. Swaps are in essence exchanges through which parties can transform the currency of their liability or of their cash flow into a preferred currency which meets their needs. Like the forward market, they are all tailor-made transactions.

The 'simulated currency loan' is a direct loan which incorporates protection against the exchange risk since the loan is denominated in one currency but reimbursements are made in a second one. The exchange risk is borne by the firm which is borrowing.

These various techniques did, indeed, exist before floating and the Group of Thirty inquiry has shown no evidence of any entirely new device having been invented to cope with the problems linked to floating. But most of the enterprises interrogated admitted that they now made more frequent use of swaps and parallel loans.

Conclusion

Our analysis might appear to lead us to the impression that firms have found reasonably satisfactory answers to the risks of floating, and that markets are well equipped. Can we then conclude that everything is for the best in the best of all possible worlds, and that all that is written about 'world monetary disorder' is only literature?

Such a conclusion would at least be realistic. The fairly generalized use of the US dollar as a vehicular and reserve currency, the development of the Euromarket, the reluctance of the major countries to allow any form of control on Eurocurrencies — be it 'monetary' or 'prudential' — make an early return to a strongly organized system for international payments very unlikely. One has to live with instability and with floating.

No country today can afford to expose its reserves for any length of time to the immense pressure of world markets which stand alert and ready to adjust their position on any currency under discussion, not only by accelerating or delaying their trading or invisible transactions operations but also simply by selling or buying the currency. Only floating, i.e. the possibility for the central bank to refine its strategy and to engineer an appropriate mix of use of reserves, interest rate policy and exchange rate variation, can restore the monetary authorities to an equal status with the market operators.

But two questions may be relevant: (a) The first relates to the possibility of facilitating access to forward cover. As we have seen, the futures markets will become more and more useful and the use of currency swaps is becoming more frequent. But the number of firms, particularly the medium and small ones, which might use such techniques will remain limited. Forward cover will remain difficult and costly and is not easily found for more than one year (not to mention the fact that, in many cases, national exchange control regulations severely curtail its access). Is it possible to devise mechanisms, at the national level, which would make this access easier and cheaper? In so doing, one should of course avoid the resurrection of systems that have been devised in some countries in the past to provide heavy equipment exporters with an insurance against exchange risks or domestic price fluctuations under the name of 'economic risks guarantees'. The main danger of these mechanisms lies in the ever-present temptation to use them as a disguise for plain subsidies — for instance, by setting the agreed reference basis at a date prior to the beginning of the contract — which are in fact tantamount to a devaluation.

(b) The second relates to the size of floating. It is often suggested that the first priority should be to limit that size. But one should make a clear distinction between central banks' interventions to smooth the exchange rate's evolution, to offset seasonal patterns in the balance of payments or to avoid temporary over-reaction to an unforeseen event, and more durable interventions, aimed at resisting an appreciation or a depreciation or at gaining time before the implementation of an adjustment programme. It is, of course, the latter which are most often referred to when one talks of reducing the size of floating and the uncertainty associated with it.

While there is general agreement that central banks' interventions can be useful in smoothing temporary exchange rate fluctuations, but with a limited effect, opinions differ widely as to the possibility of reintroducing, among the major industrialized nations, some form of commitment to maintain stability at least within agreed margins. This is what the proponents of the 'target zone' approach would like to achieve. The 'band' of possible interventions should be wide enough to give banks the means of inflicting heavy losses on the speculators, while, on the other hand, the countries participating in the arrangement would be led to take the appropriate domestic measures to keep their currency in line, at least for a reasonable period of time, with the agreed exchange parity.

In various papers, Robert V. Roosa has advocated such an approach, which would be limited initially to the currencies of the United States, Germany and Japan. The main difference from the 'pure' floating rate situation is that the three countries would undertake 'to consult, to negotiate, and within practicable limits, to act as part of a common effort to achieve balanced stability'. Once agreed upon and put in operation for a certain time, the system would permit the reintroduction of some of the most useful characteristics of the fixed rate system, such as moderating short-term fluctuations, establishing a durable benchmark for private transactions, and strengthening the discipline of the exchanges.

But, while acknowledging the value of these objectives, many would argue that, although there is room in the world for wider areas of stability, such as the one created in Europe by the EMS, it would not be possible to include the dollar in such arrangements, given its special situation and the magnitude of the pressures with which, in one direction or another, its exchange rate would always be confronted. As it has sometimes been expressed, all currencies can go back to fixed rates, but the dollar will go on floating.

In the academic world also, suggestions have been made towards achieving more stable exchange relationships. In presenting in 1984 'An International Standard for Monetary Stabilization', Professor McKinnon, pulling together many elements of his previous contributions, recommends that the monetary authorities of the three major areas, the United States, Japan, and Germany, should cooperate to stabilize the purchasing power of their currencies, and should direct their attention, not only to their domestic money supply, but also to the aggregate money stock of the three areas, calculated on a weighted basis somehow similar to the SDR formula in use since 1981 (45 per cent for the United States, 20 per cent for Japan and 35 per cent for Germany; as against 42 per cent for the US dollar, 19 per cent for the yen, and 13 per cent for the Deutschmark, the pound sterling and the French franc in the SDR). In this operation, the authorities would pay due regard to the evolution of the exchange rate. Not only would they intervene to smooth exchange rate fluctuations, but they would also adjust their monetary policy accordingly, i.e. contracting their monetary base when the dollar was weak, and expanding it when the dollar was strong. Such moves may not of course be easy to implement, as shown in such situations as that experienced in early 1984, when, in spite of the strength of the dollar, the overall evolution of activity, demand and expectations in the United States did not warrant a more expansionary monetary policy.

Lastly, as far as official thinking is concerned, no great progress has been achieved in the last four or five years towards any major change in the exchange rate system. Calls are sometimes made for 'a new Bretton Woods'. The conference of the 'non-aligned' countries, meeting in New Delhi in March 1983, endorsed the idea which later became the title of a report issued under the auspices of the Commonwealth Secretariat. With less enthusiasm, the Williamsburg Western Summit of May 1983 approved the principle of preparatory studies for such a conference, while the conclusions of the 1984 London Summit were less forthcoming, postponing consideration of the matter to 1986, and sending it back to the place where many would agree it rightly belongs, namely, the International Monetary Fund.

Even the studies undertaken after the Versailles Summit of 1982 by the deputy finance ministers did not reflect any substantial change in thinking. Their report (generally known as the Jurgensen report) concentrates primarily on the technical aspects of the use and benefits of market interventions, and does little to open the way towards anything related to the target zones approach.

Enterprises will therefore have to live with floating. They will no doubt be able to make better use of the instruments at their disposal for hedging. Governments would help them greatly if, by following in the coming years more harmonized policies (on budget deficits, interest rates, global demand management), they could avoid the excessive fluctuations, or currency misalignments, which have marked floating's first ten years.

Notes

1. R. M. Rodriguez, 'The Increasing Attraction of the SDR to Business Corporations', *Euromoney*, December 1981.

2. See IMF, *International Financial Statistics*, Vol. XXXVII, No. 5, May 1984 and *Annual Report* 1983.

3. P. Kenen, 'Exchange Rate Regimes of Developing Countries, 1974–1979', Research Memorandum, International Financial Section, Dept. of Economics, Princeton University, 10 July 1979.

4. Ronald I. McKinnon, 'Exchange Rate Instability, Trade Imbalances, and Monetary Policies in Japan and the United States' in P. Oppenheimer (ed.), *Issues in International Economics*, Stocksfield, Northumberland, Oriel Press, 1978, and *An International Standard for Monetary Stabilization*, Institute for International Economics, Policy Analyses in International Economics No. 8, Washington DC, 1984.

5. In the same way McKinnon in his 1984 book argues that the Federal Reserve System could have mitigated the inflationary explosion of the 1970s by contracting the US money supply and that it could have partially offset the strongest effects of the 1982

recession by expanding the US money supply in 1981–2 after the German (and other industrial countries') monetary supply had fallen from 1980 to mid-1982. It could be answered that such moves might not necessarily have been appropriate from the point of view of the domestic economy.

6. V. Argy, *Exchange Rate Management in Theory and Practice*, Princeton Studies in International Finance, No. 50, 1980.

7. Group of Thirty, *Foreign Exchange Markets Under Floating Rates*, New York, 1980.

8. Many elements of what is often called the 'disorder of the international monetary system' have nothing to do with the exchange rate regime and floating. One, of course, was the building up in the hands of OPEC countries with low absorption capacity of a considerable surplus (both in regard to the recycling possibilities of the system and as a percentage of the importing countries' GNP). Even though this surplus disappeared rather rapidly after the first oil shock, and even more rapidly after the second, this factor has played a considerable role in the troubles the world has known since 1974.

The second factor, whose effects would have been felt just as much under a fixed rate regime, is the technological evolution of many industries and the new international division of labour.

A third factor should not be construed as an evil of floating, since it is one of its features which can legitimately be regarded as a merit: namely, the chance that speculators may incur heavy losses from markets' endogenous up-and-down turns or from intelligent central banks' interventions. Asked by a working party of the Group of Thirty whether the functioning of forward markets had recently deteriorated, the majority of the banks interrogated answered in the affirmative but pointed out that this deterioration was, in their words, 'post-Herstatt' rather than 'post-floating'. Most crises which have affected banks in the field of foreign exchange since 1975 (Herstatt, Lugano, etc.) were of this type.

9. The four studies are: (i) P. Kenen, *Exchange Rate Variability — Measurement and Implications*, a study made under the auspices of the Group of Thirty. It considers the following 36 countries: *main industrialized countries* — United States, United Kingdom, Belgium, France, West Germany, Italy, Netherlands, Switzerland, Canada, Japan; *other developed countries* — Austria, Denmark, Norway, Finland, Australia, New Zealand, South Africa; and *developing countries* — Greece, Ireland, Portugal, Spain, Turkey, Yugoslavia, Argentina, Brazil, Mexico, Israel, Syria, Egypt, China, India, Korea, Malaysia, Philippines, Thailand, Morocco. (ii) A note by Geoffrey Bell for the Group of Thirty. (iii) Group of Thirty, 'Foreign Exchange Markets under Floating Rates', op. cit. And (iv) British North American Committee, *Flexible Exchange Rates and International Business*, Washington DC, 1981.

10. See M. C. Deppler, and R. Duncan, 'The World Trade Model: Merchandise Flows', *IMF Staff Papers*, Vol. 25, March 1978, pp. 147–206.

11. W. D. Nordhaus, 'Statement on the Decline of the Dollar', Hearings before the Subcommittee on Foreign Economic Policy, 95th Congress, 2nd Session, Washington DC, 22 June 1978, pp. 249–53.

12. *Futures Trading in International Currencies*, Chicago Mercantile Exchange/International Monetary Market, Chicago, 1977, p. 1.

13. H. Bourguinat, *Le flottement des monnaies*, Presses Universitaires de France, 1977.

14. H. Bourguinat, 'Le rebondissement du problème des monnaies de facturation', *Banque*, No. 423, December 1982.

15. Marina v.N. Whitman, *International Trade and Investment: Two Perspectives*, Princeton Essays in International Finance, No. 143, July 1981.

16. *Survey of Current Business*, August 1979.

17. Premium market for foreign investment, on which, in order to comply with the Bank of England's exchange control regulations, firms had to buy foreign exchange at a higher rate than the official rate.

18. Each loan appears as a debt in the balance sheet and so affects the firm's net exposure. The exchange risk can nevertheless be shared if the loan includes a 'topping-up clause'. (Such a clause calls for additional advances or repayments of one of the loans whenever the spot exchange rate moves past a trigger point.)

19. The swap appears as an annex to the balance sheet (balance sheet footnote item) and implies no 'translation exposure'.

4
External Adjustment in a World of Floating: Different National Experiences in Europe
Manfred Wegner*

Transition towards a new environment

In following the heated debate on the efficacy of differing monetary and exchange rate regimes, it is hard to avoid the impression that economists are often like old generals: they tend to fight battles of yesterday over and over again. The 1970s, of course, offered a unique opportunity for large-scale experiments and for testing new economic theories and policy responses. But the last ten years have also been a period of radical changes in the world economy, of worldwide stagflation and of severe and unprecedented shocks for industrial and developing countries, all of which raised very serious adjustment problems.

Two huge oil price rises have created major instabilities and large balance of payments imbalances. However, it is too simple to assume that all the major present-day economic ills can be blamed on oil. The first oil shock of 1973–4 acted more as a catalyst and accelerated a number of changes which were already in the pipeline since the end of the 1960s. The explosive growth of international liquidity, rising and divergent inflation rates and the rapid expansion of private international financial markets were all part of the story, which finally led to the breakdown of the Bretton Woods system and to the emergence of floating exchange rates. Again, it is not sufficient to assess the experience of the last decade only in relation to this new world of floating rates. Many countries pegged their exchange rates to some large currency areas, many practised 'dirty' floating, and some European countries experimented with partially pegged systems by fixing their bilateral exchange rates but floating as a block

* This chapter was written while staying as a Visiting Fellow at the Institute for International Economics, Washington, DC. The author would like to thank John Williamson and Joly Dixon for valuable comments and suggestions.

vis-à-vis the rest of the world. The period of floating also covers a vast number of reversals of policy, radical changes from fiscal expansion to monetary restraint, and—even worse—a large array of diverging policy responses among different countries and finally some attempts to coordinate policy internationally.

The decade since 1973 has been marked by a general decline in economic performance compared to the 1960s. The growth of output and productivity slowed down by more than half in the industrialized world and in turn produced a deceleration of growth by two-thirds in the volume of world trade. Unemployment rates doubled in the United States, quadrupled in Europe and rose in some countries tenfold and more. Two recessions and a long period of stagnation contributed to high budget deficits, particularly in the United States, and an adverse mix of monetary and fiscal policy led to a rise in real interest rates to levels unknown since the Great Depression. Together with the slowdown in trade, these high real interest rates have created an acute crisis in managing the debt of the less developed countries. They also threaten to abort the recent moderate economic recovery in Europe.

In this troubled world most industrial countries have struggled with large and sometimes huge balance of payments deficits due to massive changes in the terms of trade and other disturbances. External imbalances in the Bretton Woods system of the 1960s were only occasionally a restraining factor in the growth performance of the industrial countries. Their emergence was usually corrected by active demand-management policies. More persistent and 'funda-mental' disequilibria required external adjustments involving changes in the relative competitive positions through currency de- or revaluations. In Europe, the achievement of currency convertibility, the trade-creating effects of the EEC and EFTA, the alternation of boom and slower growth periods, created a virtuous circle of international and intra-European trade and domestic income growth which permitted easy real adjustments in most economies. But this unparalleled performance also contained the seeds of the breakdown of the Bretton Woods system. Growing inter-nationalization of the world economy and the increasing mobility of capital helped the transmission of inflationary disturbances. They also made the implementation and control of domestic policies more and more difficult. The open European economies were especially vulnerable to foreign imbalances and shocks. At the beginning of the 1970s the strains multiplied and became more visible. Inflation differentials and balance of payments disequilibria increased. There were recurrent exchange rate crises. Policy responses became more disparate, with realignments and exchange and capital controls. The transition toward a more flexible international monetary system became almost inevitable.

The advocates of floating exchange rates claimed that flexible rates 'would allow countries autonomy with respect to their use of monetary, fiscal and other policy instruments — by automatically ensuring the preservation of external equilibrium'.[1] Floating rates would ensure that external balance and current accounts would be kept roughly in line with fundamental economic conditions. Flexible rates would insulate economies from external influences and therefore allow them to pursue their domestic objectives without damaging the free movement of goods and capital.

Ten years should provide sufficient evidence to allow an assessment of the fundamental lessons that have been learned in adjusting to the new international economic environment. How well has the international adjustment process functioned? Have floating rates contributed to easing the pains of structural changes and have they reduced the degree of policy interdependence among open economies? The 1970s were a turbulent period, however, and no easy and clear-cut answers can be expected in a world of changing policy regimes, external shocks and rising instability. Before proceeding with a review of different policy responses in the 1970s, a broad picture of the balance of payments changes in some European countries is given below. These countries are chosen partly because they offer a wide mixture of experience in adjusting to serious payments problems, and partly because they are more trade-dependent and hence more vulnerable to external disturbances than the United States and Japan, which are often the object of economic analysis. In confronting these experiences and the different policy responses to them, we may be better able to understand the fundamental changes and the ongoing transition towards a new environment and long-term equilibrium.

Some empirical evidence on the external imbalances, 1973–83

Notwithstanding the monetarists' doubts about the meaning of 'external balance', the traditional balance of payments on current account provides a useful starting point for describing the different impacts of the two oil price shocks in the 1970s on the major country groupings and the main European countries.[2]

Current account movements can be analysed by three algebraic identities which emphasize different approaches. The 'export minus imports' identity (including services) inspires adjustments via relative price changes using the elasticity approach. The 'income minus absorption' identity interprets imbalances as the difference between national output or income generated and national absorption (expenditures) of goods and services by consumers and investors, private and public. The 'savings minus investment' identity focuses on the longer-term outcome of intertemporal choices on the part of households, firms and governments, measuring the gap between national savings and domestic investments and defining a current account deficit as 'the sum of the private financial deficit (excess of investment over savings) and the public deficit'.[3] A surplus in the current account reflects the fact that a country's savings exceed its investment requirements.

International payments adjustment and the oil price shocks

The two oil price increases in 1974 and 1978–80 were the single most important external influence on the balance of payments situation in the 1970s. For the oil-exporting countries they produced an abrupt improvement in their terms of trade and correspondingly huge current account surpluses. The counterparts of these surpluses were large deficits for the industrial and non-oil developing countries. It has been estimated that the terms of trade deterioration of nearly 10 per cent in 1973–4 and 1978–80 increased the combined oil bill of the OECD countries by about 2 per cent of GDP in 1974 and again in 1979–80.

Though the two oil shocks appeared to be similar in size and in initial impact, they produced substantial differences in the adjustment process undertaken by the major country groupings and the national economies. After the experience of the first shock, the industrial countries expected to handle the second one more smoothly, seeking to contain inflationary impulses, to avoid deflationary overreactions and to pursue a more active energy saving and substitution policy. At the same time, most observers feared that the surpluses of the oil-exporting countries would disappear more slowly because of their more cautious increases in imports.

After the first oil price increase, the large current account surpluses of the oil-exporting countries were progressively reduced in the following years and were almost completely eliminated by 1978.[4] The adjustment resulted from slower real growth of demand which caused lower exports of crude oil and, even more important, rapidly rising imports on the part of the oil-exporting countries. The two main groups of oil-importing countries reacted very differently. The industrial countries adjusted, as a group, by accepting a strong deflationary impact, with drastic import reductions during the recession in 1975 and a rapid shift of resources into net exports. The current account of the industrial world switched from a small surplus in the early 1970s to a large nominal deficit in 1974 and then back again to surplus in 1975. Table 4.1 illustrates the *real* external adjustment and the shift of about US $35 billion (at 1975 prices) into net exports between the early 1970s and 1978. The non-oil developing countries and also the smaller industrial countries, by contrast, maintained higher real economic growth rates after the first oil shock and made no progress toward real external adjustments. They therefore rapidly accumulated an enormous short- and medium-term debt burden in the following years which has threatened to become unsustainable.

At the same time, the balance between financing and adjustment in the industrial and developing countries cannot be regarded as optimal. The 1974–5 recession and restrictive policies shifted the current account deficits of the OECD countries as a whole to the developing countries. The dangers of competitive devaluations and of escalating protectionist devices were avoided, but the industrial countries paid a high price for the adjustment: slow real growth, falling investment and a steep rise in unemployment. They made an abortive attempt to 'share the adjustment burden' in a more equitable way; the 'burden-sharing' formula discussed in 1974 was that each nation should accept a current account deficit roughly relative to the increase in its oil payments. But the actual deficits of some European countries (such as the United Kingdom and Italy) had been much larger, while some other countries (such as Germany and later Japan) even experienced growing surpluses. Instead of damaging forms of adjustment like competitive devaluations or import restrictions, domestic prices and nominal exchange rates adjusted by means of varying monetary and demand policies. The industrial group as a whole probably underestimated the deflationary impact of the oil price rise and of their own policies in running aggregate demand below 'full' employment capacity.

The balance of payments performance after the second oil shock was a replay of the first, but with a much more rapid adjustment and

TABLE 4.1
Real external adjustment, 1973–83

	Real GDP growth (annual averages in percentages)		Current account as % of GDP (average)			Change in foreign balance on goods and services at 1975 prices (US $ bn)	
	1974–78	1979–83	1961–73	1974–78	1979–83	between 1970/72 and 1978	between 1978 and 1983
Oil-exporting countries	5.6	–1.5	n.a.	n.a.	n.a.	–60	–75
Non-oil developing countries	4.8	3.2	n.a.	4.1[a]	n.a.	–13	48
Industrial countries	2.6	1.6	0.3	–0.2	–0.5	35	48
of which: United States	2.8	1.2	0.4	0.1	0.3	5	3
Japan	3.4	4.0	0.5	0.6	0.2	(12)	26
EC	2.2	1.1	0.4	–0.1	–0.6	22	12

a. Excluding official transfers.
Sources: IMF, *World Economic Outlook*; EC Commission, 'Annual Economic Report, 1983–84', *European Economy*, No. 18, November 1983, Tables 7.1 and 7.2; and OECD, *Economic Outlook*, July 1984.

policy response by most of the oil-importing countries. In the two years 1980 and 1981, the real adjustment process in the industrial country group was almost completed by deflating away the deficit, thus exposing the developing countries once again to high external deficits. But external balances again deteriorated after 1981 because the developing countries tried to adjust their deficits: real exports of the industrialized countries fell and imports stagnated during the worldwide slump. The nominal and current balance improved only because the terms of trade became more favourable with falling oil prices. The experience of the European Community corresponds broadly to that of the industrial country group as a whole. It was less successful than Japan but more successful than the United States. The non-oil developing countries started their real adjustment much later but showed impressive improvements in 1982 and 1983, though the current balance is still in deficit owing to a growing debt-service burden, which has increased by more than US $50 billion since 1978.

The adjustment process in the European Community

The two oil price increases affected the industrial countries differently according to their dependence on oil imports, structure of production, initial economic conditions, diverging perceptions, macroeconomic objectives and attitudes, and different policy reactions.[5] The detailed history of the impact on income distribution, cost inflation and demand deflation is well documented elsewhere.[6] Table 4.2 shows the familiar story of the current account imbalances of the major oil-importing industrial countries in the flexible exchange rate period since 1973, in contrast to the years 1960–73.

At the risk of oversimplification, two groups of response can be distinguished within Europe, in any case up to the years 1976–7. The first group consisted of countries which were following a much stricter anti-inflationary policy stance than the rest, and which had been initiated even before the oil price rise. Countries like West Germany, the Benelux countries and Switzerland ran — sometimes vast — current account surpluses in 1974 and later, despite being large importers of crude oil. Their 'primary' oil deficits were thus overcompensated by a redistribution of the global current account 'oil' deficit at the expense of other countries. The second group, consisting of most of the other European countries (the United Kingdom, Italy, Denmark, Ireland and France) tried to ride out the

TABLE 4.2

Current account of balance of payments (% of GDP)

	US	Japan	FRG	France	Italy	UK	Neth.	Belg.-Lux.
1961–70	0.5	0.2	0.7	0.2	1.8	-0.0	0.0	0.9
1973	0.5	0.0	1.3	0.6	-1.6	-1.4	3.8	3.0
1974	0.1	-1.0	2.7	-1.5	-4.7	-4.0	3.0	1.4
1975	1.2	-0.1	1.0	0.8	-0.3	-1.4	2.3	0.3
1976	0.2	0.7	0.9	-1.0	-1.5	-0.7	2.8	0.6
1977	-0.8	1.6	0.8	-0.1	1.1	0.0	0.5	-0.7
1978	-0.7	1.7	1.4	1.5	2.4	0.7	-1.1	-0.9
1979	0.0	-0.9	-0.8	0.9	1.7	-0.3	-1.3	-2.8
1980	0.0	-1.0	-1.9	-0.6	-2.5	1.4	-1.7	-4.2
1981	0.2	0.4	-0.9	-0.8	-2.3	2.6	2.1	-4.1
1982	-0.4	0.6	0.5	-2.2	-1.6	2.0	2.6	-3.1
1983	-1.2	1.8	0.6	-0.8	0.1	0.7	2.6	-0.7
1984[a]	-2.4	2.4	0.9	-0.4	-0.2	0.5	2.7	-0.4
Mean								
1961–73	0.4	0.5	0.7	0.2	1.5	-0.0	0.5	1.1
1974–78	0.0	0.6	1.4	-0.1	-0.6	-1.1	1.5	-0.1
1979–84	-0.6	0.6	-0.3	-0.7	-0.8	1.2	1.2	-2.6
Standard deviation								
1961–73	0.4	1.2	0.9	0.6	1.6	1.0	1.4	1.2
1974–78	0.8	1.1	0.8	1.2	2.7	1.8	1.8	1.0
1979–84	1.0	1.4	1.2	1.0	1.6	1.1	2.1	1.7

a. Forecast.

Source: OECD, *Economic Outlook*, No. 35, July 1984 (Table 48).

storm by an accommodating monetary and fiscal policy, thus accepting much higher inflation rates and large external deficits. The smaller European countries of this group were already suffering persistent current external deficits, even before the oil shock.

Although the combined current account of the industrialized world recorded a surplus and the surplus of the oil-exporting countries had practically disappeared by 1978, major imbalances emerged within the OECD and also among the European countries (see Table 4.2). The hard-currency group, mentioned above, switched to deficit after 1979 (with the exception of Switzerland). France and Italy had current account surpluses in two of the three years 1977 to 1979, and the United Kingdom emerged as an oil producer and exporter after 1977, resulting in respectable external surpluses.

The adverse balance of payments effects of deterioration in the terms of trade have been met by two principal forms of real adjustment:[7] by cutting the volume of primary product imports, especially energy imports; and by increasing the traditional surplus on trade in manufactures. The members of the European Community succeeded in reducing their combined high primary goods deficit — even somewhat better than Japan — but they were much less successful in switching resources into net exports of manufactured goods between 1978 and 1982. Over the same period the Community experienced a swing from surplus to deficit on investment account (mainly servicing external debts) and a steady increase in official transfers to developing countries. Its current account in 1982 was still in deficit (0.6 per cent of GDP) in contrast to a current account surplus in 1978 (0.7 per cent of GDP), but it is expected that the deficit will be eliminated in 1984.

The story of the different performances of individual countries within the Community is quickly told. The Netherlands recorded the largest improvement, and perhaps even an overadjustment. The turn-around from deficits in 1978–80 to a current account surplus was achieved by simultaneously increasing the trade balance in primary goods (natural gas) — benefiting from the oil price rise — and manufactured goods through a combination of contractionary domestic policy and improved price competitiveness. Germany, like Japan, completed its external real adjustment by a massive increase in net exports of manufactures, overcompensating the deterioration in its balance on primary products and on invisible transactions. The United Kingdom's current account improvement and surplus in 1982 was based mainly on surplus in the energy account, and the balance of trade in manufactures deteriorated as a consequence of the steep appreciation of sterling. The United Kingdom is expected to record — for the first time in its history — a deficit in manufacturing trade in 1983, which may almost eliminate the current account surplus of previous years. Italy and the smaller countries like Belgium and Denmark made slower progress in improving their balance of trade in manufactured goods, and have had to accept a decrease in their investment income as a result both of borrowing to finance deficits in previous years, and of rising costs of debt service. France, Ireland and Greece made no progress at all during the four years from 1978 to 1982. France failed to reduce the trade deficit on primary goods and switched from a surplus in manufactured goods in 1978 to a deficit in 1982 induced by the expansionary policy in 1982, which led to a swing in the current account of 5 per cent of GDP.

Balance of payments financing, capital flows and external debts

The adjustment process after the second oil shock was considerably smoother, with inflation and real wage increases somewhat lower in 1979–80 than in the two years following the first oil shock. While the total current account deficit of the European Community was larger than in the earlier episode (as seen in Table 4.1), the distribution of these payments deficits among member countries was more balanced (see standard deviations in Table 4.2). But the former country-by-country pattern of current account imbalances has been re-established in the last few years. Germany and the Netherlands again became surplus countries (like Japan) and the former deficit countries faced even larger imbalances.

There are persistent arguments about linking the current account outcome to the savings-investment balance. Sachs emphasized that savings and investment behaviour would be an important — and sometimes even the principal — determinant in explaining the size and direction of current account positions. He tried to show that shifts in domestic investments were as important as oil import dependence in explaining recent current account patterns following the oil shock, given the apparent stability of saving rates. He (and McKinnon) claimed that declining gross fixed capital formation generated large current account surpluses in the United States, Germany and Japan and that growing capital formation (as in Norway and in the United Kingdom) was mainly financed by foreign capital flows. 'With the exception of Japan, there is a strong negative relation between the investment rates and current account position of the countries. The countries that are typically in deficit have, on average, much higher investment rates than the surplus countries.'[8]

Feldstein presents empirical evidence to the contrary. Despite the significant increase in the international mobility of capital in the 1970s, the most important source of finance for national investment is still, in his view, domestic saving. International differences in saving rates are associated with differences in investment rates, implying that 'higher levels of domestic investment do not induce foreign capital inflows but can only be financed by domestic saving'.[9]

A quick comparison of investment and saving rates from 1973 to 1982 reveals a very irregular pattern. The basic adjustment for allowing the real transfer of resources from the industrial countries to the oil-exporting countries has taken different forms. It turns out also that saving was not stable but fluctuated strongly and showed a declining trend in most European countries. The large shifts in current account performance have been heavily induced by cyclical movements in output, and changes in aggregate demand and investment are therefore closely correlated. The link between national investment opportunities and current account positions seems valid only in the very long run.

In contrast to the adjustment after the first oil shock (1974–9) when most European countries — with the exception of the United Kingdom and Italy — did not face serious payments problems, the Community remained in deficit on current account for five consecutive years after 1979. The smaller industrial countries often suffered from large external deficits but could easily finance them by borrowing. In the four years 1979–82 for which statistical information is available, the Community's accumulated current account deficit amounted to almost US $74 billion, to which should be added a net outflow of private non-bank capital of about the same size($77 billion). Table 4.3 summarizes the payments financing of some of the member countries. Over the period every member recorded a substantial basic balance of payments deficit, even countries like the United Kingdom and the Netherlands which were experiencing current account surpluses. The 'basic' deficits have been substantial in Germany, France, Italy and the United Kingdom and they have been financed in different ways. Germany and Italy preferred to resort to official long- and short-term borrowing. The use of foreign reserves played only a supplementary role in Germany. France and the United Kingdom financed their deficits mainly by means of short-term loans from banks. In most of the

TABLE 4.3
Balance of payments financing in the Community, 1979–82 (ECU bn)

	FRG	France	Italy	UK	Neth.	Belg.-Lux.	EC
1. Cumulative current account deficit	-17.9	-19.4	-16.1	22.2	2.4	-12.6	-62.1
2. Private non-bank capital (net)	-8.0	-12.1	2.3	-43.2	-6.9	-4.9	-64.8
3. Total to be financed (= 1+2)	-25.9	-31.5	-13.8	-21.0	-4.5	-17.5	-126.9
Financed by:							
4. Banks + errors and omissions	-4.5	28.9	2.6	18.2	6.8	5.9	60.4
5. Official long- and short-term capital (net)	21.1	0.5	9.6	-1.2	-0.7	9.8	48.2
6. Change in reserves (a minus denotes increase)	9.3	2.1	1.6	4.0	-1.6	1.8	18.3

Sources: Eurostat and Commission estimates; and *European Economy*, No. 18, November 1983, Table 7.8.

smaller countries financing was achieved through a combination of official borrowing and short-term borrowing from banks.

The experience of large private capital outflows in the second period of floating since 1979 confirms the contention that 'when the current account gets bad the capital account gets worse. The reason is that interest rate policies are oriented toward internal balance, which aggravates the exchange rate consequences of cyclically unsynchronized movements in economic activity in the world economy.'[10] The European countries' willingness to use interest rate policy to assist in financing current account imbalances was even more limited after 1979 when international interest rates jumped to unprecedented levels.

Policy responses and the adjustment process in Europe

Efforts at restoring balance of payments equilibria work through many channels and influences: institutions and rules, discretionary action (or inaction) by governments, monetary authorities and the private sector, and finally through market forces. The macroeconomic instruments available to national economies in facing the balance of payments deficits range from using foreign reserves, official borrowing or financing by private international banking to improving competitiveness by devaluations or through domestic price and cost performance and implementing deflationary or restrictive macroeconomic policies. Only some of these responses and reactions can be analysed in the following sections.

Exchange rates and current account imbalances

There are no simple linkages between changes in exchange rates and in current accounts. These linkages have become even more controversial since the advent of floating rates. Current account imbalances are influenced by exchange rates. A similar functional relation exists between exchange rate modifications and changes in import and domestic prices. The simultaneity of price and exchange rate determination makes it extremely difficult in practice to disentangle the causal relationship between exchange rates, domestic prices and external imbalances.

We shall analyse first the contribution that exchange rate changes can make toward reducing current account imbalances. Many of the advocates of flexible exchange rates and of the monetary approach claimed initially that exchange rates would be governed by purchasing power parity, that is, that they would stay more or less in line with relative national inflation rates thus maintaining constant price-adjusted or 'real' exchange rates.[11] But the last decade has shown clearly that there are very volatile short-term and also — even worse — more persistent deviations from this path. These deviations have been more pronounced for the major currencies and have created excessive medium-term cycles, which reflect the inherent forces of different adjustment speeds for goods and asset markets.[12]

The first 'cycles' appeared in 1973–6 in the US dollar/ Deutschmark rate. The year 1976 saw a sudden and extremely rapid depreciation of the Italian lira, French franc and pound sterling, which did not correspond to changes in the inflation rates or current account situations. The reversal of these movements in 1977/8 was much more in line with the improvements in the balance of payments and the impressive decline in the British inflation rate. In 1977–9 the US dollar depreciated sharply, culminating in the October 1978 crisis. From October 1978 until mid-1980 a period of broad stability of effective exchange rates for most of the major currencies prevailed. The year 1980/1 witnessed a marked change in the effective rate of every major currency. The US dollar, the Japanese yen and the pound sterling appreciated sharply, while the Continental European currencies in general moved sharply downward. The rise of the dollar was dramatic. In 1982 its real effective exchange rate stood at a higher level than at the beginning of the floating period. In 1979–81 the pound appreciated even more than the dollar, but fell back later. Table 4.4 indicates the maximum swings in the real effective exchange rates of some major currencies between 1973 and the end of 1983 compared to the ten years immediately prior to the floating period (using quarterly IMF statistics).

The swings were on average twice as large under floating rates, and for the independently floating pound were even more than three times larger. Careful estimates of the current misalignment (defined as 'persistent departure of the exchange rate from its long-run equilibrium level') of the five major currencies in the first quarter of 1983 led to findings of a marked overvaluation of the US dollar (+ 18 per cent) and the pound sterling (+ 11 per cent), a somewhat undervalued yen (− 6 per cent), Deutschmark (− 4 per cent) and French franc (− 3 per cent) and a similar undervaluation of most of

TABLE 4.4
Maximum swings in real effective exchange rates,ª 1963–83 (%)

	1963–72	1973–83
US dollar	14.4	36.2
Pound sterling	17.4	58.9
Japanese yen	13.7	34.6
Deutschmark	21.5	21.3
French franc	23.5	19.7
Italian lira	5.3	17.1

a. Relative wholesale prices vis-à-vis other industrial countries based on quarterly data.
Source: IMF.

the smaller industrial countries. Moreover, according to one commentator, 'There are no indications that misalignments are subsiding over time as experience with floating accumulates, if anything the reverse is true . . . Since the first quarter of 1983 misalignments have tended to increase.'[13]

There are many causes for these excessive swings in real exchange rates and for the severe misalignments: misguided interventions (as in 1974 for the Italian lira, the French franc and the pound sterling and in 1976/7 for the US dollar), market inefficiencies causing overshooting through bandwagon effects and irrelevant information on the part of market participants, and finally internationally inconsistent macroeconomic policies resulting from weak pressures to coordinate policies in a floating regime. The literature and the views on exchange rate determination are mushrooming.[14]

The monetary and asset-market approaches emphasize the dominant role of expectations, which influence exchange rate changes. Recent work has explored the role of trade and current imbalances in forming expectations concerning the future course of events and in signalling the necessary long-term exchange rate adjustments. Large current account disequilibria usually generate expectations of exchange rate changes. But if current account balances respond only sluggishly to changes in the real exchange rates and if nominal rates respond rather rapidly to trade imbalances, then self-perpetuating cycles in the exchange rates are difficult to avoid. The dominant role of expectations and 'news'[15] in a floating system is a further factor which contributes to greater instability of exchange rates and moves them away from fundamental economic conditions.

The British performance in the 1970s is another example of very marked cyclical movements in exchange rates. It combines a long deterioration of the current account balance of payments in the first half of the 1970s and a continuing depreciation of the pound until 1977, with a sustained surplus and an (over-) appreciation since then. The emergence of the United Kingdom as a net oil exporter led to a dramatic contraction of the export-oriented and import-competing manufacturing sector, compounding the British unemployment problem. The so-called 'Dutch disease' is only one cause of the 'de-industrialization' process, others being a stringent monetary policy, resulting in contraction of output in manufacturing from 1979 to 1982 by 16 per cent and of employment in this sector by 20 per cent. The sharp worsening of the British competitive position, particularly since 1979, in the non-oil manufacturing sector is mainly due to the overshooting of the real exchange rate which seriously damaged an important sector of British industry[16] and proved (as Dornbusch has said) that inflation stabilization and oil discovery make difficult bedfellows.

Assessing the costs of exchange rate misalignments is a controversial issue. A global empirical analysis is not (yet) available. But some cautious conclusions can be drawn. There can be no doubt that the real exchange rate changes of the major currencies have been excessive in leading to unjustifiably large deviations from purchasing power parities. The more open a country is, the more adverse the consequences of these excessive swings on the allocation of resources and the economic performance are bound to be. The long-term cycles of real exchange rates induce adjustment and allocation costs for firms and economies in switching from the production of tradeable to non-tradeable goods, and generate trade frictions and protectionism. Sharp declines in real effective exchange rates produce upward pressures on domestic prices and costs and reinforce inflationary expectations. Faced with an imported inflation in 1980–1 the Bundesbank was, for example, forced to counteract the risk of accelerated import price rises by a more stringent monetary policy and higher interest rates, thus damaging investment propensity. Fearing the dangers of a domestic wage/price spiral, many European countries thus adopted much more restrictive monetary policies than were warranted in view of the weak internal demand situation. The pressure to raise interest rates was, of course, more pronounced in countries with devaluation-prone currencies.

The net effect of the strong overvaluation of the US dollar since

1981–3 on the levels of output and employment in other industrial countries is still ambiguous. The impact of high real interest rates is clearly more negative for the developing countries which have suffered a sharp increase in the net cost of servicing their debts since they were largely dollar debtors. There is altogether insufficient systematic evidence as to how large the global costs imposed by exchange rate misalignments have been. But there is a growing number of economists who fear that the failure to agree on any reform of international monetary arrangements was a significant contributory factor to the worldwide stagflation and the long stagnation period since 1980/1. The former President of the German Central Bank, Otmar Emminger, argues bluntly that the excessive swings have to take much of the blame at least for the last recession.[17]

> These roller-coaster movements (of exchange rates) lasted long enough to give misleading signals for trade and investments, and they were long and strong enough to have substantial effects on domestic price levels and real growth; (and) . . . the combination of excessively high interest rates and a high dollar exchange rate spread the American recession over large areas of the world.

Table 4.5 illustrates the substantial changes in real exchange rates[18] since 1973. The direction of these changes was correct: upward for countries with strong current account surpluses and downward for countries in a weak payments position. Real exchange rate modifications have therefore undoubtedly contributed to the external adjustment process. Some pessimism concerning the size and speed of the current account reaction to changes in the real exchange rate was expressed in the early floating period up to 1978/9. The persistent surpluses despite the appreciation of the West German, Japanese and Swiss currencies from 1972 to 1978, and the large deficits of the United Kingdom in 1974–5 despite the depreciation of the pound sterling, have been regarded as evidence for a 'new' elasticity pessimism. Recent studies reveal that this pessimism is not justified, if longer adjustment periods are taken into account. There is some evidence that the price elasticities of demand for imports and exports have been slightly lower in the floating period.[19]

The sluggish response of trade to exchange rate shifts can be explained by many factors, such as cyclical and secular changes in income and productivity, trade barriers and adjustment inertia due to habits and preferences, and the slow reactions in shifting between

TABLE 4.5
Effective[a] and real[b] exchange rates (indices 1975 = 100)

	US dollar		Japanese yen		Deutschmark		French franc		Italian lira		Pound sterling		Belgian franc	
	effective	real	effective	real	effective	real	effective	real	effective	real	effective	real	effective	real
1970	118.6	140	89.8	94	78.5	90	91.7	92	127.7	98	127.2	98	94.2	92
1973	98.5	108	110.3	108	93.6	104	97.3	96	115.2	99	111.9	90	98.0	95
1974	101.0	105	103.2	109	98.4	105	90.8	89	104.0	94	108.3	95	99.1	98
1975	100.0	100	100.0	100	100.0	100	100.0	100	100.0	100	100.0	100	100.0	100
1976	105.2	105	104.2	98	104.8	101	95.6	99	82.3	89	85.6	93	101.4	102
1977	104.7	102	115.2	104	113.0	107	91.3	97	75.5	87	81.2	89	107.1	105
1978	95.7	94	141.7	118	120.1	110	91.3	94	71.1	85	81.5	94	111.1	104
1979	93.7	92	131.5	103	127.5	111	93.4	98	69.4	89	87.2	109	113.7	101
1980	93.9	93	126.5	92	128.8	109	94.4	100	67.2	91	96.1	135	114.0	97
1981	105.7	106	142.9	103	119.3	96	84.4	93	58.3	90	94.9	142	106.3	91
1982	118.1	119	134.8	95	124.3	97	76.6	90	53.8	92	90.5	137	95.9	79
1983	124.9	127	148.4	102	127.2	96	70.0	86	51.2	95	83.2	127	92.0	75

a. Changes in the effective exchange rates for 18 industrial countries (fixed weights: MERM-Model 1972 and 1977).
b. Relative normalized Unit Labour Costs.
Source: IMF, *International Financial Statistics.*

TABLE 4.6
Cumulative changes in nominal and real exchange rates vis-à-vis EMS competitors

	Real exchange rates		Changes resulting from:	
	Before EMS (1970 to 1st quarter 1979)	Under EMS 1979–1983 (1st quarter 1979 to 1st quarter 1983)	Nominal effective exchange rates	Consumer prices
FRG	+8.0	−5.3	+18.7	−20.3
France	−4.0	+0.1	−10.4	+11.7
Neth.	+17.6	−2.3	+9.9	−11.1
Dk	+6.7	−3.2	−15.2	+14.2
Belg.	+9.4	−15.6	−11.7	−4.4
Italy	−27.1	+25.0	−13.8	+44.9
UK	−16.5	+21.6	+10.9	+9.7
Japan	+33.8	+4.4	+24.6	−16.2
US	−36.8	+42.7	+44.6	−1.4

Notes: Plus signs indicate relative price increases (decreased competitiveness) and minus signs relative price declines (increased competitiveness).

The relative exchange rate and relative consumer price indices (columns three and four) are calculated in relation to corresponding EMS weighted averages.

Source: R. Triffin, 'The Future of the European Monetary System and of the ECU', Centre for European Policy Studies, Annual Conference 23–26 November 1983.

foreign and domestic goods. In the last ten years initial perverse effects, known as J-curve effects, have become notorious. Before beginning to improve, the trade balance has first worsened for 4–5 quarters after a devaluation.

The fact that floating exchange rates have contributed to these delayed and lagged effects cannot be excluded. The short-term volatility of nominal exchange rates — moving within a few months by between 20 and 30 per cent — has perhaps made it more difficult to recognize relative price changes as permanent signals for shifting resources. The effects of floating rates in the last ten years have thus not all been beneficial for the longer-term performance of the open economies of Europe. The European Monetary System (EMS), which succeeded the regional pegging of some exchange rates in the 'snake' arrangements, has provided some intra-Community exchange rate stability in contrast to the floating pound sterling, US dollar and Japanese yen. The swings in the real exchange rates of EMS currencies have been much smaller than those in other countries, thus indicating a much better purchasing power parity performance. But the more recent parity adjustments and the wide inflation differentials still existing between the EMS participants reveal growing strains due to the divergent macroeconomic policies being followed in some of the major countries.

Real wage rigidities and other obstacles to adjustment

The failure of flexible exchange rates to affect external imbalances quickly in the period after the first oil price shock can be traced to the downward inflexibility of real wages in the European countries. The adjustment process cannot work when real wages remain rigid, i.e. inflexible in the downward direction. A permanent improvement in price competitiveness by means of currency depreciation can be brought about only when real wages move correspondingly.

Most recent research in the open economy macroeconomics and empirical evidence for the 1970s leads to the conclusion that there is a fundamental asymmetry between the United States and Europe in relation to the impacts of exchange rate changes on external balances and the optimal policy mix.[20] In the United States exchange rate changes mainly affect the trade balance by changing relative prices (and output), but in Europe they have their main effect on the overall level of domestic prices without influencing the trade position. This is because of differing wage rigidities. The United States has more rigid nominal wages due to overlapping multi-year wage arrangements, whereas most European countries have shown sticky real wages due to short-term contracts, loss of money illusion, widespread wage indexation and central bargaining. Countries with sluggish real wages tend to resist devaluations as an effective external adjustment instrument. Under these circumstances the policy objective becomes one of changing wage behaviour and abolishing the negative effects of wage indexation schemes so as to make exchange rate policy more effective.

The stylized facts of sticky real wages were more or less those prevailing in most of the European countries in the 1970s. The internal and external adjustment problems of the open European economies have been aggravated by difficulties in responding rapidly to the sharp deteriorations in the terms of trade caused by the oil price crises and the successive dollar shocks. Overshooting of exchange rates resulting from asset markets adjusting more quickly than goods markets may have induced higher inflationary pressures and thus perhaps fed vicious (or virtuous) circles. The explosion of nominal wages was already beginning in Europe by the end of the 1960s, but the rise in wages accelerated with inflation after the first oil shock. The real wage growth continued even after the massive oil price rises had produced large terms of trade losses and a sudden slackening of growth in productivity. In contrast, real wages did not rise in the United States. In the years 1974–5 nominal industrial wages increased by 20 and 30 per cent per year in some European countries (Belgium, France, Italy, the United Kingdom) and as a result real product wages increased by 5–8 per cent per annum, creating a serious unemployment problem.

Under the pressure of high unemployment, real wages adjusted to the changes in the economic environment in some countries after the second oil price shock. An acute real wage problem still exists for some European countries, as indicated by the 'real labour cost gap' or declining profitability. The countries with excessive real wages are in most cases the same as those suffering from large and persistent payment deficits. Real wage resistance seems to be receding now in most countries; some have recently made progress in relaxing their wage indexation mechanisms, thus unblocking the external adjustment process.

The Belgian experience is worth examining. Real wage rigidity not only impeded the adjustment process but also damaged employment and worsened the public deficits. Belgium is a small and extremely open economy. Around 67 per cent of its GDP was exported as goods and services in 1981. The Belgian franc has been continuously pegged to some regional currency area: to the 'snake' arrangements up to 1979 and to the EMS from then on. The currency experienced an appreciation in real effective exchange rates up to 1980. Belgium entered the 1970s with a comfortable current external surplus and a low unemployment rate, but from 1976 onwards the current deficit widened, employment in manufacturing declined by more than 22 per cent during 1974–81 and the unemployment rate rose to more than 14 per cent of the labour force in 1983. Nominal and real wages rose substantially during the second half of the 1970s. Compensation per employee in industry increased in 1974–6 by 18 per cent per year (i.e. 6.5 per cent in real terms), slowing down afterwards. In the second half of the 1970s the wage level was pushed to the highest level of the industrial countries after starting from a relatively low point.

The results of the excessive (real) wage increase can be easily explained in terms of the two-sector Scandinavian model.[21] Being a price-taker in the world market, Belgium could not increase its

TABLE 4.7
Nominal and real wage compensation and 'real wage gap' (total economy)

		Average annual percentage change				
		1974–75	1976–78	1979–81	1982	1983
Nominal	FRG	9.3	6.7	6.0	4.4	3.8
compensation	France	18.1	13.3	14.1	14.5	9.7
per employee	Italy	21.5	19.5	20.7	17.1	15.6
(in national	UK	24.7	12.9	17.1	8.8	7.9
currencies)	Neth.	14.5	8.7	4.9	5.7	3.2
	Belg.	17.4	10.9	7.2	8.0	6.0
	US	8.1	7.9	9.1	6.0	5.0
Real[a]	FRG	2.6	3.0	0.9	−0.8	0.8
compensation	France	5.2	3.6	1.7	3.3	0.6
per employee	Italy	2.0	2.7	2.2	0.4	0.5
	UK	3.7	−0.2	3.1	0.7	2.0
	Neth.	3.8	2.2	−0.7	0.0	0.4
	Belg.	4.4	4.3	0.6	0.5	−1.7
	US	−1.0	1.8	−0.3	0.3	0.6

		Indices (average 1965–69 = 100)				
		1975	1978	1981	1982	1983
Real wage	FRG	108	105	105	103	101
gap[b]	France	106	107	109	108	108
	Italy	112	110	110	110	109
	UK	111	100	101	99	97
	Neth.	107	103	101	101	100
	Belg.	110	112	116	112	110
	US	103	103	103	105	103

a. Deflated by the price index of private consumption.
b. Compensation per wage and salary earner deflated by the GDP deflator, minus labour productivity.
Source: European Economy, No. 18, November 1983.

prices of tradeable goods and thus experienced a sharp profit squeeze in the open sector as the result of the appreciation of its currency and the wage explosion. Under this double pressure the manufacturing sector shed labour. Measured labour productivity growth in manufacturing was consequently the highest in Europe (1973–81: 5.9 per cent per year). The sheltered (non-tradeable) sector (construction and most services) suffered from inflationary pressures, but benefited from higher profits and investments.[22] The balance of payments situation deteriorated rapidly as a result of the second oil shock and the decline in the relative prices of tradeables. By 1980 Belgium had one of the largest current account deficits (4.7 per cent of GDP), in fact exceeded only by Ireland (traditionally a deficit country). The protracted deterioration in the payments situation increased the need to support the Belgian franc through intervention and high interest rates, further aggravating the high public deficits (1981–3: more than 12 per cent of GDP).

The Belgian authorities persistently refused to use discretionary devaluations to improve the external balance because of the fear of losing their only instrument against inflation and of entering a vicious circle. This fear was justified by the existence of widespread wage indexation schemes which passed higher import prices immediately on to higher domestic prices and wages. Special government powers, in 1982, allowed the temporary suspension of wage indexation and a reduction of real wages. This cleared the way for an 8.5 per cent devaluation of the Belgian franc within the EMS. The combined effects of the depreciation trend of all EMS currencies since 1980, the decline of relative unit labour costs during 1981–3 and the large devaluation in February 1982 have substantially improved Belgium's profitability and competitiveness (see Table 4.5). Improvements in the balance of payments are expected in 1983 and later.

Macroeconomic stabilization policy and
external adjustment

Changes in real exchange rates have been much larger during the period of floating than in the period of fixed rates. But the adjustment of balance of payments imbalances has worked efficiently and rapidly only when the changes in real exchange rates were sustained and when they were supported by differentiated movements in real demand. Some painful experience was needed to rediscover the well-known absorption approach as an important part of the external adjustment process in the floating period. The absorption approach postulates that exchange rate changes will have a lasting effect on trade and current balances only if domestic absorption is changed relative to output. A currency devaluation implies a more restrictive monetary or fiscal policy in relation to the rest of the world in order to make room for improvements in the current balance, and to allow resources to shift towards net exports. A currency appreciation requires a more expansionary policy to increase domestic demand for imported goods.

The first lesson in rediscovering the importance of supporting macroeconomic policies was brought home by the British experience in 1974–6. An accommodating monetary and fiscal policy, already started in 1971 and continued after the first oil shock, permitted a faster rise in inflation and in wage rates in the United Kingdom than in most other industrial countries. This policy did not improve, as was intended, the real growth and employment performance, but instead triggered off in 1976 a rundown of reserves, large capital outflows and a steep depreciation of the pound.[23]

The exchange rate crisis and the corresponding loss of confidence in international markets could only be stopped by a rigorous stabilization programme at the end of 1976. This consisted of spending cuts and tax increases designed to reduce the huge public deficits (the PSBR in 1975 reached more than 11 per cent of GDP). Britain was put under the surveillance of the IMF, and sterling quickly stabilized after a standby agreement with the IMF and the announcement of the restrictive policy. Most of these measures were in fact adopted already in the summer of 1976, but were not sufficient to restore confidence. Britain thus had to accept the hard fact that flexible rates did not free British policy makers from external constraints and did not provide much more room for manoeuvre in pursuing domestic objectives than did fixed rates. It was Prime Minister Callaghan in 1976 who said: 'We used to think that you could just spend your way out of a recession and increase employment by cutting taxes and boosting government spending . . . that option no longer exists, and insofar as it ever did exist, it worked by injecting inflation into the economy.'[24] And to this Chancellor Denis Healey added even more candidly in 1978: 'Some people used to see depreciation as an easy way of restoring price competitiveness. But hard experience confirms the findings of economic research that the price increases generated by a fall in the exchange rate are tending to feed through a good deal faster into rising labour costs than they used to. Depreciation can no longer be treated as a soft option.'[25]

The Bretton Woods system of fixed exchange rates prompted deficit countries to implement stronger demand-management adjustment measures than surplus countries. This asymmetry in internal disciplinary constraints reappeared in the floating regime, when West Germany continued to place higher priority on reducing inflation and implemented a much more restrictive monetary policy than its neighbours. The slower internal demand contributed strongly to its persistent large current account surpluses from 1974 to

1978 and to a substantial Deutschmark appreciation. This, in turn, helped to improve its inflation performance; the rise in consumer prices came down to 2.7 per cent in 1978. The absence of supporting demand-management policies partly explains German surpluses in this period. The gradual relaxation of the restrictive monetary policy was compensated by a more restrictive fiscal stance, when the German government tried to accelerate the reduction of the public deficit in 1977. The shift toward more accommodating policies in support of external adjustment needs was implemented only in 1979. The United States and the United Kingdom turned to much stricter monetary policies, and Germany and Japan were pushed into more expansionary fiscal policies intended to support the international adjustment process. This turn-around was part of an international concerted action in 1978, known as the 'locomotive or convoy approach', committing the German government to a budget stimulus of 1 per cent of GDP. But at the same time, it was part of launching the European Monetary System with the goal of creating 'a zone of greater monetary stability'. The current account deficits in Germany and the rest of the European Community can thus be attributed in part to the various reflationary actions, but were also caused by the first repercussions of the second oil shock. The economic story of this 'concerted action' has still to be written and is beyond the scope of this chapter.

Recent history provides two further examples of the strong combined effects of differentiated domestic growth rates and real exchange rate changes on the external balance. Germany's current account deficit turned rapidly into surplus in 1981 due to the decline of real domestic demand and a strong depreciation of the Deutschmark. After the advent of the Mitterrand government in 1981 France followed a much more expansionary demand policy than any of its neighbours. The ensuing rapid deterioration of its external position (a current account deficit approaching 3 per cent of GDP in 1982) led to two successive devaluations within the EMS and to corrective internal measures in 1982 and 1983. The policy reversal is expected to bring down domestic growth and to improve the external balance progressively.

Economic interdependence and the EMS

The German and French cases can, of course, be interpreted as examples of the stronger economic interdependence existing in a system of pegged exchange rates, where differences in national policies show up in external imbalances and losses or gains in foreign reserves. It seems useful at this stage to ask if and why the European countries had been generally less restrained under the regime of flexible than under pegged exchange rates in their pursuit of independent domestic policies. More recent views suggest that the expected insulation of national economies from outside influences and disturbances by means of flexible exchange rates can not easily be defended either on theoretical or on empirical grounds.[26] Experience has shown that flexible exchange rates confer a certain autonomy by giving central banks control over their own money supplies and by isolating countries from the world inflationary trend. The German, British and, of course, American performances since 1979 show this regained autonomy. But flexible exchange rates have not been able to protect countries against disturbances originating in international financial markets or in exogenous supply side shocks or cyclical trends abroad nor have they provided sufficient insulation against external monetary disturbances. The conclusions to be drawn from theoretical and model-building research about the operation of flexible exchange rates, and the conditions under which they efficiently bottle up the impact of external influences, are still ambiguous. The jury on flexible exchange rates has still not delivered its verdict.

The initiative to establish 'a zone of monetary stability in Europe' in 1978 was mainly political, and the European Monetary System stemmed from direct support from the German Chancellor Helmut Schmidt and the French President Giscard d'Estaing, both former Treasury Ministers. But the decision reflects even more the growing dissatisfaction with volatile nominal rates and excessive real exchange rate changes since 1977/8. The Europeans feared that their instability would seriously damage the main achievements of the European Community, namely, the free exchange of goods within the large internal market and the Common Agricultural Policy. The volume of intra-Community trade rose by 11 per cent per annum from 1963 to 1973 and by 4.3 per cent from 1973 to 1980. It covered almost 50 per cent of total trade in 1981, compared with 34 per cent in 1958 as the Community average; as regards the Benelux countries, it amounted to 70 per cent.

The establishment of the EMS was facilitated by favourable economic circumstances in 1978. It was the first year after the first oil shock when macroeconomic policy convergence showed substantial improvement. Anti-inflationary policies had been accepted by all the member states. Consumer prices increased in 1978 'only' between 3 and 4 per cent (for Germany, Belgium and the Netherlands) and 12 per cent (for Italy). The balance of payments deficits of the larger members turned into surpluses in 1977 and 1978. The official launching of the EMS in March 1979 coincided with the second oil price rise, which was followed by new inflationary pressures, prolonged economic stagnation and dramatic external monetary disturbances. It is thus difficult to assess the results of the EMS properly even after more than four years. The detailed records of the first years are presented elsewhere.[27]

The following main conclusions can, however, be drawn:

(a) The concerns initially expressed that the constraints of the system would exert deflationary pressures or impair stability-oriented policies were grossly exaggerated; the exchange rate system operated smoothly and proved to be much less rigid than was feared.

(b) The exchange rates among the major EMS countries were more stable than those among the other major floating currencies; the seven currency realignments within the EMS were relatively small — with the exception of the Belgian franc devaluation in 1982 — and tended to offset the inflation differentials, thereby avoiding overshooting cycles of real effective exchange rates.

(c) The constraints of the EMS and the pressures of market forces contributed to a stronger convergence of monetary policies and a more general use of interest rate policies, but progress toward monetary stability was slow and the participating countries had ample recourse to large external official and quasi-official market borrowing to finance their payments deficits; the temptation to fall back on capital controls and trade restrictions was able to be limited.

(d) There are growing indications that the external adjustment process has been supported by domestic adjustment programmes; the EMS countries are thus progressively accepting 'the existence of a common restraint on their fiscal policies'.[28] Recognition of the disciplinary forces imposed by the EMS became apparent in the last two years in more restrictive budgetary stances, in the suspension of widespread wage indexation systems (in Belgium and Denmark) and in the sharp correction of more expansionary fiscal policies (in France). But these changes were not sufficient to reduce substantially the divergence of inflation rates among the participating countries (between 3 and 15 per cent in 1983).

The EMS arrangements, designed as a system of fixed but adjustable exchange rates, have not lost their disciplinary effect, although currency adjustments have been used more frequently in the period since autumn 1981. The improved balance between external and domestic adjustment perhaps compensated for the recent risks of loss of credibility. The EMS and the advantages of belonging to a customs union have been instrumental in implementing painful policy changes. But the existence of a regional pegged exchange rate system will fail to protect the members from external disturbances, so long as the EMS block does not decouple itself from conflicting US monetary policies by depreciating the ECU. Such a decoupling policy implies, in turn, a more successful internal adjustment and stabilization effort. There is also evidence that the existence of the EMS has not impaired the anti-inflationary stance of more stability-conscious countries, like Germany and the Netherlands. The independently floating pound sterling and Britain's success in rapidly reducing the inflation rate are an example of a more autonomous stabilization policy[29] if one is prepared to accept the high costs of an excessive currency appreciation.

Floating exchange rates have made macroeconomic policies often more difficult to manage and imply more stable expectations and more credible and steady policies if they are to become effective. Pegged rates are not necessarily an obstacle to following a determined stability-oriented policy in the long run. In both cases, there is an advantage in policy coordination to avoid the consequences of inconsistent macroeconomic and exchange rate policies. The awareness is growing, that 'the increasing degree of economic integration in the last few decades (whether in terms of trade in goods, of trade in assets, or of socio-economic attitudes and institutions) may account partly for the increased interdependence irrespective of the exchange rate regime'.[30]

The EMS is still far from a currency union arrangement as planned earlier, and the gains in reducing the impact of internal shocks have thus been limited. Compared with the critical views expressed at the outset and taking into account the unfavourable conditions during the first years of its operation, the EMS has been a partial success story. In comparison with the expected dynamics of the first step toward monetary union and in view of the need for a stronger convergence in economic policies, the outcome has disappointed initial hopes. The EMS has not yet passed the real test and must be given a further trial period.[31] Its further progress and consolidation, and a fuller acceptance of the ECU by official authorities and private markets, and even more its development towards becoming the main 'parallel' currency of the Community countries, imply fundamental institutional and political changes for which the necessary consensus does not yet seem to exist.

Policy conclusions and the outlook
for the 1980s

The 1970s were a decade of turbulence and dramatic change. The twofold massive rise in oil prices, the strong ups and downs of inflation rates and the various reversals in economic policy were matched by large and changing current account imbalances. Even at the end of the adjustment process following the second oil shock, new external imbalances are emerging in some major industrial countries. The US current account deficit may well expand from more than $40 billion in 1983 to more than $90 billion in 1984. Its counterpart will be balance of payments improvements in some other OECD countries (particularly in Japan and in the EC). These renewed imbalances are the result of cyclical movements but also of changes in currency competitiveness due to large real exchange rate modifications. The experiences of the past decade justify the question as to whether the system of floating rates was not in itself a major source of instability during these years.

Flexible exchange rates did not fulfil the expectations associated with their introduction in 1973. The promised smooth ride has not been realized. Instead, the period under review witnessed an excessive short-term volatility of exchange rates as well as large real exchange rate swings, neither of which had been expected. These strong misalignments have severely constrained the conduct of macroeconomic adjustment policies. The old Bretton Woods system of pegged exchange rates collapsed because it was regarded as a 'permanent engine of inflation' keeping monetary authorities from pursuing anti-inflationary policies. But the industrial countries have perhaps paid a high overall price in real terms in the 1970s for winning back the 'sovereignty to choose their own inflation rates'. The extreme monetary instabilities which have dominated the period of floating have been induced by wild changes in monetary and financial policies, especially in the United States. The medium-term cycles of under- and over-valuation of the major currencies affected the real economy by impinging directly on prices, real wages and the competitive position of key sectors. After a painful learning process the open and vulnerable European economies had to accept that policy interdependence was intensified in the floating world and that dependence on the US dollar had even been strengthened rather than permitting more automony. The actual danger of a sudden dollar deterioration threatening the weak forces of the nascent recovery is the most recent example of this.

It seems a purely academic question 'to wonder whether this trip was necessary' or to speculate whether 'we would be better off today if governments had been able to defend prevailing parities in March 1973, after the second devaluation of the dollar, or the rates set by the markets at the end of 1974, after a brief "transitional" float'.[32] We rarely have the chance to make the same mistake twice, but we do have a chance to avoid similar mistakes and muddling through, which seems the policy recipe followed up to now.

Of course, the industrial countries have learned to live with flexible rates, and real exchange rate changes have contributed to moving external imbalances towards greater equilibrium. In recent years the burden of balance of payments adjustment was shared by more emphasis being put on internal restrictive policies, as well as the fact that recourse to foreign borrowing to finance large current deficits became unsustainable. Moreover, the adjustment process by means of exchange rate modifications was increasingly supported by higher real wage flexibility and the relaxation of wage indexation schemes, which had been a serious disincentive to the use of devaluations to improve external disequilibria.

Disappointment with floating rates promoted the establishment of the European Monetary System, by reintroducing the idea of a pegged but adjustable exchange rate system on a regional basis. The EMS arrangement has survived despite numerous doubts about it. The concerted exchange rate adjustments within the system have been modest, more or less maintaining purchasing power parities. The instabilities of intra-European exchange rates have remained limited relative to the fluctuations of currencies that are floating independently. Cooperation on monetary policy between the participating countries has been strengthened, though insufficiently in relation to the persistent divergence in inflation rates. Periodic realignments will continue to be necessary so long as the member countries fail to coordinate their domestic policies sufficiently. But the working of the EMS does demonstrate that some exchange rate management and monetary cooperation is possible and useful.

The lessons of floating rates in the 1970s have shown that some of the potentially negative effects of wild exchange rate fluctuations on investment and trade could have been avoided. Floating rates probably require an even closer coordination of national policies than before, and this need is growing with the emergence of a multipolar world to replace the dominance of the US dollar in international trade and finance. Many forms of international cooperation are now being discussed. They include concerted interventions in exchange markets to smooth erratic exchange rate movements, the closer orientation of monetary policies to the pursuit of more stable exchange rates or even the use of exchange rate target zones, and perhaps also a coordinated monetary approach in fixing and jointly controlling the monetary expansion of the three major reserve currencies, the US dollar, the Deutschmark and the yen.[33] All these intensified forms of cooperation in monetary and exchange rate policy imply stronger surveillance of national policies and the establishment of international institutions to exercise pressure towards coordination. But as long as countries are unwilling to sacrifice any part of their national sovereignty in economic decision-making and as long as national governments believe that 'they know best what is good for them', the industrial world will be obliged to live with the risks and disadvantages of floating exchange rates.

Notes

1. H. G. Johnson, *Further Essays in Monetary Economics*, Cambridge, Cambridge University Press, 1972, p. 199.

2. See also J. Salop and E. Spitaeller, 'Why Does the Current Account Matter?', *IMF Staff Papers*, March 1980.

3. W. M. Corden, *Inflation, Exchange Rates and the World Economy* (2nd edn), Chicago, Chicago University Press, 1981, p. 51.

4. The trade and current account balances of all countries do not sum up to zero but show a large and growing excess of deficits over surpluses ranging from $4 billion to $16 billion throughout the second half of the 1970s, increasing to $20 billion in 1980 and $89 billion in 1982. This discrepancy in the global aggregation is caused by inconsistencies including errors and omissions; substantial under-recording of investment income receipts and receipts in service payments, especially for oil exporters, understates the surplus of this group. See also IMF, *World Economic Outlook*, 1983, pp. 161–7.

5. There were other unfavourable but much less severe factors, such as the increase in prices of other raw materials and food.

6. E. R. Fried and C. L. Schultze (eds), *Higher Oil Prices and the World Economy (The Adjustment Problem)*, Washington DC, Brookings Institution, 1975; OECD, *Resource Prices and Macroeconomic Policies: Lessons from Two Oil Price Shocks*, Economic and Statistics Department, Working Paper no. 5, Paris, April 1983; M. Bruno and J. D. Sachs, 'Supply versus Demand Approaches to the Problem of Stagflation', in H. Giersch (ed.), *Macroeconomic Policies for Growth and Stability: A European Perspective*, Kiel 1981.

7. The following argument and statistical evidence draw heavily on Chapter 7, 'Balance of Payments', of the EC Commission's 'Annual Economic Review 1983–4', in *European Economy*, No. 18, November 1983; see also the study 'The Foreign Trade of the Community, the United States and Japan', *European Economy*, No. 16, July 1983.

8. J. D. Sachs, *The Current Account and Macroeconomic Adjustment in the 1970s*, Washington DC, Brookings Papers on Economic Activity No. 1, 1981, pp. 247–9.

9. M. Feldstein, 'Domestic Saving and International Capital', *European Economic Review*, Vol. 21, March–April, 1983, p. 147.

10. R. Dornbusch, 'Exchange Rate Economics: Where do we Stand?', in J. S. Bhandari and B. H. Putnam (eds), *Economic Interdependence and Flexible Exchange Rates*, Cambridge, Cambridge University Press, 1983, p. 67.

11. A large number of 'real' exchange rate indicators are now available and used in the official and academic discussion; see, for example, the IMF.

12. See J. A. Frenkel, 'Flexible Exchange Rates, Prices and the Role of "News": Lessons from the 1970s', in Bhandari and Putnam, op. cit., p. 25.

13. J. Williamson, *The Exchange Rate System*, Washington DC, Institute for International Economics, Policy Analyses in International Economics Series No. 5, 1983, pp. 35–7. In a recent congressional testimony Williamson put the overvaluation of the dollar in October 1983 at 22 per cent. See also R. McKinnon, 'Financial Causes of Friction between Japan and the United States', in E. R. Fried, P. H. Trezise and S. Yoshida (eds), *The Future Course of US–Japan Economic Relations*, Washington DC, The Brookings Institution, 1983, p. 26.

14. Bhandari and Putnam, op. cit.

15. See also the sardonic remark by Buiter in A. W. Hooke (ed.), *Exchange Rate Regimes and Policy Interdependence*, Washington DC, IMF, 1983, p. 38: '. . . it gives one very little comfort to know that asset market prices fully reflect all available information if part of that information is of the sunspot, Harry Kaufman, or other nonfundamental variety.'

16. W. H. Buiter and D. D. Purvis, 'Oil, Disinflation and Export Competitiveness: A Model of the "Dutch Disease"', in Bhandari and Putnam, op. cit; Corden, op. cit.

17. O. Emminger, *The Search for a More Stable International Monetary System — The Role of Exchange Rate Policies*, New York, Group of Thirty, Occasional Paper No. 12, 1983, pp. 21 and 24.

18. There is little agreement among economists as to which of the available indices (the IMF presents five) is the most appropriate for measuring the 'real' exchange rate or the competitiveness of a country.

19. P. B. Kenen and C. Pack, *Exchange Rates, Domestic Prices and the Adjustment Process (A Survey of Recent Evidence)*, New York, Group of Thirty, Occasional Paper No. 1, 1980; M. Goldstein, *Have Flexible Exchange Rates Handicapped Macroeconomic Policies*, Princeton, Special Papers in International Economics No. 14, June 1980.

20. W. H. Branson and J. Rotemberg, 'International Adjustment with Wage

Rigidity', *European Economic Review*, Vol. 13, May 1980. J. D. Sachs, *Wages, Profits and Macroeconomic Adjustment: A Comparative Study*, Washington DC, Brookings Papers on Economic Activity No. 2, 1979, and *Real Wages and Unemployment in the OECD Countries*, Brookings Papers on Economic Activity No. 1, 1983.

21. P. de Grauwe, 'Symptoms of an Overvalued Currency: the Case of the Belgian Franc', in M. de Cecco (ed.), *International Economic Adjustment*, Oxford, Oxford University Press, 1983.

22. The de-industrialization process was aggravated by the dual industry structure of the country: the low productivity Wallonian region with declining industries and aggressive labour unions and the high productivity Flemish part with modern industries and smooth labour relations.

23. The French franc and the Italian lira had left the 'snake' arrangements earlier in 1976 and also depreciated sharply.

24. Speech delivered at the Labour Party's annual conference in Blackpool, 28 September 1976.

25. Speech delivered at the Lord Mayor's Banquet, London, 19 October 1978.

26. R. Dornbusch, op. cit.; A. Swoboda, 'Exchange Rate Regimes and European–US Policy Interdependence', and W. H. Branson, 'Economic Structure and Policy for External Balance', both in Hooke, op. cit.

27. See EC Commission, *European Economy*, No. 12, 1982 and following years (Nos. 14, 18).

28. IMF, *Annual Report 1983*, p. 51.

29. By mid-1983 the reduction in inflation compared to 1980 had been 3 points for Germany, 4 points for France, 6 points for Italy, and 14 points for the United Kingdom.

30. Swoboda, op. cit., p. 97.

31. Emminger, op. cit., p. 26.

32. P. B. Kenen, *The Role of the Dollar as an International Currency*, Group of Thirty, Occasional Paper No. 13, New York, 1983, pp. 65 and 66.

33. R. McKinnon, *An International Standard for Monetary Stabilization*, Washington DC, Institute for International Economics, Policy Analyses in International Economics No. 8, 1984.

5
Is the Multiple Currency Standard a Destabilizing Factor?
Niels Thygesen*

Introduction

The move to floating exchange rates in the early 1970s has rekindled interest in an issue of perennial concern to policy makers and economists preoccupied with international economic issues: Does the coexistence of several national currencies in international trade and finance increase the instability of the international monetary system?

One aspect of this question has been under debate for the past 25 years: namely, the potentially destabilizing features of shifting central bank preferences for various international reserve assets. The at times uneasy coexistence of two national currencies — the US dollar and the pound sterling — and gold as the dominant reserve assets was carefully analysed on a number of occasions in the 1960s after Robert Triffin had drawn attention to the inherent instability of the gold-exchange standard in his classic *Gold and the Dollar Crisis*.[1] Attention centred at the time on the extent to which one could hope to meet the growing demand for reserve assets in the longer run through a supply of national currencies by the key-currency countries without undermining confidence in them and thereby triggering a crisis of convertibility. Preliminary steps to relieve the pressure on the reserve currencies were taken with the decisions in the late 1960s to supplement reserve creation by the allocation of a new and truly international asset, the special drawing right (SDR), and the extension of exchange rate guarantees to official holders of sterling to discourage switches into dollars.

These modest steps were hardly designed to prevent the problems of 1970–2 when the supply of dollars exploded because of growing US deficits on current and capital account. Indeed, for the first

* The author wishes to acknowledge helpful comments and suggestions from the editor on an earlier draft of this chapter.

couple of years after the suspension of the dollar's convertibility into gold, overseas official holders persisted in talking about a massive 'dollar overhang', particularly following the large interventions in support of the dollar during the final months of the fixed exchange rate regime.

Since the start of floating in 1973 the dollar exchange rate in terms of other major currencies has shown not only substantial short-run volatility, but also pronounced cyclical movements in 1973–5 and after 1977 — in the more recent period of an apparently increasing magnitude. This has occurred despite heavy central bank interventions in a number of European countries and in Japan and — on a more modest scale — by the US authorities in the 1978–81 period; observed changes in the international reserves of a number of industrial countries have — after rough allowance for valuation adjustments — become larger than during the pre-1973 period. At the same time, three national currencies, the Deutschmark (DM), the yen and the Swiss franc, have come to play a rapidly growing role in the currency component of reserves, correspondingly reducing the share of the dollar and sterling. It is natural to ask whether shifts in the official reserve holdings among the main available national currencies have on the whole been stabilizing, or whether they have, at least in some periods aggravated the cyclical swings in the main exchange rates. If the latter, the next question is obviously whether central banks could be constrained by some commonly agreed rules to avoid destabilizing switches in the future.

More recent studies of the potentially destabilizing features of the multiple currency standard focus on this aspect, namely, the contribution of central bank operations. Later in this chapter we look at some very recent studies in this area by Bergsten and Williamson and by the Group of Thirty.[2] This concentration of interest is understandable, since the central banks have a special responsibility for the international monetary system; in addition, the availability of data on official reserves poses fewer constraints than do the irregular and incomplete data relating to other dimensions of the problem.

Nevertheless, there is a certain loss of perspective if one moves straight to the role and responsibilities of the central banks. To some extent central bank operations reflect rather than determine changing international practices in the private sector. The present chapter therefore aims to place the discussion of the multiple currency standard as a destabilizing factor in a broader perspective by surveying briefly in the first two sections two other dimensions of the problem: the evolution and present pattern of currency standards in international trade, and changes in the currency composition of internationally held bank assets and liabilities. The main attributes of national monies are usually summarized under three headings: (i) the unit of account, (ii) the means of payment, and (iii) the store of value. There are good reasons for following a similar procedure in the analysis of international money: the next section will comment on the first two attributes based on studies of invoicing practices in international trade, while the following section looks at the third attribute by reviewing currency substitution in private sector portfolios. In both cases the perspective is obviously that suggested by the title of this chapter: in what sense do present practices of denominating trade contracts, effecting payments and holding assets (or liabilities) in various national currencies constitute a factor that tends to destabilize the international monetary system? After the survey in the third section of the changing official use of various currencies, a short concluding section summarizes the main points.

Recent trends in the currency composition of international trade

Since the pioneering first study of currency denominations of international trade flows by Grassman,[3] a number of researchers have tried to chart how exporters and importers in the industrial countries have modified their pattern of invoicing over the past decade of upheaval in the foreign exchange markets. It remains a difficult area primarily because the data are incomplete — they refer only to merchandise trade and not to trade in services, and they are typically collected by private research institutions or by central banks, rather than by official statistical agencies on a recurrent and internationally standardized basis. Nevertheless, the available studies do throw light on recent trends in the unit of account and possibly the medium of exchange functions of individual national currencies in merchandise trade. The following comments are based largely on a study by Page;[4] the subject of management of exchange risks by enterprises through modifications in invoicing patterns and other means is also addressed by André de Lattre in Chapter 3 of this volume.

What emerges most clearly from this and other recent studies is that the US dollar remains the only currency that is widely used in

TABLE 5.1

Percentage shares of major currencies in invoicing world exports of manufactures (approx. 1979–80)

	Country share in world exports	Currency share in world exports
US dollar	11.7	54.8
Deutschmark	11.1	14.4
Pound sterling	5.9	7.5
French franc	6.3	6.4
Dutch guilder	4.1	3.0
Belgian franc	3.6	2.6
Japanese yen	6.6	2.3
Swiss franc	1.7	2.1
Italian lira	4.7	1.9

Source: S. A. B. Page, op. cit., p. 61.

trade between third countries. While the US share of world exports of manufactures was less than 12 per cent in 1979–80, nearly 55 per cent of these exports were invoiced in dollars (Table 5.1). For some other major countries (Germany, the United Kingdom, France and Switzerland) the invoicing shares of their currencies exceed their share of world exports, but only marginally so. There appear to have been no major changes in this pattern in the 1970s; the share of sterling declined somewhat, particularly in the late 1960s and early 1970s, reflecting both the receding share of UK exports and the diminishing use of sterling in third country trade. At the same time, the role of the Deutschmark increased slightly. Otherwise, the main tendencies are that a number of smaller industrial countries have found themselves increasingly able to invoice their exports in their own national currencies, and that the role of the dollar has been pushed up by the growing relative importance of oil exports, which are almost entirely invoiced in dollars. Indeed, without this boost — the share of oil products in world exports approximately doubled between 1970 and the period just after the second oil price shock of 1979–80, from 7 to 14 per cent — the role of the dollar in invoicing would have declined slightly. Another noteworthy feature is the continuing modest role of the yen; a recent detailed study by Taguchi[5] shows that, with the exception of exports to the European Community, where the yen's share in invoicing was 55 per cent in 1981, the yen is used for setting up well below one third of Japanese export contracts. In intra-EC trade the use of the Continental European currencies — with the exception of the lira — has grown slowly and steadily, replacing sterling almost entirely and reducing the share of the dollar slightly.

A stable or slowly evolving pattern of invoicing does not preclude destabilizing features in the unit of account function of the various national currencies when exchange rates move. The main example is that of oil pricing in dollars during the major cycle in the value of the dollar in terms of other main currencies (or the SDR) since 1977. In the longer run prices of tradeable goods should adjust to the global supply-demand balance in such a way as to make invoicing practices irrelevant; if, say, oil prices in European currencies rise due to an appreciation of the dollar rather than to underlying market forces, the latter should reassert themselves by depressing the world market oil price in dollars through excess supply. But for a while there will be an 'unwarranted' rise in oil prices in the non-dollar countries, implying a terms-of-trade loss and an upward push to their domestic price levels; conversely, at a time of dollar depreciation, there is a temporary terms-of-trade gain and a reduction in the price level.

Over the 1981–3 period when the dollar strengthened in a major way vis-à-vis the European currencies and the yen, one might have expected determined efforts on the part of the non-dollar countries to protect themselves against this terms-of-trade worsening and instability — some European policy makers deplored it as a 'third oil shock' — by pushing the use of other units for invoicing, either their own currency or a basket of currencies, such as the SDR, or for the Europeans the European Currency Unit (ECU). Numerous statements have been made by prominent officials about the desirability of such a change of practice, but very little appears to have happened. The exporters of oil and other raw materials or intermediate products have clearly been unwilling to move significantly in this direction, although they had already begun, during the 1970s, to diversify on the financial side into non-dollar currencies in their official reserve policy. There remains considerable scope for moving further towards the use of non-dollar currencies and baskets in invoicing, but whether it will be easier to achieve this when the dollar is weakening remains to be seen.

An intensification of the move towards letting the exporter prevail in the choice of invoicing currency, as witnessed, for example, in intra-EC trade, would hardly be optimal in the sense of stabilizing the exchange markets and helping the international adjustment process. To illustrate this one might compare two benchmark cases: one in which all exports are invoiced in the exporter's currency and another in which a single international unit, say the SDR, has penetrated into all trading contracts. As a basket, the SDR will tend to be a centre of gravity for exchange rates and not to move in cycles of the size and persistence experienced with the dollar in recent years.

Again, the difference in invoicing practice between the two benchmark cases is likely to be unimportant in the long run, as prices reflect underlying market trends. But in the short run of 6 months or so during which the terms of exporting cannot in practice be easily modified — usually referred to as the contract period, though it may often extend beyond the formal length of trading contracts — the adjustment process will depend in an important way on invoicing practices as described, for example, by McKinnon.[6]

In the second benchmark case, the pure SDR standard, a change in the SDR value of the exporter's currency will immediately trigger a change in the relative price of tradeables and non-tradeables in the exporting country and induce a shift of productive resources in the direction indicated by the movement of the SDR exchange rate: towards the production of tradeables in a devaluing country and conversely in a revaluing country.

In the first benchmark case, with trading contracts set in the exporter's currency, the adjustment of production is delayed more universally. Although producers will obviously look beyond the relatively short duration of export contracts of typically 3 to 6 months and begin to plan in the light of the likely longer-run relative prices to which the exchange rate adjustment points, there is no immediate inducement to change.

This difference between the operations of the adjustment mechanism in the two benchmark cases is to some extent offset on the import side. If one looks at an isolated exchange rate adjustment, confined to the SDR value of the exporter's currency, the relative price between imports from that country and domestic prices (in the various importers' currencies) will change by less under the pure SDR standard than in the first benchmark case of trade contracts in the exporter's currency. On the import side, substitution will therefore be triggered more quickly in the first benchmark case. But since the responsiveness tends to be greater on the supply (exporter) side than on the demand (importer) side, the net effect of the fragmented invoicing pattern is to delay quantity adjustment in international trade flows.

This is a source of concern. It will take longer for depreciation to show up in an improvement in the current balance of payments, or for appreciation to curtail an external surplus. This will in turn make financial markets nervous and encourage speculation in further exchange rate adjustments. The existence of a so-called 'J-curve effect' — namely, perverse current account responses over the initial six- to twelve-month period after an adjustment — is a destabilizing phenomenon which has contributed to the breakdown of the Bretton Woods system and to the size of the swing in exchange rates in recent years. For example, J-curve effects protected the German current account from worsening in periods of Deutschmark appreciation and exposed it further when the D-Mark was temporarily depreciating in 1980–1; the impression of weakness of the French franc has been magnified through J-curve effects following the 1981–3 devaluations, and — most dramatically — the inevitable worsening of the US current account has been delayed by J-curve effects throughout the phase of remarkable dollar appreciation in 1981–4.

The relevance of the present discussion to evaluation of the multiple currency standard is the following: there has been a slow but unmistakable trend towards the proliferation of national currencies as invoicing units in international trade, permitting the share of exports that are invoiced in the exporter's home currency to climb — for most smaller European currencies to levels around 50 per cent, for larger industrial countries much higher. Were it not for the increased share of dollar-invoiced oil and other energy products in world trade, the role of the dollar would no doubt have declined. This role has also been sustained since 1980–1 by the strength of the dollar, which has removed some of the incentives to exporters in other currency areas for switching from the dollar as an invoicing currency. But a trend towards a more limited dollar role must be expected to emerge with a decline in the real oil price and a weakening of the dollar. The issue is then whether the international adjustment process would be best served by pushing in the direction of one or other of the two main options, 'benchmark cases', referred to above, and, in particular, whether movements towards increasing fragmentation of invoicing practices, which is by far the likelier outcome, are desirable.

While such a process may be viewed favourably by most national policy makers — acceptability of one's national currency in international trading contracts is regarded as a seal of approval — and by exporters who find it convenient to extend their preferred domestic monetary unit, it may well have some costs for the international system as a whole by delaying the adjustment of trade flows to a new constellation of exchange rates. The point should not be exaggerated; contract periods probably average less than 6 months, and other factors — changes in the composition of trade, the existence of trading companies acting as a buffer between the rest of the world and domestic producers (or consumers) and oligopolistic practices — may all be more important quantitatively. But one must be careful in limiting the impact of any potentially destabilizing factor on the international monetary scene.

The choice of invoicing currency is clearly not a process which is easily influenced by governments. But nor is the impact of government policies confined to the indirect one of making the respective currencies for which they are responsible more stable in purchasing power and hence more attractive as contracting units. Governments do influence the choice of invoicing currency by the way in which they administer official export financing schemes and by their attitude to capital movements. The more they insist on the exclusive use of the national currency in export financing and the more they restrain the scope for holding working balances in other currencies, the greater the encouragement to the use of the national currency in invoicing. While a protectionist attitude to the national currency may often be justified on other grounds, it is not without cost to the international system if the governments of a large number of countries succeed in raising the share of their respective currencies in the invoicing of their own exports.

If exporters, backed in most cases by their governments, were to be dissuaded from this move towards fragmentation in the currency denomination of trade flows, what could be advocated as a superior alternative? Of the two main globalist options — increasing the use of one national currency (the dollar) or a common basket standard (the SDR) — the latter would have the advantage of spreading the adjustment more symmetrically among countries. But invoicing in a basket has made very little headway in recent years, despite the instability of the main currency relationships. This is understandable in view of the limited facilities for lending and borrowing in SDRs; developments of these financial dimensions have to go hand in hand with increasing use of a basket unit for invoicing. What one might have expected was a greater readiness on the part of governments to agree to extended use of the SDR in areas where intergovernmental negotiations are a decisive influence on trading practices — commodity agreements, state trading, fares and rates subject to intergovernmental approval etc. The fact that such a trend towards increasing use of the SDR basket has not been observable after a decade of increasingly unstable exchange rates is impressive testimony to the difficulties of introducing international monetary reform.

Similar reflections are inspired by the regional experiences in Europe. The pattern of currency invoicing is more fragmented between national currencies than at the global level because of the very limited role of the dollar in intra-EC trade. There is very limited evidence so far of any emerging readiness to use the ECU for invoicing purposes, though some suggestions for trying to encourage its adoption for energy and possibly other raw materials and intermediate imports into the Community have been made by French officials over the past couple of years. But in the meantime no specific progress has been made towards checking the proliferation of the use of national currencies. The argument that such steps are desirable is, however, weaker than at the global level in view of the greater cohesiveness of the intra-European part of the global exchange rate structure. As the European Monetary System appears to be moving towards greater cohesiveness in intra-EC exchange rates, the difference between invoicing in ECU and in any component currency obviously fades away.

The multi-currency composition of private portfolios

Recent interest in the contribution of shifts in the currency composition of private sector portfolios to international financial instability has focused on two subjects: (i) outright currency substitution and (ii) the demand-supply balance on the markets for bonds denominated in various currencies. Though not unrelated, they can be discussed separately.

Within the last decade the notion of currency substitution has attracted growing attention; see, *inter alia*, the studies by Brittain and McKinnon.[7] It has been inspired by the observation that the income velocity of money has become more unstable in recent years in some of the main industrial countries, particularly in the United States. Although some of this instability has proved to be explainable on a country-by-country basis, notably by bringing in additional measures of the opportunity costs of holding money and hence allowing for a rapid rate of innovation in domestic financial markets, other elements seemed to be linked to monetary developments abroad. More specifically, at times when the US money supply accelerated relative to income, this often coincided with a decline in the money-to-income ratio abroad, particularly in Germany. In short, there is a negative association between movements in velocities around their trend levels. It seems *a priori* a plausible hypothesis that this association is produced by shifts in the currency composition of the working and other liquid balances of international corporations and non-bank financial institutions in response to changing expected returns and risk evaluations.

The implications of these shifts for exchange rate instability are worrying in themselves, if they can be shown to be significant relative to current account imbalances and to capital flows in other less liquid forms. But they become particularly destabilizing, if policies in which monetary targets play a major role are applied in the two countries between whose currencies the reshuffling of balances is taking place, as is in principle the case since the mid-1970s in the United States and Germany. If the focus of monetary policy is to rely on a stable domestic demand function for an aggregate which comprises an internationally shiftable component, policy errors will be committed. If international corporations and non-bank financial institutions shift some of their liquid holdings out of dollars and into Deutschmarks in anticipation of a DM appreciation, as happened in 1977–8, and the US authorities stick to a pre-announced course of monetary aggregates by feeding additional liquidity into the US banking system, while the German authorities tighten policy to mop up excess liquidity, the stage is set for a perpetuation of the currency shift. Conversely, when during several phases from 1980 onwards currency preferences shifted in the opposite direction, as the prospects for a strong dollar encouraged shifts out of most European currencies and the yen, symmetrical reactions of tightening in the United States and (temporary) relaxation in Germany will perpetuate the movement of the Deutschmark/dollar rate away from any underlying equilibrium.

The main remedy in a situation where such shifts are becoming important is to suspend the monetary targets for a while and pay more attention to exchange rates as intermediate objectives. In fact, the German and US monetary authorities have shown considerable flexibility in permitting their main monetary targets to drift well beyond their stated target intervals, though they have not been prepared to move in the direction of developing objectives for their exchange rates. To the extent that currency substitution is important, the basic message of McKinnon and others who have seen outright currency substitution as a major cause of exchange market instability, is relevant; this implies a greater element of external orientation in monetary policy, with non-sterilization of exchange market interventions as a central element.

There is little doubt as to the basic reasons why financial assets in some currencies gradually displace those denominated in others; see, for instance, the survey of the theory of currency competition by Vaubel and the recent theoretical and empirical study by Padoa-Schioppa and Papadia.[8] The market share of a commodity depends on its perceived quality, and that applies to currencies as well; financial institutions and multinational firms who are in a position to substitute between holdings in several currencies will prefer the higher-quality ones. As Padoa-Schioppa and Papadia argue, a natural indicator of quality is the inflation rate and its variability, the two being typically positively associated. Empirical studies taking this starting point have thrown useful light on the penetration of external currencies into domestic use in high-inflation countries, for example, 'dollarization' in Mexico, Argentina and other Latin American economies.

Similar reasoning can be applied to the changing currency pattern in the Eurobanking system, in which a wide range of agents are faced with a choice between the dollar and other major international currencies. A look at the most recent three-year period for which data are available shows that the share of the dollar on both the deposit (liabilities) and lending (asset) side of the Eurobanks' balance sheet has stabilized in the 75–80 per cent range, whereas this ratio was declining prior to 1980 (Table 5.2). Though the period since mid-1982 has been an exceptional one with a very low rate of growth in international bank activity, due, among other things, to a sharp deceleration in lending to developing countries and smaller payments disequilibria in the rest of the world, there is preliminary evidence that a perceived improvement in the 'quality' of the dollar has been accompanied by a reassessment by unconstrained portfolio-holders of the previous strategy to move towards a lower share of dollar-denominated assets.

Currency substitutions between national monetary domains or between different denominations in the Eurobanks have become important elements in international monetary linkages, but substitution between national securities markets remains more important quantitatively. Bond substitution dominates for several reasons; capital liberalization has proceeded further than for deposits in the domestic banking system, the yield on bonds is generally more attractive, and movements in bond prices tend to be inversely related to those in the exchange value of the currency in

TABLE 5.2

Currency breakdown of international banking activity 1980–3 ($ bn)

	Assets					Liabilities				
	Changes[a]					Changes[a]				
	1980	1981	1982	1983	End-1983	1980	1981	1982	1983	End-83
Total	241.2	264.8	175.6	108.4	1,753.9	242.3	237.7	125.8	116.5	1,702.1
in domestic currency	69.7	99.8	129.4	50.0	569.4	39.3	48.6	76.2	56.2	415.8
in foreign currency	171.5	165.0	46.2	58.4	1,184.5	203.0	189.1	48.9	60.3	1,286.3
of which:										
US dollars	125.6	118.0	19.6	33.1	902.1	152.9	148.4	35.5	30.8	1,005.6
Deutschmarks	14.1	15.8	8.1	10.0	121.5	14.0	10.2	1.0	9.4	111.7
Swiss francs	16.1	11.2	3.5	2.7	57.8	19.0	15.8	-3.0	4.7	61.8
Pound sterling	1.2	3.7	0.2	0.6	12.0	7.4	0.3	-0.9	-0.5	14.1
Japanese yen	2.6	6.6	0.3	1.3	17.0	-1.0	5.8	1.8	4.0	21.2
Dutch guilders	-0.1	1.6	1.5	3.0	10.7	0.5	2.1	2.0	2.5	11.5
French francs	4.9	-1.0	1.2	3.2	9.7	4.6	-0.2	1.6	2.3	11.2
Other and unallocated[b]	7.1	9.1	11.8	4.5	53.7	5.6	6.9	10.9	7.1	49.2

a. At constant end-of-quarter exchange rates.

b. Including external positions of banks in the United States and of their branches in the five major offshore centres in currencies other than the US dollar.

Source: Bank for International Settlements, *Fifty-Third Annual Report*, Basle, 1984.

which they are denominated, thus providing a hedge which is lacking in the case of bank deposits. Private capital movements between bonds denominated in different currencies are typically much larger than private banking flows. Both of them dwarf the shifts in central bank assets; and central banks are constrained by cooperative arrangements which are absent among private agents. These considerations suggest that the potential for destabilization through shifts in private portfolios is far greater than that arising from shifts in central bank official reserves. But since the focus of the present chapter is on the latter, the following section will be concerned only with official behaviour.

The role of national currencies in official international reserves

The inherent instability of an international monetary system in which official international reserves comprise holdings of several national currencies in addition to extraneous assets has long been recognized. It was analysed first and most perceptively by Robert Triffin in the late 1950s[9] and subsequently became a constant preoccupation of policy makers and international institutions for at least a decade from the early 1960s. But the scene has changed so much in the past 20–25 years, with respect to both the exchange rate regime and the process of reserve creation, that it requires some justification to draw close parallels between the concerns of, say, the early 1960s and those of today.

The inevitable instability in the process of reserve creation under the Bretton Woods system of largely fixed exchange rates which prevailed prior to 1971 can be succinctly stated in the form of the so-called Triffin Dilemma. To rely on reserve creation through the external deficits of the then reserve-currency countries as a supplement to additions to monetary gold reserves through gold production 'is haphazard and does not ensure that changes of world reserves are neither excessive nor deficient', to quote an important contemporary survey of academic views.[10] In the face of gradual inflation the official gold price was being overtaken by the costs of producing new gold. At the same time, the reserve-currency countries could not and should not be relied upon to continue running deficits of a size adequate to meet the world demand for reserves. Indeed, both the United States and the United Kingdom were officially committed to a policy of reducing their external deficits through a combination of measures to strengthen the current account and, particularly, to restrain capital outflows.

The prospective inadequate size and the unstable composition of international official reserves were the two horns of the Triffin Dilemma. In the words once more of the same Bellagio group, 'Since the system necessitates a progressive increase in the ratio of liquid liabilities of the reserve-currency countries to their gold holdings, it creates a growing threat to the value of the reserve holdings of other countries with the result that confidence in the stability of the system is undermined.'

This fear of sudden conversion crises, of an implosion of reserves, caused by holders of sterling trying to convert into dollars or by holders of dollars trying to convert into gold, was regarded as a more imminent threat than the opposite danger of a petering out of the supply of reserve currencies. The UK authorities were already from 1961 onwards engaged in complex negotiations with other major industrial countries to protect sterling against the exchange rate impact of fluctuations in the official reserves held in the overseas sterling area — the so-called Basle Agreements.[11] The share of sterling in official currency reserves was still above one third in the early 1960s. Clear danger signals could also be detected in the US external position: the ratio of US short-term liabilities to the gold stock had risen from less than one half in the early 1950s to the 1.5–2.0 range ten years later. (Incidentally, it remains in that range today with the increase in the gold price approximately matching the growth in US liabilities to official holders;[12] with gold valued at the old official price [\$35/ounce], US short-term liabilities exceed short-term assets by a factor of six.)

In retrospect, the analysis of the Triffin Dilemma with its emphasis on the instability of a multiple reserve asset standard proved correct, though its main proponents greatly underestimated the ability of policy makers to bolster the stability of the system through unilateral efforts or multilateral improvizations. The main surprise was the extent to which an increasing role for the dominant reserve currency, the US dollar, proved manageable for nearly another decade after official reform efforts had been launched in 1963–4. In the process the convertibility of the dollar into gold became increasingly circumscribed, though its formal suspension was delayed till President Nixon's announcement of August 1971. The main efforts were directed at limiting, through increasingly tight and mandatory regulation, the scope for capital outflows from the United States.

The parallel traumatic experience of phasing out sterling's

reserve-currency role left a deep mark on UK official and academic thinking about the international monetary system. This helps to explain the espousal of floating in the early 1970s and the coolness towards participation in efforts towards European monetary integration involving this time at the EC level a potential new European reserve asset, with the formation of the EMS in 1978–9.

It is instructive in the present context to review briefly not only the diagnosis of the inherent instability of the multiple reserve currency system under the conditions of the early 1960s, but also the main proposals made for its reform. In their lucid summary of the main assumptions underlying the possible reform options, Machlup and his colleagues in the Bellagio Group reviewed four ways of assuring the availability and composition of international reserves to match the need for them in a rapidly growing world economy:

(i) transition to flexible exchange rates;
(ii) a major revaluation of gold in terms of reserve currencies;
(iii) centralization of reserve creation through the IMF; and
(iv) a widening of the range of reserve currencies, i.e. an explicit move towards an extension of the multiple reserve currency system.

This list is not exhaustive — it omits, notably, an international standard and reserve asset based on a selection of internationally traded commodities — but it does contain the main options that have been under discussion and put into effect since then.

When faced with a situation in which the demand for reserves seems likely to outstrip what can be supplied in a stable way through existing reserve creation mechanisms, two main approaches are conceivable, focusing either on a reduction in demand or an increase in supply. The first of the four options listed focused on the former, the other three on the latter. Over the past fifteen years all four roads towards reform have been pursued, some by explicit design, others by passive acceptance of strong market forces. And yet, as I shall argue below, the basic problem of an unstable multiple reserve currency standard is still with us in a form not basically different from that of twenty years ago.

Greater reliance on *exchange rate flexibility* in the adjustment of international payments was clearly perceived as a method of diminishing the need for international reserves. Through the more frequent and larger de- and revaluations of the major European currencies which began in 1967, the Smithsonian realignment in

1971, which also brought wider bands of fluctuations around parities, to the introduction of floating in 1973 and its formal acceptance in the Second Amendment to the IMF Articles of Agreement agreed upon in 1976 and ratified in 1978, the international monetary system has, indeed, been reformed in this direction to a degree which no observer had foreseen. The surprise is the limited extent to which this has reduced the demand for reserves. A number of empirical studies, most recently by Frenkel,[13] reveal a considerable stability in reserve demand. In his study of reserve behaviour in 22 industrial and 32 developing countries between 1963 and the end of the 1970s, Frenkel does find a statistically significant downward shift in reserve demand around the time of the transition to floating in 1973, but it is of minor proportions and the demand for reserves continues to be well explained by the same variables which were used to explain holdings in the fixed rate period (income level, degree of openness measured by the import propensity, and observed variability of reserves in the recent past). Most countries obviously still feel a need to maintain sizeable reserves to relieve the exchange rate of their currencies from the full burden of adjustment.

The option of allowing a substantial *increase in the gold price* in order to enlarge existing monetary stocks relative to likely external payments imbalances, and to assure future additions to stocks through new production, has also been exercised, though — as in the case of exchange rate flexibility — more by default than by design. The gold price has fluctuated in recent periods around a level some ten to twelve times that of the official price prior to the US suspension of dollar convertibility in 1971 ($35/ounce). Measured at the market price, the largely unchanged volume of monetary gold at present constitutes close to half the world's total gold, IMF and currency reserves; the share is well above that for the industrial countries which hold approximately 80 per cent of all monetary gold.

The experience of sharp fluctuations in the market price of gold as well as agreements among central banks to limit its transferability have, however, underlined its gradual transformation from a reserve to a speculative asset. The risk of massive destabilizing conversions into gold which so preoccupied participants in the reform debate of the 1960s has been eliminated, but the enormous rise in the book value of gold has not eased the demand for more readily usable currency reserves and hence the risk of destabilizing shifts between reserves denominated in different currencies. Gold is likely to remain on the books of central banks in a passive role, at least as long as any risk of a renewed surge of inflation is not generally thought to have been eliminated. At times it has been used as collateral by sovereign borrowers — Italy in 1976 and some Latin American countries in the early 1980s — and Portugal was recently reported to have sold a small share of its monetary gold to repay a BIS loan. These remain exceptions, however, to its recent largely passive role in the international monetary system.

The preferred option in the reform debate of the 1960s was the *centralization or internationalization of reserve creation* through the IMF. Indeed, that was the only option carefully examined at the official level as exemplified in the Ossola Report of 1965,[14] which was the first step leading to the decision to create a genuinely international reserve asset, labelled special drawing rights (SDR), at the 1967 Annual Meeting of the IMF. By entrusting part of international reserve creation to collective international decision-making it was hoped to remedy the imbalance between demand and supply and to stabilize reserve composition.

For several reasons the process has had far more limited effects than would have been required to achieve these objectives.

First, the amounts agreed upon for SDR allocation have been very modest. At present, after two triennial periods of allocations in 1970–2 and 1979–81, global official holdings of SDRs amounted to little more than 5 per cent of world monetary reserves excluding gold and only 2–3 per cent including gold (at market value).

Second, while the initial decision was motivated by a desire to *supplement* reserve creation in the 'haphazard' form of external deficits in the reserve-currency countries, no provision was made for the absorption of excessive reserve creation in this or other forms — except, obviously, to the modest extent that allocations could be stopped in this eventuality. When it became clear in the 1970s that the threat to international monetary stability lay in excessive rather than in inadequate reserve creation, and hence more in inflation than in deflation in the international economy, the focus of international debate shifted to the scope for *substituting* SDRs for currency reserves. But it proved impossible, for reasons to be discussed further below, to agree on the terms to be offered to holders of dollars (and, in principle, other reserve currencies) to induce them to engage in large-scale substitution, and the plan for a Substitution Account in the IMF for official holders had to be put into cold storage at the April 1980 meeting of the IMF Interim Committee.

Third, the effort to introduce the new asset had to struggle for about a decade with determined opposition from the United States to endowing it with the attractive qualities necessary to ensure that it would be willingly held. The entire emphasis at the beginning was to create a substitute for gold; hence the SDR was defined in terms of gold, and a minimal interest rate was set on net creditor and debtor positions. After the unit's definition had been changed to that of a basket of currencies in 1974, it took a few more years to adjust the interest rate to the market level, namely, an average of interest rates on the component currencies. Hence it is only recently that the SDR has become, from the viewpoint of holders, an asset competitive with reserve currencies; in the meantime demand for it had to be underpinned by complicated provisions regarding limits up to which creditors were obliged to accept SDRs in settlement.

For all these reasons, discussed much more fully by Corden[15] and Kenen,[16] it can be argued that the main significance of the SDR allocations still lies in their being the thin end of the wedge of real monetary reform. So far they have only marginally affected the level and composition of world monetary reserves. In particular, they have done little to mitigate the instability of the multiple reserve currency system.

Before turning to the present nature of that instability and the scope for containing it, some remarks on the fourth and final policy option, that of openly *encouraging a move towards a multiple reserve currency system* with a wider range of currencies, are appropriate. While most observers have always been critical of this approach, regarding it as potentially more unstable and complex than the other main options listed, advocates have emphasized the beneficial effects of extending a reserve-currency role beyond the dollar and sterling. In particular, they have argued that such a process would subject additional countries to the discipline required of suppliers of reserve currencies; and it would meet the transactions needs in international trade and private capital movements more closely than a system in which central banks held only one or two currencies (in addition to gold and possible IMF assets).

This line of reasoning hardly looks persuasive. Whether reserve-currency status is an especially disciplining factor remains an open question, regardless of the exchange rate regime. It clearly was an important constraining factor on UK policies in the 1960s, but it has been much less so on the United States. While some countries might appreciate sharing the 'exorbitant privilege' of financing an external deficit through the issue of liabilities denominated in their domestic currency, they would typically want the process of decentralized reserve creation to be guided by rules that protected them against sudden shifts out of their currencies. One would then move in the direction of the suggestion made in the reform debates of the 1960s by the Dutch negotiators,[17] i.e. to harmonize the composition of international reserves among countries. Through such guidelines for reserve composition and/or settlement among central banks one might have envisaged, within the then prevailing system of fixed exchange rates, a gradual and controlled move towards currency diversification, which would also contain safeguards for those countries that had recently joined the ranks of reserve-currency suppliers.

Yet the difficulties of controlling such a process remain forbidding. Even in the mid-1960s proponents of the scheme thought that it would require full-scale gold guarantees to assure acceptability of a wider role for existing and new currency assets. And the basic premise that beneficial effects on the stability of domestic policies would emerge from the disciplining impact seems highly questionable. The initial effect, at least, might well be the opposite, as a new reserve-currency country felt freer to run external deficits while other countries were building up their holdings of reserve assets denominated in that currency. It is possible that a system in which one country provides the bulk of the world's currency reserves at least has the merit of focusing attention on the balance of reserve supply and demand more clearly than would the alternative and more complex systems.

In any case the option of deliberate encouragement of the evolution of a multiple reserve-currency system as a method of enlarging and stabilizing world monetary reserves has been overtaken by events. Basically, the evolution has taken place more rapidly without encouragement — and even in the face of opposition from some of the new suppliers of reserve currencies — than one could have imagined (see below). Furthermore, a simpler way of creating conditional reserves has been used through quota increases in the IMF where all member countries contribute to reserve creation by transferring their own currencies to the Fund. Finally, most of the new large reserve holders, outside the circle of industrial countries which held 75–80 per cent of the world's currency reserves in the early 1960s, have come to appreciate the freedom which the present choice in reserve composition offers them. The issue in the 1980s is not, therefore, to revive some scheme for harmonization of reserve composition, but to add stabilizing features to the multiple reserve-currency system which has evolved in a decentralized and unplanned way. The main danger in the 1980s of flexible exchange rates and an easing of the reserve constraint for most countries through the vastly increasing scope for sovereign borrowing, is no longer primarily that of reserve implosion, though reserves could still shrink in a destabilizing way through large payments surpluses in one or more of the reserve centres. The main danger is now excessive exchange rate instability, aggravated by switches in official reserves.

Recent studies by the Group of Thirty and Bergsten and Williamson help to put these problems in perspective.[18] They start from the fact that, despite the massive increase in the amounts of outstanding dollar reserves, the dollar share of total currency reserves dropped over the decade up to the end of 1983 by 9 percentage points, and the share of sterling dropped to about one third of the 6-7 per cent observed in 1972. As shown in Table 5.3, the combined share of the two traditional reserve currencies declined appreciably, namely, from 85 to 72 per cent of total identified official currency reserves. Nearly all of this shift in composition occurred, however, within shorter time spans — for the dollar in 1978–80, for sterling in 1973–6 — and the process of diversification has subsequently been halted, even slightly reversed. During 1982 world reserves contracted for the first time in a decade, as many developing countries and some large oil exporters reduced their official holdings of reserve currencies. Though the reduction mainly took the form of lower dollar balances in the Eurobanking system, there was also a contraction (at constant exchange rates) in some of the new reserve currencies. The Bundesbank has calculated the reduction of Deutschmark balances at $4 billion. At current exchange rates the figure was close to $6 billion, reducing the share of the Deutschmark by a couple of percentage points in 1982. This was beyond the small decline already registered in 1981, which was due entirely to valuation adjustments. The process of diversification out of the dollar was therefore temporarily checked in 1982 and it was not resumed in 1983.

While the diversification procedure went on prior to 1981, the corresponding gains were made largely by three newer reserve currencies, the Deutschmark, the yen and the Swiss franc, in that order of importance. Since the period of maximum diversification corresponds roughly to phases of depreciation for the two traditional reserve currencies and appreciation for the new ones, the major question is whether central bank reserve switching has aggravated rather than dampened the exchange rate instability of these particular periods.

Bergsten and Williamson find some evidence in support of this

TABLE 5.3

Share of national currencies in the SDR value of total identified official holdings of foreign exchange, selected end-years 1972–83[a]

	1972[b]	1975	1976	1977	1978	1979	1980	1981	1982	1983
All countries										
US dollar	78.4	79.4	76.5	77.9	75.6	72.8	66.7	69.4	68.5	69.1
Pound sterling	6.5	3.9	1.8	1.7	1.7	2.0	3.0	2.2	2.5	2.6
Deutschmark	5.5	6.3	9.0	9.2	11.0	12.6	15.1	13.2	12.5	11.9
French franc	0.9	1.2	1.6	1.3	1.2	1.4	1.7	1.4	1.4	1.2
Swiss franc	1.1	1.6	2.3	2.4	2.3	2.7	3.2	2.8	2.7	2.4
Dutch guilder	0.3	0.6	0.9	0.9	0.9	1.1	1.3	1.2	1.0	0.8
Japanese yen	—	0.5	2.0	2.3	3.2	3.5	4.2	4.1	4.2	4.2
Unspecified	7.3	6.5	5.9	4.3	4.2	4.0	4.8	5.7	7.2	7.8
Industrial countries										
US dollar	87.3	87.3	87.0	89.0	86.2	83.5	77.6	78.7	77.1	77.4
Pound sterling	3.9	1.1	0.8	0.8	0.7	0.7	0.8	0.8	0.9	1.0
Deutschmark	2.6	4.0	6.2	5.6	8.0	9.8	14.5	13.1	12.8	13.4
French franc	—	0.1	0.5	0.3	0.4	0.6	0.5	0.5	0.4	0.3
Swiss franc	0.8	0.9	1.1	1.0	1.3	1.6	1.8	1.8	1.8	1.5
Dutch guilder	0.2	0.3	0.6	0.5	0.5	0.6	0.7	0.8	0.6	0.5
Japanese yen	—	0.2	1.8	1.6	2.1	2.5	3.4	3.6	4.2	4.7
Unspecified	5.3	6.2	1.9	1.1	0.8	0.7	0.7	0.7	2.3	1.1

a. ECUs issued to members of the European Monetary System since 1979 in exchange for US dollars are regarded as still held in that currency because of the temporary nature of the swap arrangements; analogously ECUs issued against gold are not counted as exchange reserves.

b. End of March 1973.

Source: IMF, *Annual Report 1984*, p. 61.

hypothesis. Though central banks in both the industrial and the non-industrial countries — the only breakdown available in the data published by the IMF — appear on the whole to have been faithful to the strategy of 'leaning against the wind', namely, of selling currencies which were appreciating vis-à-vis the SDR and buying depreciating currencies, their behaviour has been less stabilizing in the more fundamental sense of containing movements away from equilibrium, represented by medium-term trends in the effective exchange rate. The evidence suggests that there have, indeed, been some examples over the 1974–81 period of destabilizing changes in reserve composition for both industrial and non-industrial countries. Among the clearer examples are the move out of sterling in late 1976, when the UK currency was weakening fast, and the build-up of Deutschmark and yen balances during the phase when these currencies were rising vis-à-vis the dollar in 1977–8.

As the authors are careful to point out, these calculations are at most only suggestive. The data refer to quarterly changes in exchange rates and reserves and do not permit the short-run detailed analysis of central bank actions required for assessing their impact on exchange rate stability. Such data are not publicly available, and the general conclusions from examining them, published as a by-product of the study of exchange market interventions undertaken by the monetary authorities of the seven main industrial countries, the so-called Jurgensen Report,[19] do not throw light on particular periods. Data would also have to be disaggregated by country to decide whether the observed changes in aggregate composition to some extent reflect a reshuffling of reserves between central banks with different patterns of reserve holdings. For example, EMS member countries have tended to maintain a dollar share in their total currency reserves of around 90 per cent, while OPEC members (and non-oil developing countries) hold little more than two thirds of their currency reserves in dollars. An OPEC payments surplus vis-à-vis the industrial countries will accordingly reduce the overall dollar share. More modest differences in reserve patterns exist within each major group of countries, and the effects of such underlying factors would have to be eliminated from the data before one could appropriately label the observed shift in reserve composition as destabilizing. Finally, it should be realized that observed shifts do not always or even typically indicate an active central bank policy of intervention to change the composition; they will often merely reflect the decision of other agents, private or public, with respect to the currency denomination of trade contracts, borrowing or lending.

Despite these caveats Bergsten and Williamson's analysis is indicative of a worrying feature of international monetary developments over the last decade, namely, that central banks have at times magnified the size of medium-term swings in the exchange rates between the main internationally used currencies. However, they soon console their readers that this influence has been marginal; drawing on a couple of the leading models of international economic linkages, they conclude that the impact in any one quarter is likely to have been less than half a percentage point on the exchange rates involved. These are minor effects compared to departures from medium-term equilibrium in the 20–25 per cent range as measured by the authors. But these optimistic calculations neglect the impact on exchange market expectations of more effective central bank cooperation to limit to the minimum any destabilizing effects of official actions on already excessively volatile markets; in that sense they certainly represent an underestimate of the potential damage.

The two studies by the Group of Thirty throw useful light on official thinking in the main reserve-holding countries. In particular, the answers from 22 central banks to the Group's questionnaire on reserve management give an impressive qualitative illustration of the motives for the past process of reserve diversification and its likely extension in the 1980s.[20]

On the basis of the frank responses given — the identity of individual respondents singled out for quotation is not disclosed — there is wide agreement on the main cause of diversification: the breakdown of the fixed rate system. Whereas the demand for reserve currencies prior to 1971 seems to have been guided primarily by transactions motives and some inertia, notably in relation to sterling, general portfolio considerations — obtaining the best possible combination of yield and stability — have come to the fore since the advent of floating. The long period of negative US interest rates net of measured inflation, combined with considerable volatility in the dollar exchange rate in terms of most other internationally traded currencies, had a major impact not only on private investors, but also on central banks.

This admission of active management vindicated the rapidly growing literature which has tried to apply traditional methods of portfolio selection to the analysis of observed central bank behaviour.[21] Most of these studies have concluded that diversification still has a long way to go based on the currency and interest rate experience of the first 5–8 years of floating; according to these considerations, it would have been optimal to allow the dollar share to drop at least another 10–15 percentage points below the approximate 70 per cent reached in the early 1980s. However, these calculations are *ex post*, assuming knowledge of the actual movements in exchange rates and interest rates. If one reassesses the problem, taking into account that central banks, like other investors, have to forecast the expected returns and the exchange risks associated with diversification, the gains to be expected from a diversification strategy are drastically reduced.[22] No matter what methods are used for forecasting exchange rates, the uncertainties have been such that serious 'errors' in reserve management are unavoidable. There could be no more vivid demonstration of this than the shift in the yield on dollar assets after 1980, which could not have been in any way accurately anticipated. Gains from diversification are not easy to obtain.

A second important motive for diversification of official reserves is the desire to obtain a currency mix which approximates the structure of the country's external indebtedness. A number of sovereign borrowers have deposited the proceeds of their foreign loans in the central bank in the currency in which they were raised. Some central banks also report that they look to the currency composition of private external short-term debt in deciding on their reserve holdings. The continuing dominant role of the dollar in interventions assures the US currency of a disproportionately large share of short-term official currency assets.

Though some other motives for diversification are also occasionally mentioned by the respondent central banks, protection of yield and matching to liabilities well illustrate that central bank reserve behaviour is led largely by developments in financial markets and in national policies in the main countries which determine the qualities of the candidate currencies. The questionnaire survey also brings out clearly that most central banks are reconciled to this state of affairs, to which they see no feasible or even desirable alternatives. This does not mean that the impact of central bank actions on reserve composition is confined to the indirect, though major, one of determining the relative stance of national monetary policies which is the major influence on the use of various currencies in private financial and trading contracts. The national monetary authorities *can* constrain the evolution towards a full-fledged multiple reserve-currency system, namely, a system which merely reflects evolving currency practices in the private markets (and the impact of monetary policies thereon). They can do so collectively or individually, as the following three illustrations may clarify; the discussion should bring out the elements for assessing why the constraints have been set where they are and whether they contribute constructively to the stabilization of international monetary relations.

Collectively the main industrial countries were considering a major initiative to constrain reserve switching when the negotiations on a Substitution Account in the IMF were undertaken in 1979–80. The scheme was inspired by the sharp depreciation of the dollar and the prospect of continuing large US current account deficits — myopic as these worries may appear with the benefit of hindsight. Concerns about a 'dollar overhang' reappeared, fed by and feeding reserve diversification into assets denominated in other currencies with associated deflationary pressures on the economies concerned through appreciation. There appeared to be possible common ground between the main reserve currency issuer, the United States, which was anxious to limit further dollar depreciation, and the large European and Japanese official dollar-holders and issuers of substitute reserve currencies. And there was at least no active opposition from the rest of the IMF constituency which was favourably disposed towards any initiative that could be expected to contribute to greater exchange rate stability.

Yet the scheme had to be shelved for two main reasons. The first was that the oil price shock of 1979–80 was worsening the current account positions of the non-energy producers, removing some of the reluctance of Germany, Japan and others to move to a growing reserve-currency status, as they now experienced a need for foreign borrowing and found it convenient to borrow in their domestic currency. As the United States was in any case unprepared for linking the issue of substitution to any commitment to 'asset settlement', i.e. using reserve assets rather than dollar liabilities as the means of settling payments imbalances, one might say that there was, by 1980, a near-consensus not to implement the accompanying reform of the international monetary system (i.e. asset settlement) to which the substitution idea had originally been linked in the reform debate of 1972–4 within the Committee of Twenty. However, this might not in itself have been decisive in blocking the proposed Substitution Account; to link the two elements is a political decision rather than a logical necessity. So a *second* consideration took the front of the stage.

No formula for sharing the currency risk involved could be devised that was at the same time acceptable to both dollar-holders and the US Congress. The former group remained unpersuaded by the calculations of the US Treasury, the IMF staff and others, see for example, the plea for the Substitution Account in the Group of Thirty[23] and Kenen's more dispassionate analysis,[24] that the risk of losses for the proposed facility was sufficiently small to make exchange rate guarantees — anathema to US legislators — by the United States on the Account's dollar assets superfluous.

Over the four years since the scheme foundered, dollar holders have registered a gain of more than 25 per cent by holding dollars which have appreciated strongly against the SDR while yielding at the same time a higher interest rate during much of the period. It is not surprising that there has been no expression of interest in substituting SDRs for dollars in official holdings. But it is easily predictable that the proposal will re-emerge once the dollar begins to depreciate. The attitude of the US authorities is then bound to be even less forthcoming than it was in 1979–80; to have any chance of arriving at an agreement, the European, Japanese and OPEC holders of dollars will have to start from the assumption that next time they will themselves have to bear a significant part — or all — of the exchange risk. Even in these circumstances it would seem to be in the interest of the authorities of the main substitute currencies to consider carefully a collective move towards an increased role for the SDR through substitution facilities for a sizeable part of their dollar holdings. Otherwise the international economic debate over the next few years is likely to take on an additional note of acrimony, as politicians and central bankers watch their official holdings of depreciating dollars grow while they intervene to control and smooth the appreciation of their own currencies.

If such a global initiative proves not to be feasible as may well be the case, regional plans with a similar purpose might be envisaged. In particular, the members of the EMS have the necessary facilities, though in embryonic form. But again, past experience does not suggest that they are likely to put the efforts required into such an initiative.

When the EMS was set up in 1978–9 one important element was a limited and temporary move towards reserve pooling, in that the participating central banks agreed to deposit 20 per cent of their gold and dollar reserves with the European Fund for Monetary Cooperation (FECOM) in return for credits denominated in the basket European Currency Unit (ECU), to be revalued quarterly on the basis of observed developments in the market price of gold and the dollar exchange rates of the ECU's component currencies. Formally, the arrangement is a three-month renewable swap; since the central banks have accordingly not really diversified into ECU by giving up possession of their gold and dollars, it seems justified to exclude this cosmetic operation when calculating the composition of reserves (see the footnote to Table 5.3).

The participants obviously had the option of giving that arrangement more permanent shape, of enlarging the amount and of extending its reserve substitution features to other holders, either central banks outside the EMS or selected private financial institutions. The fact they have rejected it — or rather not even considered it seriously — along with more modest initiatives proposed by the European Commission to raise the limits within which EMS central banks are obliged to accept ECUs in settlement — is strong evidence that European officials are less unhappy with the multiple reserve-currency system than their often sharp criticism and expressions of concern indicate. It would have been particularly logical to complement the efforts of the German authorities to restrain the private and official use of the Deutschmark, during the period when particular emphasis was given to them, by building up facilities for holders — in the first instance official — to invest in attractive and marketable assets denominated in ECUs and issued by a European institution or by national governments in the EMS countries. But in fact, in the case of the ECU, no official encouragement has been given to its development into a reserve currency for the members, not to speak of non-EMS countries; if anything, its official use has begun to lag behind its increasing use in the international bank and bond markets.

The two illustrations of the failure of collective initiatives may be supplemented by some final comments on national attitudes in the countries which issue the currencies competing with the dollar (and the SDR- and ECU-currency baskets) in official and private portfolios. Again a survey by the Group of Thirty[25] is useful in offering in condensed form the views of major present or past officials from Germany, Japan, Switzerland and the United Kingdom. Basically, the survey leaves the impression that these currency issuers have moved from determined opposition to reserve-currency status — in the case of the United Kingdom, detailed policies for phasing out official sterling balances — via passive acceptance to efforts at exploiting it while containing the destabilizing impact. But the full consequences of this change of attitude are not observable in the figures for either official or private use, because it has occurred during a period when the attraction of the dollar was exceptionally strong. If maintained over the next few years of potentially sizeable dollar depreciation and continuing exchange rate volatility, the effects are likely to become far more visible.

The change in attitude has been the product of two main factors: a recognition that reserve diversification even at the official level is a difficult process to control, and reassessment of the costs and benefits of reserve-currency status.

The former difficulty is due primarily to the existence of markets in the substitute reserve currencies outside their frontiers. Placements in these markets, though they could be curtailed by explicit or implicit understandings with other central banks, were initially seen by the issuers as preferable to purchases of domestic assets, since a direct impact on domestic monetary conditions was absent. But the exchange rate impact was not, and gradually the reserve issuers came to see direct acquisitions or, preferably, tailor-made, non-market issues of domestic-currency liabilities as easier to monitor. The proportion of total official holdings held outside the country of issue remains a useful indicator of the extent to which the new reserve-currency countries have resisted the process; according to BIS statistics it is highest for the Swiss franc (75–80 per cent), around one half for the Deutschmark, one fifth for sterling, and one tenth for the yen. Since the reserve centres hold virtually all of their currency reserves with each other, the degree of diversification into the external banking system by other official reserve holders remains well above the figures mentioned.

The reassessment of costs and benefits has sometimes taken place within short periods of time in the light of the balance of payments position. Germany may be quoted as the prime example. While an article by the Bundesbank in its *Monatsberichte* of November 1979 argued firmly that it was in the interest of neither Germany nor the rest of the world to allow a 'highly unstable structure' of several reserve currencies to develop, the tone had changed significantly less than a year later. The Governor of the Bundesbank still wrote critically about such an evolution,[26] but his article emphasized the need for developing, through consultations between the reserve-issuing central banks, adequate safeguards against rapid diversification, which might otherwise be inevitable. And in his contribution to the study by the Group of Thirty[27] Dr Rieke of the International Monetary Affairs Department of the Bundesbank continued in the same direction of reluctant acceptance of diversification, while consoling himself that the reserve role of the Deutschmark would be 'narrowly circumscribed by the role of the dollar which continues to have all the attributes of a leading reserve currency, whereas the Deutschmark is largely used only as an investment currency and less so for transaction and intervention purposes'.

This view, underlining the leading role of private usages of a currency in determining its reserve status, also summarizes the main conclusion of the present chapter. But it remains an open question whether the constraints arising out of these differences between currencies are adequate as a safeguard against future important shifts towards the Deutschmark and other non-dollar currencies, once the period of exceptional strength of the dollar is over. The quality and uses of currencies evolve over time, as do the types of financial outlets they offer to investors. Conditions have been particularly propitious in most respects for users of the US currency: inflation has been sharply reduced since 1980, improving confidence in the long-run stability of dollar assets, and financial innovations have proceeded rapidly to offer holders a wider range of opportunities than are available in the markets for financial assets denominated in other currencies. This has temporarily increased the comparative advantage of the dollar and has helped to check and modestly reverse the process of official diversification out of dollar holdings. But there is no reason to expect these factors to be permanent.

To improve the safeguards of which the Bundesbank Governor and others have spoken so insistently, it would be preferable to undertake some advance planning, rather than to await an urgent need to contain a renewed process of reserve diversification. One major element in such planning is the reconsideration of organized large-scale substitution arrangements into SDRs to underline the aim of moving towards a more stable and centralized system of reserve holdings and creation. But the authorities of the reserve-currency countries could also make an important contribution by collective action to encourage the use of the SDR (and possibly the ECU) in the international bank and bond markets and in trading contracts for raw materials and other major internationally traded goods. Only by influencing these underlying determinants — and by limiting the extreme volatility of exchange markets — can the authorities hope to establish the safeguards against the potentially destabilizing features of a multiple reserve currency system which they claim to favour.

Conclusion

The present chapter has taken a broader look at the issues involved than is usual in trying to answer the question asked in the title. Starting from the premise that private and official uses of different currencies are closely interrelated, it has looked at two private and one official dimensions of the multiple currency standard — with special emphasis on the latter.

There is evidence of increasing fragmentation in the use of currencies in trading contracts, i.e. in the private unit of account and means of payments functions. Though the role of the dollar as the only truly international currency in this respect remains basically untouched (the data are not the most recent ones), a number of other currencies have become more widely used, particularly as a result of pressure from exporters for the use of their own currencies in invoicing. This entails costs as well as benefits: the calculation is not as favourable to systemic stability as is often perceived.

An often-neglected element on the cost side is that the proliferation of national currencies in invoicing delays the start of the adjustment process of exporters following exchange rate changes, relative to the situation in which all trade is invoiced in one international unit. On the benefit side, it must be counted that once the main international unit becomes unstable in terms of a larger number of other currencies, its use as a unit of account in international trade imposes short-run terms-of-trade fluctuations on the rest of the world. The main example of this is the continued global use of the dollar in invoicing oil and most raw materials. It is surprising that the efforts by the rest of the world to shift to a more predictable standard have not become more visible over the past few years of turbulence in exchange markets.

As regards the second dimension, the relative role of national currencies in private financial markets, the chapter briefly reviews discussions about currency substitution and capital mobility more generally. It is argued that currency substitution does occur, though it is far less significant than shifts between bond holdings in various currencies. Its occurrence has particular destabilizing features because it distorts the monetary signals on which most central banks rely in monitoring their monetary policy, namely, their monetary aggregates. This could, however, be remedied by focusing on a different target, notably the exchange rate. Yet it raises the issue of whether liberalization of short-term capital movements has not been taken too far, so long as monetary policies continue to be as uncoordinated as they have been in the past few years.

The third dimension — the use in official reserves of various national currencies — has been on the international financial agenda for at least the past two decades. Prior to 1971 the main destabilizing feature of the system was seen to be the risk of haphazardly rapid or slow reserve creation globally and shifting inflationary and deflationary pressures on the reserve issuers as diversification proceeded or receded. The official response was centralized reserve creation (SDRs), but in reality all of the main options discussed in the 1960s came to be pursued, more by default than by design. The multiple reserve currency system remains with its inherent instability now centred on the risk of aggravating short-run volatility and medium-term swings in exchange rates through official reserve switching. Most observers consider that no real alternatives exist.

Recent studies of central bank reserve behaviour suggest that central bank reserve shifts have not infrequently contributed to moving exchange rates away from their medium-term equilibrium, but that the quantitative effects have been negligible as compared to the observed swings in rates. Nevertheless, there remains considerable scope for improving the stability of the system, particularly if the monetary authorities were prepared to bolster any limitations on their own reserve behaviour by encouraging wider use of new composite assets in private trade and financial markets. Since usage in the private sector is largely ahead of official practices, trying to constrain the latter without acting to influence the former could well be self-defeating.

Notes

1. Robert Triffin, *Gold and the Dollar Crisis*, New Haven, Yale University Press, 1960.

2. C. Fred Bergsten and John Williamson, *The Multiple Reserve Currency System: Evolution, Consequences and Alternatives*, Washington DC, Institute for International Economics, Policy Analyses in International Economics Series, No. 9, 1984; Group of Thirty, *Reserve Currencies in Transition*, and *How Central Banks Manage Their Reserves*, New York, 1982.

3. Sven Grassman, *Exchange Reserves and the Financial Structure of Foreign Trade*, Farnborough, Saxon House, 1973.

4. S. A. B. Page, 'The Choice of Invoicing Currency in Merchandise Trade',

National Institute Economic Review, London, November 1981.

5. Hiroo Taguchi, 'A Survey of International Use of the Yen', *BIS Working Papers*, No. 6, Basle, 1982.

6. Ronald I. McKinnon, *Money in International Exchange*, Oxford, Oxford University Press, 1979.

7. Bruce Brittain, 'International Currency Substitution and the Apparent Instability of Velocity in Some Western European Economies and in the United States', *Journal of Money, Credit and Banking*, May 1981; Ronald I. McKinnon, 'Currency Substitution and the Instability in the World Dollar Market', *American Economic Review*, June 1982, and *An International Standard for Monetary Stabilization*, Washington DC, Institute for International Economics, Policy Analyses in International Economics Series No. 8, 1984.

8. Roland Vaubel, 'Free Currency Competition', *Weltwirtschaftliches Archiv*, September 1977; Tommaso Padoa-Schioppa and Francesco Papadia, 'Competing Currencies and Monetary Stability', *CEPS Working Documents No. 2*, Brussels, Centre for European Policy Studies, June 1983, reprinted in Rainer Masera and Robert Triffin (eds), *Europe's Money*, Oxford, Oxford University Press, 1984.

9. Triffin, op. cit.

10. Fritz Machlup et al., *International Monetary Arrangements: The Problem of Choice*, Report in the Deliberations of an International Study Group of 32 Economists (the Bellagio Group), Princeton NJ, International Finance Section, 1964, p. 81.

11. Cf. McMahon in the Group of Thirty, *Reserve Currencies in Transition*, op. cit.

12. Cf. the calculations of the net reserves of the main currency issuers in Robert Triffin, 'How to End the World "Infession": Crisis Management or Fundamental Reforms?', *CEPS Working Documents No. 1*, Brussels, Centre for European Policy Studies, June 1983, reprinted in Masera and Triffin (eds), op. cit.

13. Jacob Frenkel, 'International Liquidity and Monetary Control' in G. von Fürstenberg (ed.), *International Money and Credit: The Policy Rules*, Washington DC, IMF, 1983.

14. Group of Ten, *Report of the Study Group on the Creation of Reserve Assets*, (Ossola Report), Rome, 1965.

15. W. Max Corden, 'Is There an Important Role for an International Reserve Asset such as the SDR?', in G. von Fürstenberg, op. cit.

16. Peter B. Kenen, 'The Use of the SDR to Supplement or Substitute for Other Means of Finance', in G. von Fürstenberg, op. cit.

17. S. Posthuma, 'The International Monetary System', *Banca Nazionale del Lavoro Quarterly Review*, September 1963.

18. Bergsten and Williamson, op. cit.; Group of Thirty, *Reserve Currencies in Transition* and *How Central Banks Manage Their Reserves*, op. cit.

19. *Report of the Working Group on Exchange Market Intervention* (the Jurgensen Report), Paris and Washington DC, 1983.

20. Group of Thirty, *How Central Banks Manage Their Reserve Assets*, op. cit.

21. Cf., for example, Abraham Ben-Bassatt, 'The Optimal Composition of Foreign Exchange Reserves', *Journal of International Economics*, May 1980; Rudiger Dornbusch, *Exchange Rate Economics: Where Do We Stand?*, Brookings Papers on Economic Activity, 1980: 1, Washington DC, 1980; Jorge Braga de Macedo, 'Portfolio Diversification Across Currencies' in R. Cooper et al., *The International Monetary System Under Floating Rates*, Cambridge Mass., MIT, 1982.

22. Cf. John T. Cuddington and Jeremy A. Gluck, *Exchange Rate Forecasting and*

the *International Diversification of Liquid Asset Holdings*, Seminar Paper No. 245, Stockholm Institute for International Economic Studies, April 1983.

23. Group of Thirty, *Towards a Less Unstable International Monetary System: Reserve Assets and a Substitution Account*, New York, 1980.

24. Peter B. Kenen, 'The Analytics of the Substitution Account', *Banca Nazionale del Lavoro Quarterly Review*, December 1981.

25. Group of Thirty, *Reserve Currencies in Transition*, op. cit.

26. Karl Otto Pöhl, 'The Multiple Currency Reserve System', *Euromoney*, October 1980.

27. Group of Thirty, *How Central Banks Manage their Reserves*, New York, 1982, p. 23.

6
The Creation of International Liquidity
Michel Aglietta

The need for adequate international liquidity to meet developing international commercial and financial relations has been a major concern since the end of World War I. In order to restrict the use of gold, a means of settlement based on a few key currencies was fostered by the Genoa conference of 1922. However, this mixed gold-exchange monetary system did not withstand international payments imbalances caused by the divergence in prices in the key-currency countries, by the continuous fall in the price of raw materials, by the sterilization policies governing imports of gold into the United States, and subsequently by the refusal among the countries of the gold block to hold reserves in the form of liquid credits in pounds sterling.

After World War II, the ambitious reconstruction of the international monetary system put into effect at Bretton Woods was designed to apply the lessons learnt from the international monetary collapse of the 1930s and to overcome the bilateralization of international trade resulting from the proliferation of exchange controls. The Bretton Woods agreement allowed countries to pursue national aims of fostering growth and achieving full employment within the context of renewed interdependence. However, autonomy of national economic policies, currency convertibility and fixed exchange rates were not necessarily compatible. The first was liable to cause disequilibria in the balances of payments, thereby jeopardizing the other two. The Bretton Woods agreement provided for credits from an International Monetary Fund to finance temporary deficits and authorized modifications in parities to correct structural disequilibria. It did not, however, make any institutional provisions to adjust the growth of international liquidity to meet the needs incurred by the expansion of the world economy.

The history of international liquidity since 1945 has been an eventful one, dominated by a series of palliatives imposed to overcome the lack of a common set of rules and the absorption of international means of payment. These successive palliatives have been the distinguishing features of the various systems of international monetary creation. Curiously enough, the end of each decade has marked the passing from one monetary system to another and hence a change in the forms of external constraints to which countries have been subjected.

At the end of the 1940s, the last illusions about the chances of a rapid return to currency convertibility had disappeared, while the shortage of dollars in Europe reinforced the practice of bilateral trade and caused a proliferation of quantitative trade restrictions. The combination of American public aid and a multilateralization of debts resulting from bilateral imbalances in intra-European current account payments enabled these obstacles to be overcome with the setting up of the European Payments Union. However, the rapid restoration of European competitiveness, together with the increase in direct investments by American firms in Europe after the end of the Korean war, greatly accelerated the internationalization of the dollar. By the end of the 1950s, Robert Triffin could detect a complete change in the monetary landscape. The overvaluation of the dollar caused an excessive increase in dollar credits held by non-residents, which in turn threatened its convertibility into gold.

Attempts were made to counter this threat by a combination of decisive changes: the restoration of the convertibility of the currencies of the major industrial countries, the substantial, if incomplete, lifting of restrictions on international capital movements, the creation of the gold pool, the tacit recognition by the central banks of the Group of Ten that they must use great caution before exercising their right to request conversion of their dollar credits with the American Treasury into gold, the revaluation of the Deutschmark, and successive regulations to halt the deficit in the American balance of net liquid assets. This monetary system was remarkably successful in the early 1960s, but the rise in inflation in the United States accentuated the dollar's overvaluation, letting loose a flood of capital, the excess of which over the demand of private non-residents resulted in conversions on the exchange markets which monetary authorities were less and less able to absorb without losing control of their own money supply. The innovation of this monetary system was the rapid expansion of the Eurodollar market. In return, the latter became the vehicle, though not the cause, of the abandonment of the system at the turn of the 1970s.

The death throes of the Bretton Woods system lasted from the collapse of the gold pool in the spring of 1968 to the abandonment of dollar-gold convertibility in August 1971. An explosion of international liquidity followed during the 1970s under the aegis of the private banking system. An economy of international indebtedness developed, increasingly dissociated from the dollar supply by the US balance of payments deficit and provided the means for monetizing deficits worldwide following the first oil crisis. The world economy had found an endogenous method of expanding liquidity in the form of international bank credit in dollars. But if this expansion had become relatively unrelated to the US balance of payments in quantitative terms, it remained highly sensitive to the monetary conditions obtaining in the United States. Thus the change of direction in US monetary policy at the end of the 1970s gave rise to the crisis of international indebtedness into which we are now plunged. This crisis has shown up the limits to the expansion, on a world scale, of private credit which is not bound by international monetary rules.

This brief summary underlines the fact that the regulation of international liquidity is a vital question which is still unresolved. The present chapter attempts to analyse the significance of this question and what lies at stake in it. In the next section we shall look at the factors affecting the demand for international liquidity. We shall then describe its expansion, the forms it has taken and the sources of its counterparts. We shall then try to characterize the relationships between international liquidity and national monetary policies, studying the choices that have faced countries since the end of the 1960s in terms of holding reserves under the constraint of financing balance of payments deficits. The final section discusses the problem of the control of liquidity.

Factors affecting the demand for international liquidity

Liquidity is a concept which can be precisely defined in theory, but which it is difficult to pin down statistically. This is true on a purely national basis; the international dimension therefore provides even greater statistical difficulties. The problem lies in the potential nature of liquidity, which is a concept related to uncertainty. Any asset is liquid which enables an economic agent to settle a transaction whereby he acquires goods, services or securities, or to settle a debt.

The instruments of liquidity are therefore those which are immediately accepted means of settlement in the economic sector concerned. But they are also all those assets which can be converted immediately into these means of payment at negligible cost and without risk of loss of capital.

Thus, liquidity is not a strictly functional concept. Supply and demand for liquid assets depend on financial organization, and in particular on the innovations modifying the range of assets proposed to customers, and on the depth and resilience of the secondary financial markets in attenuating price fluctuations caused by the transactions of agents who are trying to remodel their portfolios. Supply and demand for liquid assets also depend on the perceptions which economic agents have of uncertainty. Not the least of the paradoxes of liquidity is that its sphere of influence is restricted when there is a trend in its favour. When uncertainty about the future grows, financial assets which had previously been considered virtually perfect substitutes for means of payment are no longer so. The excess sales from all those rushing to convert them cause a fall in exchange rates and hence the capital losses which underlay the original change in market opinion.

The history of international financial relations offers many examples of this. Thus, in the last quarter of the nineteenth century and the beginning of the twentieth, cyclical fluctuations were accompanied by financial disturbances; monetary stability was considered sacrosanct, however, and prospects for growth in international investment remained unshaken. Fluctuations in short-term interest rates were not therefore transmitted to long-term interest rates, which demonstrated a general tendency to decline, thus holding out the hope of capital gains on long-dated stocks. As financial centres such as London and Paris were well equipped to assess the risks and had effective secondary markets, first-category international obligations were the highest form of potential liquidity. In contrast, over the past fifteen years of persistent inflation which has affected the whole structure of interest rates, there has been a burgeoning of short-term financial innovations in an attempt to reconcile the immediate availability of international means of settlement and inflation-linked safeguards against capital losses.

These remarks do not question the traditional analysis of liquidity in terms of motives of transaction, precaution and speculation, but they do reveal two things: the forms in which liquidity may be held vary and also the respective influences of the different motives.

International assets are therefore all the assets which are said to be liquid and which are held by private economic agents or by official institutions in monetary metal, supranational fiduciary currency or foreign currency. As any asset in foreign currency is a liability for dealers of the issuing country, a distinction must be made between gross liquid assets and net liquid assets. Worldwide net liquid assets in principle include only stocks of monetary metal and the cumulative total of *ex nihilo* creations of supranational money; but, in a world economy with highly developed international financial relations, the demand for liquidity is significant only for gross liquid assets. The factors determining this demand may be categorized as follows:

(a) *the determinants of international trade which directly affect transaction reserves.* These are the global growth rates of countries and the degree of openness of economies to international trade which affect the growth rate of international trade relative to world output. Transaction reserves, defined as proportions of imports determined by these trends, correspond to a stock view.

(b) *the distribution of payments deficits requiring financing.* This type of determinant on demand for liquid assets combines transactional and precautionary motives. Above all, however, it expresses the tensions which underlie international relations, especially the degree of discordance between national economic policies. Demand for liquid assets reflects the dilemma between financing and adjustment. It also affects the international distribution of liquid assets. In practice, if deficit countries become indebted to finance their deficits, the liquid assets accumulate at the surplus poles, thus changing their significance as they exceed transactional and precautionary reserves. They then obey the speculative motive which inspires the choice of portfolio in terms of a search for yield and a cover for risk. However, countries may become indebted beyond their foreseeable financing requirements in order to create precautionary reserves against uncertainty. In that case, international liquidity depends not simply on the total of the deficits, but also on the volatility of the balances over time. This latter variable has all the more effect because it concerns countries which do not have the capacity to borrow in their own currency in order to meet unforeseen changes in their balance of payments.

(c) *determinants of the international financial order which affect the distribution of liquid assets in terms of the currency in which they are held, and which encourage either savings or additional demands for international reserves.* The efficacy of a system of payments depends on its centralization and the existence or otherwise of a single means of settlement. This is the role of money as a public good. A plurality of convertible currencies safeguards the cohesion of multilateral payments, but the exchange risks lead to crossed holdings of liquid assets in the different currencies used as means of settlement. If effective long-term exchange markets do exist, the liquid assets necessary for the operation of the payments system tend to take the form of interbank deposits. When financial operations are taken into account, it can be seen that crossed deposits are minimized when the currency of settlement is also that in which international exports of capital are made, with a single financial centre managing the international transfer of payments. Conversely, if the regulation of international investments and the financing of international investments are done in different currencies, exporters of capital, or more probably their bankers, will hold deposits in the currency of settlement on the books of banks of the country issuing the money. From these deposits are subtracted the purchases of securities in the rest of the world by savers in the capital-exporting countries. This relationship will give rise to crossed deposits if the commercial banks of the capital-exporting country finance this export by selling their own money to the banks of the country of the currency of settlement, being that in which the importers of capital receive the transfer of funds. Conversely, if the composition of private deposits by agents from the capital-exporting country is financed by a reduction in the reserves held by the central bank of that country, another important phenomenon occurs in the formation of international liquidity: the substitution between private liquid assets and official reserves.

These opening remarks are intended solely to draw attention to the different scenarios and to the apparent proliferation of deposits which occur when international liquidity is created primarily as the result of very heavy banking activity.

The expansion of international liquidity and its counterparts

The traditional perspective for measuring the expansion of international liquidity is a limited one, consisting in observing the progression as a whole and the composition of official reserves. The progression in total reserves since World War II is illustrated in Table 6.1. This shows a slow and fairly regular increase up to the end of the 1960s, an explosion of growth in the 1970s and a dramatic

TABLE 6.1
International reserves (end-of-year positions, $ bn)

	1945	1955	1960	1965	1970	1975	1980	1982
Reserves by components								
Gold[a]	33.3	35.0	38.0	41.5	37.2	35.7	40.0	39.8
(gold holdings by the US)	(20.1)	(21.7)	(17.8)	(14.0)	(11.1)	(11.6)	(11.2)	(11.2)
Currency	14.3	18.1	18.6	25.4	45.5	162.4	378.3	325.0
(US/official institutions liabilities)	(4.2)	(7.3)	(11.1)	(15.8)	(23.8)	(80.7)	(157.1)	(164.0)
SDRs and reserve positions in IMF[b]	—	1.9	3.6	5.4	10.8	25.0	36.5	47.6
Total reserves	47.6	55.0	60.2	72.3	93.5	223.1	454.8	412.4
World exports during the year	34.2	87.0	118.3	170.5	286.8	812.4	1,876.4	1,704.1
Ratios (in %)								
Share of direct US liabilities in currency reserves	29.4	40.3	59.7	62.2	52.3	49.7	41.5	50.5
Currency/Total reserves	30.0	32.9	30.9	35.1	48.7	72.8	83.2	78.8
Total reserves/world exports	139.2	63.2	50.9	42.4	32.6	27.5	24.2	24.2
Currency/world exports	41.8	20.8	15.7	14.9	15.9	20.0	20.2	19.0

a. Gold is valued at official prices: $35 per oz before 1980, and at $42 per oz thereafter.
b. The components of the reserves other than gold are expressed in dollars by conversion of the IMF statistics valued in SDRs, employing the following parities for the dollar/SDR: 1,000 up to and including 1970; 1,171 in 1975; 1,275 in 1980; and 1,103 in 1982.
Source: IMF, *International Financial Statistics.*

contraction after 1980. It was the currency component of the reserves which was responsible for these contrasting movements. The evolution of gold was static and its importance decreased, not simply quantitatively, but primarily because it ceased to be the ultimate means of settlement between central banks. It therefore no longer occupies more than a peripheral place in international monetary relations, although it is no less disruptive, as will be seen later. The reserves connected with the monetary role of the IMF are shown to have progressed strongly after each of the oil crises, when the Fund became involved in financing the deficits of an increasing number of countries. Nevertheless, their totals were overestimated in the official figures; in fact, the reserve positions of the IMF include not only credits granted by the Fund, which increase the global total of international reserves, but also transfers to the Fund of gold and SDRs already owned by countries which are simply substituting one form of reserve for another. In 1980, the total reserves connected with the IMF were overestimated by about $11.5 billion in the official report; nevertheless, this figure was retained in order to provide a series based on the same definition since 1945.

A closer examination by period gives some other interesting indications. Up to the mid-1960s, the share of currency in total reserves was quite stable, but there was a marked decrease in the share of reserves in international trade, and in particular a rapid progression in the direct liabilities of the United States to foreign official institutions. With the deficits in the current account balances of the deficit countries representing cumulative annual totals not exceeding 3 per cent of the total current transactions worldwide, we get a fairly clear idea of the monetary system which had gradually imposed itself since the time when a multilateral payments system was re-established.

The decline in the pound sterling, the initial weight of US external trade as a proportion of world trade and then the rapid expansion in the foreign activities of US companies resulted in the dollar becoming the principal means of settlement. The main determinants in the demand for liquid assets were global growth and the interdependence of trade relations. Fixed exchange rates and the absence of major current account deficits restricted the need for precautionary reserves. Improvements in communications and the development of payments by bank transfer reduced the need for reserves as compared with transactions, as had occurred previously with the integration of domestic banking systems. This obviously explained the change in the ratio of currency reserves to world exports from 20.8 per cent in 1955 to 14.9 per cent in 1965. But it did not explain the initial fall in the ratio after 1945, which resulted purely from the accumulation of liquid credits during the war by non-belligerent countries with key-currency countries, which provided the finance for purchases when normal commercial relations were re-established. During this period, the principal source of international reserves was the US balance-of-payments deficit. The USA's increased financial liabilities to foreign official institutions were essentially due to the monetization of the deficit in its non-monetary operations, principally at that time net exports of public and private long-term capital, followed by conversion on the exchange markets by private agents in receipt of these dollars.

Nevertheless, in the second half of the 1960s, increasing concern was expressed about the viability of this system of international monetary creation. Table 6.1 shows two of the indices of this. The reduction in the ratio of currency reserves to international trade revived the spectre of a lack of reserves, for, although the ratio of total reserves remained high, gold, which was the essential alternative to currency, was concentrated in the central banks of the most powerful surplus countries other than the United States. When official US liabilities exceeded the US gold stock in 1965 and the gold pool concentrated its supplies to calm the market, the circulation of gold between central banks was in fact virtually frozen, with the exception of periods when the Bank of France purchased gold against dollars in 1965 and 1966.

A deeper cause for concern at that time was the fact that a system of monetary creation based on the payments deficit of one single country was not necessarily compatible with the financing requirements of the rest of the world, once trade started to diversify and the relative economic weight of the country issuing the principal source of reserves declined rapidly. While a concerted official solution to the problem of diversification had been sought with the invention of Special Drawing Rights (SDRs), the system was simultaneously being transformed through bank competition. The spectacular result is illustrated by two developments: between 1965 and 1980, the ratio of currency reserves to world exports rose from 14.9 to 20.2 per cent, while the share of US liabilities to foreign official institutions fell from 62.2 per cent to 41.5 per cent of the total amount of official currency reserves.

But Table 6.1 by no means tells the whole story of the explosion in international liquidity in the 1970s. Two factors intervened to change the previously held idea of liquidity radically: the soaring increase in the market price of gold and, above all, the large growth in bank credits. The quantitative incidence of the first factor can be illustrated by óne figure. Whereas world reserves of monetary gold in 1980 were $40 billion at the conventional price of $42 per ounce, they exceeded $600 billion at the market price! This enormous discrepancy had no direct effect on liquidity, however, since gold, excluded from interbank settlements, became the most illiquid of all reserves. But a gold stock valued at the market price might well be seen as a guarantee of creditworthiness by the banks. Thus, speculation in gold and the excessive expansion of dollar credit feed one another if the dollars spent by borrowers accumulate in the hands of a small group of creditors who seek to dispose of them on the margin in order to balance the composition of their portfolios.

Table 6.2 extends the definition of international liquidity and relates the forms in which it is held to the sources of its creation. Thanks to the statistical information supplied by the BIS, which has done its best to distinguish interbank deposits from those of other categories of depositors, it is possible to draw up a table of international liquidity according to the same principle as that for national liquidity, by measuring money supply and its counterparts. We need not point out that the quality of the statistics is very inferior, that heterogeneous sources have had to be combined and that the statistical coverage is incomplete.

The principal merit of Table 6.2 is to bring out clearly the considerable change which has occurred in international monetary creation. From 1970 to 1982 the share of the monetization of the US deficit in the whole of its non-monetary operations fell from 47 per cent to 12 per cent of the total sum of international liquidity in currency. Among these liquid assets, private agents' deposits grew more rapidly than official reserves. This change may be seen as the transfer from *exogenous* monetary creation, in terms of the financing requirements of the world economy, because it is linked to fluctuations in the US balance of payments, to *endogenous* monetary creation through a banking system responding flexibly to the demand for credit. The efficacy of this system, simply from the point of view of the improvement in the degree of liquidity in the world economy, is illustrated by the evolution in the ratio of private bank assets to world imports, excluding US imports. This ratio has continued to increase since the first oil crisis, rising from 10 per cent to 20.7 per cent in 1982. Lastly, the capacity for adaptation in the supply of international credit is attested by the changes that have

TABLE 6.2: International liquidity and its counterparts (end-of-year rates)

I—Counterparts by source	1970	1974	1975	1976	1977	1978	1979	1980	1981	1982
Operations (in $ bn)										
Eurobank credits	28	134	168	200	242	289	354	411	470	498
External credits of banks located in the USA	7	14	16	18	20	33	46	58	81	107
Monetization of the deficit of US non-monetary operations	31	62	53	58	89	117	130	107	90	83
Overall total	66	210	237	276	351	439	530	576	641	688
Share of monetization of US deficit in total creation of liquidity (%)	47.0	29.5	22.4	21.0	25.4	26.7	24.5	18.6	14.0	12.1

II — Liquid assets by forms of holding and categories of holder	1970	1974	1975	1976	1977	1978	1979	1980	1981	1982
Operations (in $ bn)										
Deposits in Eurobanks										
private	—	62	62	77	89	120	156	199	261	275
official institutions	—	38	51	64	73	84	120	139	126	98
various	—	25	34	32	51	65	95	62	67	107
Total	38	125	147	173	213	269	371	400	454	480
Private deposits in banks located in USA	4	8	10	11	12	14	16	17	23	41
Official reserves deposited in the USA	24	77	80	92	126	156	143	159	164	167
Overall total	66	210	237	276	351	439	530	576	641	688
Private banked assets/world imports excluding US imports (%)	—	10.2	10.0	11.0	11.1	12.7	12.8	12.9	17.4	20.7

The credits and deposits of the Eurobanks are currency operations with non-bank traders of the banks reporting to the BIS and of subsidiaries of American banks in the Caribbean, together with currency loans and currency deposits of Eurobanks with their resident customers. The credits and deposits of banks located in the USA involve operations with non-resident non-bank traders.

Sources: BIS and *Federal Reserve Bulletin*; IMF, *International Financial Statistics*.

occurred since 1979. Whereas the sudden change in US monetary policy caused a long recession and a rise in interest rates which completely reversed the position of non-monetary operations in the US balance of payments, producing a drastic contraction in this source of international monetary creation, the increase in bank loans on the part of the Eurobanks and then of banks located in the United States nevertheless allowed the growth of liquidity to continue. This example of interdependence between the counterparts of international liquidity shows that the world economy has found a system of private credit which corresponds to its commercial and financial integration. At the same time, a new problem has come to light: that of regulating such a system.

International liquidity and national monetary policies

The empirical analysis of the sources and components of international liquidity brought out in the previous section stresses the salient features. Bank loans in currency and the monetization of the US balance of payments deficits are the two sources; agents and official monetary institutions are holders who behave in different ways when the pace of growth in international liquidity is abruptly changed.

The overall importance of dollar-denominated assets induces us to adopt the method followed by McKinnon.[1] In a first approximation, the interdependence between national money stocks through the accumulation or decumulation of international reserves can be studied in a simplified framework. It entails the assumption of a world economy made up of two zones: on the one hand, the United States; on the other, the set of all the other convertible-currency countries.

In this schematic presentation, the asymmetry between the United States and the rest of the world is taken to the extreme. American residents do not hold assets denominated in the currencies of the rest of the world, while the residents of the rest of the world, obviously including subsidiaries and affiliates of US firms, have a portfolio which is diversified according to the relative yields anticipated from dollar assets and from assets in the currencies of the rest of the world. The US monetary authorities do not hold reserves in foreign currency, while the official institutions of the rest of the world hold all their reserves in dollars.

The Eurodollar appears as an extension to the system of dollar credit. The resources for this lie principally in the deposits of American and foreign private agents and in those of part of the rest of the world's official reserves, the other part being invested in the United States itself. Consequently, the Eurodollar's effect on the overall sum of international liquid assets is not mechanical; it cannot be measured by means of a stable monetary multiplier, the base for which would be determined by the net assets of the Eurobanks with the American banks. Its effect is, however, very considerable and is expressed by way of a more intense competition for the supply of credit and for the capture of deposits. This globalized competition, based on the pivotal US interest rate, acts to stimulate the demand for credit.

Our view therefore is that this source of endogenous monetary creation obeys the principle of 'loans make deposits'. The deposits which the Eurobanks and the banks located in the United States apparently recycle are only the counterparts of the loans which they have granted. The demand for credit by the rest of the world and the response which the banks make to it become the main determinants in the growth of international liquidity. This does not mean that the global amount of international liquidity and the world money supply are uncontrollable. Such control would imply close collaboration between the US monetary authorities and those in the rest of the world. Since monetization of the American deficit is passive, because it results from the dollar's status as an international currency, this coordination depends on a delicate compromise: steps need to be taken to prevent the real rate of exchange between the dollar and the currencies of the rest of the world from being affected by sharp overvaluation or undervaluation. However, this exchange rate management prevents the money supply of the rest of the world from being controlled; it is the aggregates of internal credit which need to be controlled. Thus the three driving forces of liquidity are domestic credit in each zone and monetization of the American payments deficit.

We are therefore led to conclusions similar to those of McKinnon in his study published in 1984 by the Institute for International Economics:[2] to decide on desirable changes in internal credit in each zone; and to stabilize exchange rates within a range compatible with the long-term development of competitiveness. The difference is that McKinnon bases himself on a law of one price. We, on the other hand, follow Williamson[3] in considering a range for the exchange rate which would enable us to avoid the systematic monetization of balance of payments deficits. This means seeking a baseline balance which would not tend to follow a divergent course when the exchange rate was in the appropriate range. Finally, it is preferable not to try to neutralize the variations in the external component of the rest of the world's money supply. Official reserves and private deposits in dollars by agents from the rest of the world evolve in opposite directions when a change in relative profitability modifies the agents' holdings of dollar deposits.

The experience of the 1970s and the first years of the 1980s with a world economy linked by international credit not only leads to some basic principles of monetary cooperation. It also reveals the channels whereby disturbances in US monetary policy are transmitted to the outside world. An increase in US interest rates compared with those of the rest of the world contracts international liquidity but not always the world money supply. It all depends on the cumulative balance of the US balance of payments. If there is a cumulative deficit, there is a contraction in the world money supply. A move in interest rates in the opposite direction has an ambiguous effect. Everything depends on the respective elasticity of the demand for credit in dollars and in the currencies of the rest of the world. Finally, an anticipated dollar depreciation stimulates the expansion of international liquidity and an anticipated appreciation inhibits it. If the United States has a cumulative deficit, the world money supply exhibits the same movements. And if that deficit increases for reasons exogenous to US monetary policy without the latter reacting — an attitude known as 'benign neglect' — international liquidity increases correspondingly if American residents do not re-deposit on the Eurodollar market.

What conclusions can be drawn when the United States adopts a monetary regulation to control the supply of money directly? A restrictive US monetary policy causes an increase in the nominal interest rate and an anticipated appreciation of the dollar. Private residents of the rest of the world tend to substitute the dollar for other deposits. In response to this movement, central banks accept the loss of reserves and raise their interest rates, which in turn causes a decrease in the demand for credit in the rest of the world. For these two associated reasons, the decrease in reserves and the reduction in loans, the money supply of the rest of the world contracts as a reflection of the restriction on US monetary objectives. Thus, any inflationary or deflationary movement in the United States is amplified by the asymmetrical structure of the international monetary system, as was observed first in one direction and then the other at the end of the 1970s and the beginning of the 1980s.

The sole compensating force, which intervenes only after long, uncertain periods, is the current account deficit in the United States caused by long-term appreciation. Such a deficit, which does not affect the American money supply if the latter is exogenous, is the source of dollar creation which, for the part converted into foreign currency, helps increase the money supply of the rest of the world. International liquidity is thus increased by the amount of the US current account deficit. This effect partly softens the deflationary influence of the reduction in demand for credit in the rest of the world, without, however, neutralizing it entirely if US monetary policy remains restrictive.

International liquidity and deficit financing

The approach followed up to now is inadequate because it is a global one. The rest of the world is a heterogeneous mixture of countries which have reacted very differently to the major changes in international economic relations. Resuming our analysis of the factors in the demand for international liquidity, it might be said that the financing of current account deficits and the uncertainty induced by the generalization of floating exchange rates have replaced the need for transaction reserves related to the expansion in international trade. Furthermore, the ratios in Tables 6.1 and 6.2, describing the global relationships between different measurements of liquidity and world trade, become difficult to interpret in the 1970s. Two facts must be taken into consideration which markedly distinguish this period from the previous one. Whether measured in SDRs or in dollars, the total current deficits of deficit countries have increased substantially in absolute terms compared with the average for the 1960s. Even when related to the world total of current flows, the total current account deficits increased from a mean level of less than 3 per cent in the 1960s to more than 5 per cent in the 1970s. In addition, the variability of this indicator was very much greater, with a peak of almost 8 per cent in 1974–5. Moreover, there was a huge contrast in the development of world trade between the 1960s and the 1970s. In the first period, the volume of trade grew faster than the volume of world GDP, whereas the unit value of trade was less than world inflation and remained remarkably stable even up to 1968. In the second period, it did not increase more than the growth in world GDP, itself considerably slowed down, while the unit value increased distinctly faster than world inflation, which was itself very much higher.

Looking at all these things together, it is impossible to ignore the ceaselessly reiterated diagnosis made by Robert Triffin: namely, that the deregulation of the sources of international liquidity is to a large extent responsible for generalized world inflation. The move towards international monetary creation endogenous to countries' financing requirements has weakened the adjustment constraints of the balances of payments by monetizing the deficits of the whole world. If there appears to have been no overliquidity, this should be no cause for surprise. By systematically financing deficits, the international monetary system legitimized inflationary competition for a share of world revenue which had declined in volume. The response to the oil price shocks was a fall in the dollar and a rise in the prices of manufactured goods. The apparent combination of a soaring increase in liquidity and an expansion of world trade in nominal terms was simply the consequence of the operation of an economy of international indebtedness.

A detailed analysis of balance of payments financing is necessary to justify these hypotheses, but considerable statistical difficulties arise here. In fact, the current world balance of payments drawn from statistics published by the IMF reveals a cumulative deficit of almost $330 billion over the period 1974–82, more than a third of which (about $125 billion) was for 1982 alone. Figures of this magnitude destroy the credibility of any analysis of the financial mechanisms which attempt to cover these deficits. In fact, it is not possible to make sense of a situation which describes a generalized current deficit in all the major economic zones in the world. The problem is no longer one of statistical imperfection but of consistency in international economic relations. It is possible to form some idea of its scope by noting that the $125 billion deficit in 1982 was greater than the total OPEC surpluses during the second oil crisis and that it amounted to the total debt of Brazil and Mexico for the same year, 1982.

The precondition for serious analysis is therefore a statistical study designed to harmonize current balances on the basis of world equilibrium. A first step in this direction was undertaken at the Centre d'Etudes Prospectives et d'Informations Internationales (CEPII),[4] and the result is presented in Table 6.3. The basic conclusion to be drawn is that current account receipts were heavily undervalued in the OECD countries, especially in those whose banking systems participated in international financial mediation (United States, United Kingdom, France, West Germany, Japan, Switzerland). Detailed analysis of the operations contributing to the

TABLE 6.3
Correspondence between the unharmonized and harmonized current accounts in $ bn
(excluding cumulative reinvested profits 1974–82)

	UH	H
US	−87.9	−1.5
France	−19.2	+6.6
Japan	+19.5	+49.1
West Germany	+3.3	+24.9
Italy	−21.3	−9.9
Belgium + Netherlands	−7.9	+25.3
UK	−3.6	+32.3
Alpine countries	+16.3	+40.3
Southern Europe	−86.7	−81.2
Scandinavian countries	−53.5	−40.4
Other industrialized countries (Canada + ANZSA)	−70.0	−53.8
OPEC	+330.2	+340.8
Mexico	−40.9	−40.7
Brazil	−78.5	−77.3
Other Latin American countries (non-OPEC)	−57.8	−50.8
Africa (non-OPEC and non-South Africa)	−64.5	−60.2
Rapidly developing SE Asian countries	−28.0	−25.0
Other non-OPEC Asian countries with market economies	−40.4	−33.8
Central Europe	−71.9	−69.6
Other socialist countries	+21.0	+19.2
International organizations	+16.7	+26.6
World total	−327.3	0.0

UH = unharmonized current accounts from IMF statistics.
H = harmonized current accounts after CEPII adjustments.

Source: CEPII.

formation of current accounts confirms this observation. Receipts of interest and dividends are poorly recorded; this explains the rapid increase in the statistical differential from 1980. The undervaluation of income from capital increased with the rise in interest rates, the substantial increase in credit in the second oil crisis, and the proliferation of financial operations directed through sectors which escaped any control (offshore and international banking facilities). The counterpart to this underestimation of current receipts was an underestimation principally of the exports of long-term capital other than direct and portfolio investments from the countries mentioned above. Lastly, errors and omissions remaining after the major current and capital operations had been reconciled on a world scale represented flows which were not recorded either by the issuing or the receiving country; this primarily involved unrecorded entries of capital from Middle East and Latin American countries.

The results presented below summarize the analyses based on harmonized balances of payments, in other words, they are in balance in accounting terms on a world scale. An attempt is made to characterize the positions of the main debtor countries and zones in the international monetary system. In the previous section, the overall observation of the growth in international liquidity enabled a distinction to be made between an initial period comprising a rapid increase in currency reserves up to the second oil crisis and the accompanying change in US monetary policy, followed by a second period characterized by a contraction in that category of reserves. Such a break illustrates a radical change in the system of international monetary creation, and it is important to understand how this has had repercussions on the constraints on financing disequilibria in balances of payments in the world economy. In order to do this, we have examined the relationships between the variation in net reserves and current balances on the one hand, and recorded private capital flows and current balances on the other. These relationships were studied for each of the two periods in cross section, using the division into countries and zones described in Figure 1.

Figures 1 and 2 clearly show the unity of the period 1969–78. They indicate that the transformation of the system of monetary creation, characterized by the rapid expansion in international bank credit, is the significant factor in the study of international liquidity. The first oil crisis has come to be part of the monetary relations which were thus established in a way which confirms and strengthens them, not which calls them into question.

Figure 1 studies the relationship established at that time between the variation in net reserves and the current accounts of the countries or zones. Four conclusions can be drawn from this:

(a) the exceptional position of the United States. The dollar being the means of international financing, the accumulation of dollar reserves provides stability only to the extent that certain foreign official institutions agree to hold a growing amount of outstanding debts on the US Treasury. This increase was on average almost $22 billion per year.
(b) the current balance of the United States is in deficit to the extent of approximately $4.5 billion per year. But this source of liquidity creation is very much less than the accumulation of dollars held by

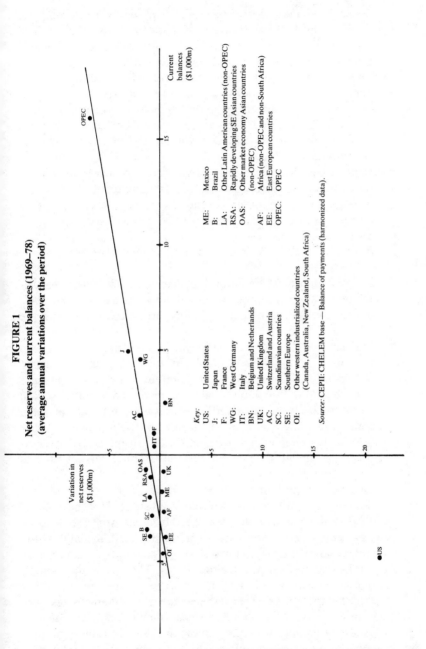

FIGURE 1

Net reserves and current balances (1969–78)
(average annual variations over the period)

Variation in
net reserves
($1,000m)

Current
balances
($1,000m)

Key:		
US:	United States	
J:	Japan	
F:	France	
WG:	West Germany	
IT:	Italy	
BN:	Belgium and Netherlands	
UK:	United Kingdom	
AC:	Switzerland and Austria	
SC:	Scandinavian countries	
SE:	Southern Europe	
OI:	Other western industrialized countries	
	(Canada, Australia, New Zealand, South Africa)	

ME:	Mexico
B:	Brazil
LA:	Other Latin American countries (non-OPEC)
RSA:	Rapidly developing SE Asian countries
OAS:	Other market economy Asian countries
	(non-OPEC)
AF:	Africa (non-OPEC and non-South Africa)
EE:	East European countries
OPEC:	OPEC

Source: CEPII: CHELEM base — Balance of payments (harmonized data).

the central banks of other countries. The supply of international liquidity has therefore been an international credit process which was very much more than just the counterpart of the American economy's external operations in goods and services.

(c) outside the United States, no country has had significantly negative net reserves despite the very wide spread of current balances. This clearly indicates that monetary financing of deficits has prevailed over adjustments to absorb those deficits. Several countries have managed to borrow sufficiently to gain reserves despite considerable deficits.

(d) a precise positive relationship exists between the variation in net reserves and the current balances. The reserve distribution clearly distinguishes those countries which have free reserves, gained by current surpluses (particularly OPEC, Japan, West Germany and Switzerland), from the others which have borrowed reserves, France and Italy being in the centre between the two groups.

Figure 2 confirms this relationship, despite statistical discrepancies in the registration of capital flows, and shows the expected decrease in the relationship. The net capital-exporting countries, with the exception of the United States, are the countries with free reserves.

In the period 1979–82, no relationship can be established between variations in reserves and current balances (Figure 3). Certain countries lose reserves, and others continue to borrow to increase them, while at the same time financing increased deficits. But the decisive change from the period 1969–78 is the abrupt turn-about in the situation of the United States. Instead of continuing to increase substantially its liabilities to foreign official institutions, it increases them only minimally to the extent that the variation in its net reserves becomes slightly positive.

One very important conclusion can be drawn from this. The system of monetary creation which was substituted for the collapse of the Bretton Woods system was freed from the American balance of payments as regards the amount of liquidity made available to the world economy. But it remained closely dependent on the monetary conditions in force in the United States. The systematic monetization of deficits by international credit was a system which was favourable to debtors because the negative real interest rates were supported by the US inflationary expansion. The abrupt change in US monetary policy from the autumn of 1979 interrupted this process under the worst possible conditions, given the accumulated indebtedness. The halt in the global progression in reserves in a

FIGURE 2

Current balances and movements of private capital (1969–78)
(average annual variations over the period)

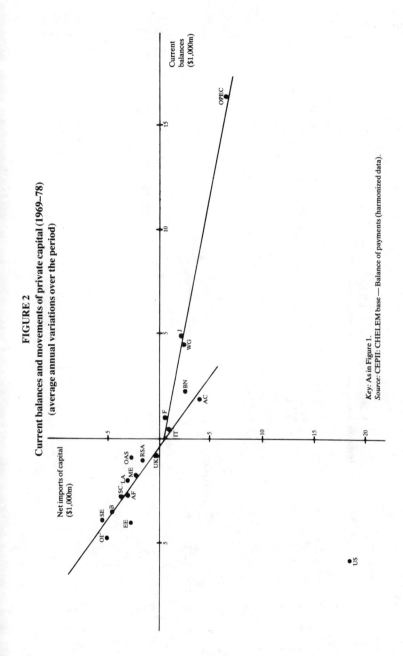

Key: As in Figure 1.
Source: CEPII: CHELEM base — Balance of payments (harmonized data).

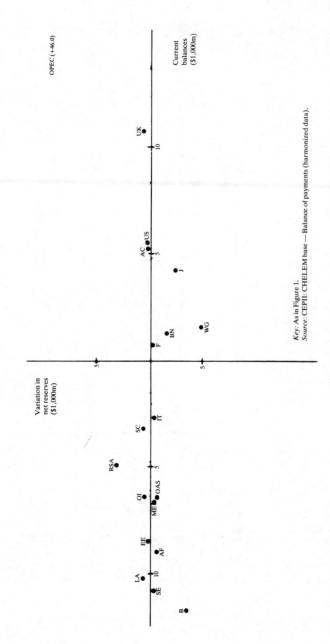

FIGURE 3

Net reserves and current balances (1979–82)
(average annual variations over the period)

Key: As in Figure 1.
Source: CEPII: CHELEM base — Balance of payments (harmonized data).

situation where current disequilibria were exacerbated following the second oil crisis, raised the problem of monetary adjustment in dramatic circumstances. The countries which had been in surplus and which had previously accumulated free reserves, such as West Germany or Japan, accepted a sudden monetary contraction before rapidly returning to surplus. The temporary loss of reserves was one of the counterparts of this deflationary policy. The OPEC countries did the same after the fall in the price of oil. But other industrialized or developing countries which were structurally in deficit found themselves in a very much more delicate situation because on the one hand their reserves were borrowed and not free and because on the other they were a guarantee of their future creditworthiness. Among these countries, reactions varied greatly. Some, such as the Scandinavian countries and the rapidly developing Asian countries, maintained a good financial profile. They were able to continue to borrow beyond what was necessary to finance their current deficits and to accumulate reserves. Others, however, such as Brazil or the African countries, lost reserves despite their financial fragility.

The question then arises as to whether we are now about to witness a destruction of the framework of indebtedness such as took place in the 1930s. At that time, in fact, capital began to flow from debtors to creditors, from deficit countries to surplus countries, with the United States draining the gold reserves of the entire world. Figure 4 allows a negative response to be given to the question. Even if the spread is greater than in the period 1969–78 (Figure 2), it can be seen that the countries are situated only in the second and fourth quadrants, indicating that over the period 1979–82 private capital flows continued to be in the direction of the deficit countries and away from the surplus countries. American banks in particular lent larger sums than ever before. Admittedly, in 1983 the net exports of capital from American banks ceased, but the United States returned to a position of deficit on current account.

Table 6.4 breaks down the sub-periods even more precisely, distinguishing the years preceding and following the two oil crises. It isolates the years 1981–2, during which the symptoms of grave financial difficulties began to manifest themselves for a number of debtor countries. The abruptness of the reaction of traditionally surplus countries (Japan, West Germany and Switzerland) was clearly apparent. These countries continued to export capital, but they had drawn massively on their reserves to accompany a drastic deflation. This substantial monetary contraction enabled them to return to a more surplus position than ever on their current accounts

FIGURE 4

Current balances and movements of private capital (1979–82)
(average annual variations over the period)

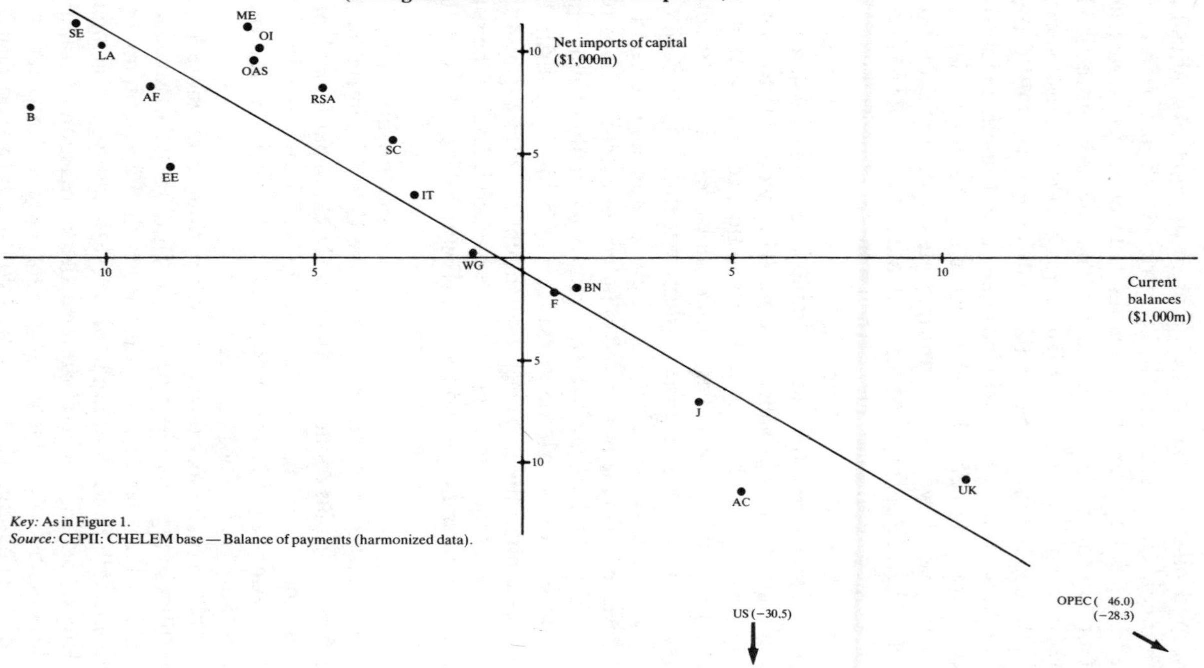

Key: As in Figure 1.
Source: CEPII: CHELEM base — Balance of payments (harmonized data).

TABLE 6.4

Variations in international reserves analysed from balances of payments ($ bn and mean year for each period)

Operations by countries and groups of countries	1969	1970–3	1974–8	1979–80	1981–2
United States					
Adjusted reserve assets	+1.2	−1.8	+0.8	+1.6	+4.4
Reserve liabilities	−0.2	+20.2	+27.3	+2.2	+2.7
Net reserves	+1.4	−22.0	−26.5	−0.6	+1.7
Current balance	−1.5	−4.2	−5.9	−6.8	+17.7
Net capital exports	−4.4	+15.7	+24.2	+20.6	+48.3
Errors and omissions	+1.5	+2.1	−3.6	−26.8	−26.3
Japan + West Germany + Switzerland					
Adjusted reserve assets	−1.7	+9.2	+11.1	−18.1	+2.0
Reserve liabilities	0	+0.8	+4.0	+4.0	−6.1
Net reserves	−1.7	+8.4	+7.1	−22.1	+8.1
Current balance	+6.2	+6.3	+16.4	−12.5	+28.6
Net capital exports	+9.2	+1.2	+14.4	+13.1	+23.8
Errors and omissions	−1.3	−3.3	−5.1	−3.4	−3.3
United Kingdom					
Adjusted reserve assets	+0.2	+1.3	+1.8	+1.9	−3.4
Reserve liabilities	−0.6	+1.2	+3.0	+13.3	−16.5
Net reserves	+0.8	+0.1	−1.2	−11.4	+13.1
Current balance	+1.3	+0.3	−2.0	+4.2	+17.2
Net capital exports	+0.7	0	−0.4	+17.4	+4.2
Errors and omissions	−0.2	+0.2	−0.5	−1.8	−0.1
France + Italy + Belgium + Netherlands					
Adjusted reserve assets	−1.0	+2.2	+2.6	+5.4	−6.8
Reserve liabilities	+0.2	−0.4	+3.3	+2.3	+0.2
Net reserves	−1.2	+2.6	−0.7	+3.1	−7.0
Current balance	+3.4	+3.9	+3.4	−0.5	−1.2
Net capital exports	+4.3	+1.4	+6.0	−2.4	+3.0
Errors and omissions	+0.3	−0.1	−1.9	−1.2	+2.8
Other industrialized countries					
Adjusted reserve assets	−0.4	+5.2	−0.2	+2.5	0
Reserve liabilities	0	0	+0.3	−0.3	0
Net reserves	−0.4	+5.2	−0.5	+2.8	0
Current balance	−7.0	−1.3	−20.5	−17.1	−23.8
Net capital exports	−2.9	−6.5	−24.0	−23.1	−22.2
Errors and omissions	−3.7	0	+4.0	+3.2	−1.6
Non-OPEC developing countries					
Adjusted reserve assets	+1.6	+3.1	+6.1	+5.1	−6.1
Reserve liabilities	0	0	0	+0.5	+2.2
Net reserves	+1.6	+3.1	+6.1	+4.6	−8.3
Current balance	−3.7	−7.1	−17.8	−44.9	−56.4
Net capital exports	−5.2	−8.3	−27.5	−50.3	−62.5
Errors and omissions	−0.1	−1.9	+3.6	+3.8	+14.7
OPEC					
Adjusted reserve assets	+0.3	+2.1	+11.8	+19.6	−5.9
Reserve liabilities	0	0	0	0	0
Net reserves	+0.3	+2.1	+11.8	+19.6	−5.9
Current balance	+0.1	+3.8	+31.1	+78.6	+13.4
Net capital exports	−1.8	+0.7	+15.7	+35.7	+20.6
Errors and omissions	+1.6	+1.0	+3.6	+23.3	−1.3

Note: The variations in reserve assets are counted (+) when they are gained by the country. The net capital exports and errors and omissions are counted (+) when there is a positive variation in the assets for a country. The relationships are therefore:

net reserves = assets − liabilities
= current balance − net capital exports − errors and omissions

Source: CEPII: CHELEM base — Balance of payments.

from 1981–2. The other Continental EC countries (France, Italy, Belgium and the Netherlands) did not improve their external accounts so rapidly. They tried initially to overcome the second oil crisis by borrowing more than their current deficits. But with current balances very sensitive to the recession among their partners and to the rise in the dollar, and with, in addition, the resumption in capital outflows attracted by US interest rates, they had to accept heavy losses in reserves which weakened their currencies in the period 1981–2.

Finally, the non-OPEC developing countries suffered a catastrophic deterioration in their current balances under the triple effect of the decline in the terms of trade for their exports, the recession in the major Western countries and the increase in financial charges on their accumulated debt. The mistrust shown by the commercial banks towards the most heavily indebted countries was reflected in the latter period in a net increase in loans of less than the current deficit. Losses in reserves were the result. In contrast, the other industrialized countries, which had been traditionally very much in deficit since the first oil crisis, were able to continue to finance their worsened current deficit by borrowing. Among them, mention must be made of the extraordinary position of the United Kingdom which benefitted from a short-lived speculative boom in favour of the pound at the time of the second oil crisis, whence the strong increase in its reserve liabilities, reversed in the subsequent period. Lastly, OPEC saw its capital export capabilities and its reserves develop hand in hand with the fluctuations in the oil market.

Conclusion: the problem of regulating international liquidity

The study we have just made of the creation of international liquidity indicates that the regulation of this process remains an unresolved problem. The fluctuations between excess and shortfall in liquidity arising from the asymmetric structure of the international monetary system cause large disequilibria in exchange rates between the principal currencies. These currencies occupy positions which are more complementary than substitutable in the systems of international monetary creation which have taken over from the system of the gold-dollar standard. This complementarity is illustrated by the flow-chart below (Figure 5) which describes the relations between the dollar and the Deutschmark.

FIGURE 5

The interdependence of international financial and monetary relations

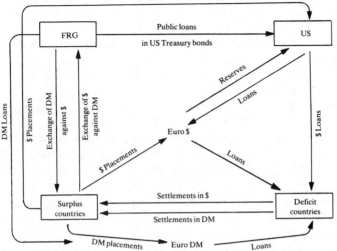

Source: CEPII, 'Economie mondiale: la montée des tensions', *Economica*, 1983, p. 32.

Contrary to the expectations of the supporters of flexible exchange rates, their institution did not spontaneously introduce greater symmetry into the system. The dollar standard continues to exist because the Deutschmark is grafted on to the dollar circuit. Apart from West Germany's own external transactions, there is no area in which the Deutschmark would exercise all the functions assigned to an international medium of payment. International liquidity was created principally by dollar loans to deficit countries from American banks and Eurobanks.

During the phase of strong expansion in international liquidity from 1974 to 1980, these loans served to pay surplus countries either directly in dollars or in another currency (the Deutschmark in the example in Figure 5) after conversion on the exchange markets. Among these surplus countries, OPEC has accumulated liquid assets very much greater than its transaction reserves and has adopted a course of diversification of its assets: investments in Eurodollars, US financial securities, Deutschmarks after conversion on the exchange markets. The position of West Germany is then clear. Constrained by the pressure exerted on the dollar/ Deutschmark exchange rate, German monetary policy closes the dollar circle when the differential between the financing needs of debtors and the investment choices of creditors exerts pressure on exchanges, for which private speculators cannot compensate without a dollar collapse. By defining its mediation between Deutschmark appreciation in terms of the dollar and absorption of dollars invested in American Treasury bonds, the Bundesbank establishes a compromise between monetary expansion and large variations in real exchange rates. It is an agent of global regulation of the international monetary system.

This was the mechanism in force before the radical change in US monetary policy. Although this mechanism was far from perfect given its inflationary tendency, it at least had the advantage of including a compensatory force restricting the one-way movements of dollars. That is now no longer the case. The irresistible attraction of the dollar has upset a number of flows and opened the way for the internationalization of currencies other than the dollar. The demand for dollars is fed by debtors forced to increase their present debt to honour the servicing of their past debt, the real value of which, measured in terms of the purchasing power of their exports, has increased considerably. Added to this is the demand of all those who borrow in other currencies and convert their borrowings into dollars to invest them in the United States. Lastly, the German financing requirement during 1980–1 is covered by Deutschmark loans, part of which constitute credits convertible into dollars. OPEC no longer provides a counterweight to this demand for dollars since the time when its current surpluses virtually disappeared. The international monetary system is therefore abandoned without any compensatory mechanism to the vagaries of US monetary policy, and the supply of liquidity to the goodwill of the US banks. Insofar as other currencies continue to become internationalized, they no longer do so as a complement to the dollar, in other words, at the instigation of dollar holders wishing to diversify their assets. They do so by the direct indebtedness of the issuing country at the instigation of its borrowers or by loans in its currency to foreign debtors. The consequence is that rival circuits to that of the dollar may be formed in a system which is rendered unstable by the extreme fluidity of capital movements when financial arbitrage does not correspond to the relative rates of internationalization of different currencies.

Although it is thus possible to detect certain recent trends towards a multiple currency system, these trends are occurring under the worst conditions of instability, relating to the banks' fragility in the face of the potential insolvency of their debtors, the lack of structural creditors capable of replacing OPEC as a counterbalance to structural debtors, and the uncertainty about the future direction of the dollar in the light of a rapidly expanding US current account deficit. Recent experience has amply shown that it is not possible to establish a reliable mechanism between an ordered growth in international reserves to allow the development of the world economy, and the establishment of symmetrical and graded constraints affecting both surplus and deficit countries to contain and if possible reduce the disequilibria between the balances of payments. On this subject, whole libraries of plans for reform have gone unheeded. In this conclusion, we are not attempting to offer new proposals or to pass judgement on those which have been made, but simply to draw some lessons from the empirical analysis carried out in this study.

First of all, we should remember one truism which the partisans of pure floating exchange rates insisted on ignoring: money does not manage itself of its own accord. That applies on an international as well as a national scale. To believe that floating exchange rates would perform the miracle of reconciling each country's complete freedom to follow an economic policy of its choice and at the same time benefit from the interdependence between nations is a delusion. Those who hoped to resolve the reserve problem by eliminating its raison d'être should reflect on the causes of the explosion in reserves with floating rates and not treat this phenomenon as proof that exchange rates were not allowed to float sufficiently.

Secondly, we should mention one further truism: any strengthening of interdependence implies mutual constraints and responsibilities in national economic policies, which involves taking the situation and preferences of other countries into account. The world economy has undergone a prodigious advance in private financial inter-dependence over the last twenty years, but international monetary cooperation between the governments of the main currency countries has considerably regressed, with the notable exception of the European Monetary System.

If we accept these two truisms, it may be feared that international monetary relations have entered a critical phase, illustrated, on the one hand, by total uncertainty about the future development of the dollar, and, on the other, by the hidden international financial crisis which is managed on an *ad hoc* basis. The world economy needs an official monetary control compatible with the degree of financial interdependence which it has attained. Without it, it is highly likely that this degree of interdependence will be reduced by barriers to capital movements which countries will be forced to impose in arbitrary fashion as soon as financial instability threatens the foundations of their economies and their social equilibrium.

Experience and prudence suggest a pragmatic approach to establishing elements of monetary cooperation. Recent trends towards a multiple currency system do exist. Such systems are unstable if they are not tightly managed, because they encourage permanent competition between currencies to fulfil the functions of a vehicle, on the one hand, and of the ultimate settlement of debts, on the other, in which the currency has the status of a public good. Any monetary system needs a central pivot in order to conform to this status. If nothing is constructed in its place, a decline in the predominance of the dollar might very well aggravate the chronic instability which we are facing, rather than improve it.

In the 1970s, the central banks of some strong-currency countries played a *de facto* stabilizing role. But this involved a situation in which the dollar and the other strong currencies fulfilled complementary functions, and not a true multiple currency system in which the currencies were competing for the same functions. In order to diminish the importance of settlement problems and to intervene directly in the creation of international liquidity, it was seen as desirable to establish compatibility in the rates of increase in the internal credit of the major countries. But the proposal made in 1974 by McKinnon[5] to restrict this to a tripartite agreement between the United States, Japan and Germany is probably inadequate today. The monetary organization of Europe seems to be a precondition for the viability of a three-currency system on a world scale. As Triffin has constantly reiterated, this organization implies the development of the European Currency Unit as a parallel currency. That involves accustoming private traders to the use of ECU in credits as well as deposits, so that the banks can establish a system of payments and an interbank market of credits in ECUs, and at the same time progressing towards the second phase of the EMS which would make the official ECU a payments currency in its own right between the European central banks.

Although the extreme uncertainty about the future development of the dollar has encouraged timid approaches towards a multiple currency system, the persistent problems of indebtedness for the greater part of the present decade have brought out another trend: the return to power of the official institutions, central banks and international institutions, in financial relations between debtor countries and private creditors. This growing mediation is occurring on a step-by-step basis and unwillingly, but it may hold much in the way of promise. Combined international reserves in the last few years have progressed more rapidly than international currency liquidity, though admittedly from a very modest base.

The injection of these reserves was related to operations by the International Monetary Fund as a lender of last resort with the currency resources at its disposal. It also took the form of compensatory financing to soften the destabilizing effects of upheavals in the world business cycle, when these upheavals threatened to cause a depression in countries whose export receipts were particularly sensitive to price variations over which they had no control. These initiatives did not affect the traditional responsibilities of the IMF. They extended its operations, which nevertheless remained strictly circumscribed by the contributions to which the member countries issuing currency for use as loans were prepared to agree.

The proposal to promote the SDR to the rank of a direct payment asset between central banks and to facilitate its use in private financial transactions is completely different. It was advanced by J. Polak and P. Kenen,[6] whose suggestions are similar in substance, even if they differ as to the institutional measures to achieve this aim. The promotion of the SDR meets a need which has been clearly demonstrated. Countries need to keep own reserves, i.e. free reserves, and not simply reserves attached to loans which have an unfortunate tendency to run dry just when they are most needed. SDRs are not reserves which are the counterpart of a country's liabilities. They are created *ex nihilo* and are allocated to countries. If therefore the SDRs could progressively replace currency reserves and not be supplementary to them, a large step would have been taken towards collective control of the development of international liquidity. Certainly, this evolution by the IMF towards the status of a central world bank in its own right will not happen overnight. But necessity knows no law. The severity of the financial problems inherited from the unbridled competition between the private banks may cause decisions to be taken which will lead to it. As the attraction of a reserve instrument is closely linked to its use in settling debts, the fundamental decision according to Kenen is to allow central banks to intervene on the exchange markets in SDRs, since interventions are the mechanism by which official settlements are made. This implies that private agents should learn to use the SDR, which they would do if the central banks, through their interventions, restricted the variation in its fluctuations compared with those of national currencies. There remains, then, the formidable problem of defining the rules by which SDRs would be issued, freed from the present straitjacket of discretionary allocations.

Notes

1. R. McKinnon, 'Currency Substitution and Instability in the World Dollar Standard', *American Economic Review*, Vol. 72, No. 3, June 1982.

2. R. McKinnon, *An International Standard for Monetary Stabilization*, Institute for International Economics, Policy Analyses in International Economics No. 8, Washington DC, 1984.

3. J. Williamson, *The Exchange Rate System*, Institute for International Economics, Policy Analyses in International Economics, No. 5, Washington DC, 1983.

4. J. Oliveira-Martins and C. Leroy, 'Les désajustements mondiaux de balances de paiements', *Economie Prospective Internationale*, CEPII, No. 17, 1st quarter 1984.

5. R. McKinnon, *A New Tripartite Monetary Agreement or a Limping Dollar Standard*, Princeton Essays in International Finance, October 1974.

6. J. Polak, 'Thoughts on an International Monetary Fund based fully on the SDR', pamphlet No. 28, Washington DC, IMF, 1979; P. Kenen, 'The Use of the SDR to Supplement or Substitute for other Means of Finance', in G. von Fürstenberg (ed.), *International Money and Credit, The Policy Rules*, Washington DC, IMF, 1983.

7
The Role of International Banking
David T. Llewellyn

A particular feature of the international monetary system in the 1970s was the substantially increased role that came to be played by international banking and the consequent shift in the balance of roles of the *official* and *private* sectors.

In terms of the provision of international liquidity, the financing of the transfer of real resources to less developed countries, and balance of payments financing, the international banking sector increased its role both absolutely and relative to the traditional official sector. Analyses of the international monetary system of the 1950s and 1960s would not normally encompass the international banking sector. Analysis of the 1970s and early 1980s cannot ignore it, as the system developed a dual structure (official and private sectors) with overlapping and competing roles. During the 1970s the private international banking sector became an integral part of the international monetary system and came to adopt roles previously regarded as within the province of the official sector.

The increasing role of international banking was manifest in terms of the substantial increase in the volume of the banks' external assets in major financial centres, the rise in the proportion of external assets and liabilities in their total balance sheet positions, the relative shift from trade financing to more direct balance of payments financing, and the substantial rise in the number of banks participating in international lending business. At the end of 1982 the volume of cross-border domestic and Eurocurrency assets of banks in the BIS reporting area amounted to $1,627 billion (against $126 billion in 1971). On the basis of BIS estimates of double-counting associated with interbank redepositing, the volume of net international bank credit outstanding is given as $985 billion at the end of 1982. A World Bank estimate suggests that in 1978 there were ten times more banks participating in the syndicated Eurocredit market than in 1972.

The themes of this chapter relate to the implications for the international monetary system of the increasing role of international banking and the shift in the roles of the official and private sectors. This was not a consciously planned change in the structure of the international monetary system, but developed for two main reasons: (i) traditional mechanisms did not develop in line with the increased demand for external financing following the rise in the absolute size of payments imbalances, and (ii) it was consistent with the changing portfolio objectives and behaviour of banks that occurred at the same time. In the process a new *confidence problem* analogous to that originally defined by Triffin in the 1960s emerged in the early 1980s. This might be held to justify a reconsideration of the respective roles of the private and official sectors for the future. The debt problems that emerged in the 1980s in turn induced an official sector response which produced a 'tandem system' with cooperative roles for the two sectors.

World economy context

The development of international banking over the 1970s occurred in the context of substantial changes in the world economy with the conjuncture of inflation and recession, greatly increased payments imbalances between countries, the structural aspects of two sharp rises in the price of oil, and sometimes volatile exchange rates and interest rates. Tables 7.1–7.3 give the evolution of payments imbalances over the 1970s, with the aggregate current account deficit of developing countries rising from $11.6 billion in 1973 to $97 billion in 1982. Between 1974 and 1981 non-oil primary product prices rose by less than 50 per cent, while the prices of manufactured goods more than doubled and oil prices rose by close on 1,000 per cent.

Trends and developments in international banking interact with the world economy, with causality working in both directions. Autonomous developments in the world economy impinge upon the international banking sector through their effect upon confidence, through the supply of and demand for the intermediation services of international banking, and through interest rate movements. The rise in the absolute size of international payments imbalances (Table 7.1) and the structural change in financing (Tables 7.2 and 7.4) were major factors in the development of the international banking sector. Over the period 1973–82 (Table 7.1) industrial countries in aggregate had a cumulative deficit of only $4.5 billion, though it ranged from a deficit of $45 billion to a surplus of $30 billion. The cumulative OPEC surplus of £465 billion had, as a counterpart, an

TABLE 7.1
Summary of payments balances on current account, 1973–82[a] ($ bn)

	1973	1974	1975	1976	1977	1978	1979	1980	1981	1982[b]
Industrial countries	17.7	−13.9	17.9	−2.6	−5.7	29.8	−10.2	−44.8	−3.7	11.0
Canada	—	−1.6	−4.6	−4.0	−4.0	−4.0	−4.3	−1.9	−5.8	−5.0
United States	9.1	7.6	21.2	7.5	−11.3	−10.9	4.9	8.4	11.0	5.0
Japan	0.1	−4.5	−0.4	3.9	11.1	18.0	−8.0	−9.5	6.2	13.5
France	−0.1	−4.9	1.0	−4.9	−1.6	5.2	3.0	−6.3	−6.6	−6.5
FRG	7.1	13.0	7.6	7.7	8.5	13.4	0.1	−8.8	−1.0	10.5
Italy	−2.2	−7.6	−0.2	−2.6	3.1	7.9	6.4	−9.5	−7.3	−6.5
United Kingdom	−1.3	−7.2	−2.9	−0.6	1.5	4.5	1.3	11.5	19.8	12.5
Other industrial countries	5.0	−8.7	−3.9	−9.6	−12.9	−4.3	−13.7	−28.7	−20.0	−12.5
Developing countries										
Oil-exporting countries	6.7	68.3	35.4	40.3	30.8	2.9	69.8	115.0	70.8	25.0
Non-oil developing countries[c]	−11.6	−37.0	−46.5	−32.0	−28.3	−39.2	−58.9	−86.2	−99.0	−97.0
By analytical group										
Net oil exporters	−2.6	−5.1	−9.9	−7.7	−6.5	−7.9	−8.5	−11.0	−20.6	−23.0
Net oil importers	−9.0	−31.9	−36.6	−24.3	−22.8	−30.6	−48.8	−72.7	−80.5	−74.0
Major exporters of manufactures	−3.7	−19.1	−19.6	−12.2	−7.9	−9.9	−21.5	−32.4	−36.0	−31.0
Low-income countries	−4.0	−7.5	−7.5	−4.1	−3.6	−7.5	−10.0	−14.5	−14.3	−15.0
Other net oil importers	−1.3	−5.2	−9.5	−7.9	−11.3	−13.2	−17.4	−25.8	−30.2	−28.0
By area										
Africa[d]	−2.1	−3.5	−6.9	−6.1	−6.6	−9.0	−9.7	−12.7	−13.3	−13.0
Asia	−2.4	−9.6	−8.9	−2.6	−1.6	−6.1	−12.6	−22.5	−24.8	−27.0
Europe	0.3	−4.3	−4.7	−4.1	−7.6	−5.2	−8.5	−10.9	−7.9	−6.0
Middle East	−2.6	−4.5	−7.0	−5.4	−5.2	−6.5	−8.5	−7.8	−9.0	−12.0
Western hemisphere	−4.7	−13.5	−16.4	−11.9	−8.7	−13.2	−21.3	−33.1	−41.5	−35.5
Total[e]	12.8	17.4	6.8	5.7	−3.2	−6.5	0.7	−16.0	−31.9	−61.0

a On goods, services and private transfers.
b Figures are rounded to the nearest $0.5 billion.
c The People's Republic of China, which is both a net oil exporter and a low-income country, is included in the total (from 1977 onward) but not in the subgroups.
d Excluding South Africa.
e Reflects errors, omissions and asymmetries in reported balance of payments statistics on current account, plus balance of listed groups with other countries (mainly the USSR and other non-member countries of Eastern Europe and, for years prior to 1977, the People's Republic of China).

Source: IMF, *World Economic Outlook*, 1982.

TABLE 7.2
Non-oil developing countries: current account financing, 1973–82ᵃ ($ bn)

	1973	1974	1975	1976	1977	1978	1979	1980	1981	1982
Current account deficitᵇ	11.6	37.0	46.5	32.0	28.3	39.2	58.9	86.2	99.0	97.0
Financing through transactions that do not affect net debt positions										
Net unrequited transfers received by government of non-oil developing countries	10.1	13.0ᶜ	11.8	12.0	14.9	17.2	23.0	24.1	26.3	27.8
SDR allocations, valuation adjustments and gold monetization	5.4	6.9ᵉ	7.1	7.4	8.3	8.2	10.9	12.3	12.9	13.6
	0.4	0.7	−0.6	−0.2	1.3	2.1	2.8	1.8	−0.2	—
Direct investment flows, net	4.3	5.3	5.3	4.7	5.3	6.9	9.2	10.0	13.6	14.1
Net borrowing and use of reservesᵈ	1.5	23.9ᶜ	34.7	20.1	13.4	22.0	35.9	62.1	72.7	69.2
Reduction of reserve assets (accumulation—)	−9.7	−2.4	1.9	−13.8	−12.4	−15.8	−12.4	−4.9	−1.6	−4.0
Net external borrowingᶜ	11.2	23.3ᶜ	32.9	31.2	25.8	37.8	48.4	67.1	74.3	73.2
Long-term borrowing	11.7	19.5ᶜ	26.6	27.9	26.5	35.3	37.9	45.5	55.8	59.4
From official sources	5.4	9.3ᶜ	11.4	10.8	12.6	14.2	15.4	20.5	20.2	22.3
From private sources	8.3	13.7	15.3	19.3	23.0	27.9	33.1	31.4	37.0	38.5
From financial institutions	7.1	12.6	13.8	17.0	19.4	23.9	32.4	30.1	35.5	37.0
From other lenders	1.2	1.1	1.5	2.4	3.6	4.0	0.8	1.3	1.5	1.5
Residual flows, netᶠ	−2.0	−3.5	−0.1	−2.3	−9.2	−6.9	−10.6	−6.4	−1.4	−1.4
Use of reserve-related credit facilitiesᵍ	0.2	1.7	2.5	4.4	−0.1	0.5	−0.6	1.7	5.4	6.0
Other short-term borrowing, net	0.2	5.2	6.4	12.2	0.8	4.7	10.5	19.9	13.1	7.8
Residual errors and omissionsʰ	−0.8	—	−2.7	−11.2	−1.1	−2.5	0.5			

a Excludes data for the People's Republic of China prior to 1977.
b Net total of balances on goods, services, and private transfers, as defined in the Fund's *Balance of Payments Yearbook* (with sign reversed).
c Excludes the effect of a revision of the terms of the disposition of economic assistance loans made by the United States to India and repayable in rupees and of rupees already acquired by the US Government in repayment of such loans. The revision has the effect of increasing government transfers by about $2 billion, with an offset in net official loans.
d That is, financing through changes in net debt positions (net borrowing, less net accumulation — or plus net liquidation — of official reserve assets).
e Includes any net use of non-reserve claims on non-residents, errors and omissions in reported balance of payments statements for individual countries, and minor deficiencies in coverage.
f These residual flows comprise two elements: (i) net changes in long-term external assets of non-oil developing countries and (ii) residuals and discrepancies that arise from the mismatching of creditor-source data taken from debt records with capital flow data taken from national balance of payments records.
g Comprises use of Fund credit and short-term borrowing by monetary authorities from other monetary authorities.
h Errors and omissions in reported balance of payments statements for individual countries, and minor omissions in coverage.

Source: IMF, *World Economic Outlook*, 1982.

aggregate deficit of $536 billion for non-oil-exporting countries. This distribution arose largely because developing countries attempted to maintain aggregate demand in the face of the tax effect of the oil price rise while industrial countries tended not to do so. In effect, the deficit was shifted to the less developed countries.

Conversely, portfolio decisions made by international banks have powerful implications for the world economy mainly through their effects upon the balance of pressures as between balance of payments adjustment and financing, the transfer of real resources, and the economic and financial implications of the growth of external debt.

Overall, the evolution of international banking over the 1970s meant that this sector became an integral part of the world economy. This can be illustrated in a few obvious ways. Firstly, its recycling of oil-related surpluses prevented what might otherwise have been a more substantial world recession had oil-importing countries been required to cut oil consumption in the context of financing constraints. Secondly, it contributed to the substantial expansion of world trade through the provision of trade-related finance. Thirdly, it shifted the balance of pressures as between adjustment and financing of payments imbalances towards the latter. Given the size of some of the world's payments imbalances, this might be viewed as appropriate though it might also be argued that the shift was excessive. Fourthly, the international banking sector contributed to a substantial transfer of real resources to developing countries and thereby contributed to their development. To the extent that this international financial intermediation allocated world savings to where rates of return were highest, it would in the process have contributed to world economic growth. The international banking sector intermediated between surpluses and deficits in the world economy on a massive scale. In the process, international business became more important to the banks and a higher proportion of their balance sheet positions.

A contrary view is that the role of international banking has not been unambiguously beneficial in the world economy. Firstly, by providing financial intermediation services to oil importers and exporters (i.e. allowing and facilitating the financing of oil-related deficits) international banking might have validated the rise in the price of oil. Had oil-importing countries been unable to finance the deficits, the price of oil would probably have been reduced. There might nevertheless be some doubt about whether a lower oil price would in practice have emerged without major economic dislocation. A second line of argument is that international banking activities and the ease of financing delayed necessary balance of payments adjustment. Thirdly, in some cases the ease of finance induced excessive consumption expenditure and uneconomic investment projects.

Combined with the larger balance of payments deficits, there were substantial shifts in the pattern of developing country financing. Firstly, the deficits were increasingly financed through borrowing rather than through the use of reserves. Secondly, non-debt forms of financing (aid and autonomous capital inflows) declined in relative importance. Thirdly, the proportion of debt incurred against banks rose sharply over the decade as the private sector came to displace the traditional official sector in balance of payments financing. At the same time international bank lending tended to shift from private to public sector borrowers, from short- to long-term assets, from fixed to floating interest rates, and from trade-related to balance of payments financing. Thus, compared with earlier periods of borrowing, two specific structural shifts developed over the 1970s: from bonds to bank credit and from the official sector to the private sector.

Implications

This development of international banking had substantial implications for the international monetary system in several dimensions. The change in the balance of pressures as between balance of payments adjustment and financing had two dimensions. To the extent that it became easier to finance deficits, and governments had confidence in future financing facilities, there was correspondingly less pressure on them to adjust their balance of payments. Whether this is regarded as beneficial depends upon whether the balance of pressures for adjustment versus financing was previously optimal. In principle, this could be indicated by the extent to which the enforced pursuit of balance of payments objectives caused domestic objectives to be sacrificed (in either an inflationary or deflationary direction) or involved quick-acting measures (such as control mechanisms) which in general have adverse welfare implications. Whatever the starting position, given the nature and size of the increased deficits over the 1970s, some shift towards easier financing was generally appropriate. A second dimension is that the change in the balance of pressures as between adjustment and financing had a distribution effect in that it moved more towards financing for those countries with ready access to bank finance. Not only did the increased financial intermediary role of banks alter the global balance of pressures as between financing and adjustment, it did so differentially as between countries.

Cohen also notes that in some cases access to bank credit had an adverse effect on the efficiency of the adjustment process itself and the mechanisms chosen.[1] It also altered the conditions under which financing facilities were made available. In general, private banks are not able to impose general policy conditionality on loans, whereas the IMF invariably does impose such conditionality. Many deficit countries developed a strong preference for 'non-conditional' finance during the 1970s to the extent of being prepared to pay considerably higher market interest rates for funds, compared with charges levied by the IMF. This was reinforced by the larger amounts and longer maturities frequently available on bank finance compared with IMF facilities. On the basis of a series of case studies of different borrowing countries, Cohen makes a distinction between those which used access to credit markets to postpone needed adjustment and other countries which adopted an integrated approach and developed a borrowing strategy as part of a programme of balance of payments adjustment. Some countries appear to have used borrowing as a substitute for adjustment, while in other cases it was complementary. If efficiency of adjustment is measured in terms of the costs imposed by particular adjustment mechanisms, Cohen observes that efficiency had in some cases been reduced by borrowing because, by delaying the ultimately necessary adjustment, the eventual adjustment mechanism had to be more severe and costly.

A further implication of the increased role of international banking is that the significance of the adequacy or otherwise of international liquidity, which was a central feature in debate about international monetary arrangements in the 1960s, became less clearly defined. As countries' access to borrowing facilities expanded, so their financing need for 'owned liquidity' declined. At the same time, the proportion of owned reserves held with private sector institutions grew steadily over the decade.

The growth of international banking facilities clearly altered the mechanisms of financing, with the important implication that a higher proportion of financing of payments imbalances had as a counterpart the build-up of market-related external debt. This in turn produced a fifth major implication in the form of a new

TABLE 7.3

Non-oil developing countries: outstanding use of Fund credit, 1973–82 ($ bn)

	1973	1974	1975	1976	1977	1978	1979	1980	1981
Total outstanding use of Fund credit by non-oil developing countries	1.2	2.8	4.8	8.0	8.0	8.0	8.3	9.5	14.9
By analytical group									
Net oil exporters	1.1	0.1	0.1	0.9	1.1	1.1	1.0	0.8	0.8
Net oil importers	0.1	2.6	4.7	7.2	7.0	7.0	7.3	8.7	14.1
Major exporters of manufactures	0.2	0.5	1.2	2.4	2.4	1.8	1.4	1.9	2.7
Low-income countries	0.5	1.5	2.1	2.2	2.0	1.9	2.1	2.7	4.7
Other net oil importers	0.4	0.6	1.4	2.5	2.6	3.2	3.7	4.2	6.8
By area									
Africa	0.2	0.4	0.6	1.5	1.7	1.9	2.0	2.3	3.9
Asia	0.5	1.5	2.1	2.5	2.2	2.2	2.2	3.1	6.0
Europe	0.1	0.3	0.8	1.6	1.6	1.7	1.9	2.4	3.3
Middle East	0.1	0.2	0.4	0.6	0.7	0.8	0.6	0.4	0.2
Western hemisphere	0.4	0.5	1.0	2.0	1.9	1.4	1.5	1.3	1.6

Source: IMF, World Economic Outlook, 1982.

confidence problem in the early 1980s. Concern developed over the debt-servicing capacity of developing countries and over the implications for banks which in many cases had become heavily exposed to developing countries in general and to some countries in particular. This issue is addressed in more detail in a later section of this chapter.

A final implication, related to the confidence problem, is a change in the role of the International Monetary Fund. During the 1970s its lending capacity was not increased in line with the demand for balance of payments financing facilities. But neither was its actual lending increased in line with its capacity (Table 7.3). Many deficit countries chose to borrow from banks rather than the Fund. The influence of the IMF in balance of payments adjustment was thereby lessened. But in the early 1980s, as more countries encountered debt problems and borrowing constraints, use of Fund resources increased substantially.

The role of the Fund then changed in two major respects. Firstly, it was lending increasingly to debtor countries which had become less creditworthy in private markets. Secondly, it came to play an important role in easing the strain on the international banking system by coordinating debt-rescheduling operations. As part of these arrangements, new funds were provided by banks which also agreed to reschedule their claims on debtor countries on condition that the debtor country also borrowed from the IMF. This in turn meant that the banks secured the advantages pertaining to the conditionality provisions applied by the Fund on its own lending. Something of a partnership role emerged, with the banks providing funds on the basis of the IMF's conditionality.

An analytical framework

In considering the banks' possible future role, a framework is set in which analysis of the factors underlying the banks' expanding role during the 1970s can be made. This is the more important given the key role international banking has come to play in the international monetary system. The international banking sector performs financial intermediation services on an international scale in a similar way to domestic financial institutions within national economies. The analysis therefore needs to focus upon two broad sets of forces: (i) basic flow of funds factors and (ii) the determinants of the supply of financial intermediation services by particular institutions. In turn, the former considers the pattern and volume of surpluses and deficits together with the portfolio preferences of surplus and deficit sectors. A more comprehensive review of this analytical framework is given elsewhere.[2]

The fact that the volume of international financial imbalances rose during the 1970s does not in itself explain why any particular channel of financial intermediation (by banks, for example) was expanded. Banks are not passive agents in financial intermediation and have a choice about accepting deposits, making loans and providing intermediation services. To concentrate exclusively on the size of surpluses and deficits, and the portfolio preferences of the relevant agents, makes the implicit and unwarranted assumption that banks have no portfolio objectives or constraints and that the supply of intermediation services is infinitely elastic. But just as banks' portfolio objectives and constraints are relevant in the determination of the volume and terms of international lending, so the pattern and volume of flow of funds from non-banks must be considered since banks cannot determine the volume and price of lending independently of the portfolio preferences of their customers.

The traditional analysis of international banking has exclusively emphasized supply factors (based upon credit-rationing models) or demand factors (volume of bank lending determined by balance of payments financing requirements). In an integrated approach, banks are not passive agents in the international flow of funds but have balance sheet objectives and act aggressively to secure them. They are presumed to seek to balance the risk-adjusted marginal rate of return on domestic and external assets and to fund in the cheapest markets. The supply and demand for international banking funds cease to be exogenous and independent of banks' own portfolio behaviour. Total planned assets (domestic and external) are funded at the lowest price, though the banks' liability management will itself determine deposit interest rates. In this sense it is misleading to postulate OPEC deposits as funding bank lending to oil-importing countries as if the volume of OPEC deposits was independent of the terms offered by banks. These terms are important and determined by objectives with respect to the acquisition of external assets. Thus, banks can be viewed as funding assets rather than lending exogenous deposits.

Banks are ultimately asset-driven in that they are motivated by a desire to acquire earning assets. With the development of sophisticated liability management techniques and an efficient international interbank market, they develop strategies to fund assets. In this sense the international intermediation process can be described as banks funding (from domestic and international sources) their international loan portfolio rather than as lending external deposits. Banks borrowed from OPEC in order to finance oil-importing countries rather than loaned exogenously determined OPEC deposits. In the final analysis banks' portfolio behaviour is positive on both sides of the balance sheet, with the volume of business determined partly by the interaction of two interest rate elasticities: with respect to customers' demand for loans and supply of deposits.

The flow of funds component of the integrated approach includes the structure of financial surpluses and deficits (both within countries and between countries), and the portfolio preferences of surplus and deficit sectors. The factors influencing the supply of financial intermediation services can be divided between (i) efficiency considerations, (ii) the portfolio objectives and preferences of financial institutions, and (iii) their portfolio constraints, notably capital and regulations.

The central conclusion is that, when analysing the factors behind the increasing role of the private banking sector in the international monetary system, the focus of attention needs to be wider than the size of balance of payments imbalances. The portfolio preferences of surplus and deficit agents need to be incorporated and in this sense it must be presumed that banks, having a choice, willingly took upon themselves this particular role because of their own portfolio objectives and perceptions of risk. It cannot legitimately be maintained that they were themselves passive agents or that their increased role can be ascribed simply to the rise in the size of international payments imbalances. They had the option not to provide international financial intermediation services which, had they exercised that option and had there been a limit on alternative financing mechanisms, would have meant that the *ex ante* payments imbalances would have had to be adjusted.

The 1970s role

The factors behind the expansion of international banking have been extensively analysed elsewhere. Taking a broad perspective, five sets of forces are identified: (i) the absolute size of financing imbalances rose substantially in the 1970s in part due to oil price rises but also to other factors; (ii) the supply of traditional finance did not expand in line with the size of financial deficits; (iii) there was a discernible shift in portfolio preferences by both deficit and surplus sectors towards intermediation by banks (OPEC's desire for liquidity and deficit countries' desire to preserve their stock of foreign exchange reserves and to avoid the conditionality provisions being the more obvious examples); (iv) banks' portfolio preferences and strategies also changed, with the development of international business and lending becoming part of their strategic objectives; and (v) the regulatory climate was conducive, especially, but not exclusively, from certain off-shore financial centres. It was the interaction of these pressures that produced a decade of unprecedented expansion in international banking.

Current account imbalances rose during the 1970s both in absolute size and as a proportion of GNP.[3] As we saw in Table 7.2, in the period 1973–82 the cumulative current account deficit of non-oil-exporting developing countries amounted to $536 billion, having risen from $11.6 billion in 1973 to close on $100 billion in 1981 and 1982. To the extent that reserves were too low to be regarded as an effective financing instrument, and that there was a demand to increase reserves over the same period, the cumulative financing need amounted to $611 billion.

In general, the supply of non-bank financing facilities did not rise in proportion to current account imbalances. Before the 1970s current account deficits were financed predominantly by flows of official aid and direct investment. During the 1970s both rose in absolute terms and both remained at the same proportion of donors' GNP. But as current account surpluses and deficits rose as a proportion of GNP, traditional sources did not keep pace. Net direct investment inflows to developing countries were expanded during the 1970s from $4.3 billion to $14 billion but as a proportion of the aggregate current account deficit declined from 37 to 15 per cent (Table 7.4). In terms of the definition of the financing requirement in Table 7.4, non-debt sources of finance rose by only $8 billion while the financing requirement rose by $70 billion. Non-debt sources financed 34 per cent of the total financing requirement in 1973 but only 16 per cent in 1982. Similarly, long-term borrowing by developing countries from official sources (governments and development agencies) expanded in absolute terms from $5.4 billion to over $22 billion, but again as a proportion of the total financing requirement it declined from 32 to 25 per cent. The data record only *ex post* transactions and do not indicate the supply potential of these

TABLE 7.4

Financing requirement and financing of non-oil developing countries, 1973–82 ($ bn)

			1973	1974	1975	1976	1977	1978	1979	1980	1981	1982	1973–82
(a) Financing requirement													
	(1)	Current account	11.6	37.0	46.5	32.0	28.3	39.2	58.9	86.2	99.0	97.0	535.7
Plus	(2)	Increase in reserve assets	9.7	2.4	-1.9	13.8	12.4	15.8	12.4	4.9	1.6	4.0	75.1
Less	(3)	Net direct investment	4.3	5.3	5.3	4.7	5.3	6.9	9.2	10.0	13.6	14.1	78.7
Equals	(4)	Total financing requirement	17.0	34.1	39.3	41.1	35.4	48.1	62.1	81.1	87.0	86.9	532.1
(b) Financing account													
	(5)	Non-debt transactions	5.8	7.6	6.5	7.2	9.6	10.3	13.7	14.1	12.7	13.6	101.1
		(i) Net unrequited transfers	5.4	6.9	7.1	7.4	8.3	8.2	10.9	12.3	12.9	13.6	93.0
		(ii) SDR allocations, etc.	0.4	0.7	-0.6	-0.2	1.3	2.1	2.8	1.8	-0.2	—	8.1
	(6)	Net external borrowing: non-banks	4.2	13.8	19.0	16.3	6.6	14.0	16.0	37.0	38.8	36.2	201.9
		(i) Long-term from official sources	3.4	9.3	11.4	10.8	12.6	14.2	15.4	20.5	20.2	22.3	142.1
		(ii) From non-bank private sources	1.2	1.1	1.5	2.4	3.6	4.0	0.8	1.3	1.5	1.5	18.9
		(iii) Use of reserve-related credit[a]	0.2	1.7	2.5	4.4	-0.1	0.5	-0.6	1.7	5.4	6.0	21.7
		(iv) Other (including errors and omissions)[b]	-2.6	1.7	3.6	-1.3	-9.5	-4.7	0.4	13.5	11.7	6.4	15.2
	(7)	Net external borrowing: banks	7.1	12.6	13.8	17.0	19.4	23.9	32.4	30.1	35.5	37.0	228.8
	(8)	Total financing	17.1	34.0	39.3	40.5	35.6	48.2	62.1	81.2	87.0	85.8	531.8

a Use of IMF credit and short-term borrowing by monetary authorities from other monetary authorities.

b Errors and omissions in balance of payments accounts and minor omissions in coverage together with: (i) net changes in long-term external assets of non-oil LDCs and (ii) residuals and discrepancies arising from mismatching of creditor-source data taken from debt records with capital flow data from balance of payments records.

Source: Adapted from IMF, *World Economic Outlook*, 1982.

sources. Nevertheless, with the exception of borrowing from the IMF, it is reasonable to conclude that developing countries maximize their financing from official sources and net direct investment inflows. To this extent the residual financing requirement is met through net bank borrowing which rose from $7 billion in 1973 to $37 billion in 1982. Banks increased their share of international financial intermediation and there was a distinct preference for bank finance on the part of deficit countries. At the same time, banks' new portfolio objectives were consistent with meeting it.

Portfolio preferences of surplus and deficit sectors also enhanced the role of the international banking sector. Surplus agents channelled funds through banks largely because banks offered liquidity but also because of the general advantages of indirect financial intermediation (economies of scale, more diversified portfolios, different maturity preferences of lenders and borrowers, the belief that there are lenders of last resort to banks but not to states) compared with the position where surplus sectors lend directly to those in deficit. The lending capacity of the IMF was not increased proportionately to the rise in members' total financing requirement. But neither were its facilities fully utilized. This suggests a portfolio preference for bank financing as an alternative to borrowing from the IMF. This became pronounced during the 1970s partly in order to avoid the Fund's conditionality provisions but also because, compared with bank borrowing, the amounts individual countries were able to borrow from the Fund were limited. The IMF came to be viewed as a lender of last resort. However, as mentioned earlier, its facilities became more important in the early 1980s as banks became increasingly constrained in making further loans and required borrowers to submit to IMF programmes.

Emergence of problems

As a result of the form of financing during the 1970s the long-term external debt of non-oil developing countries rose from $96 billion in 1973 to over $500 billion by 1982 and further to $620 billion by the end of 1983. At the same time the proportion owed to banks rose from 14 to 35 per cent. Overall, but especially for large borrowers, debt service ratios rose sharply over the decade. For low export growth countries, for instance, the debt service ratio (DSR) rose from 16 per cent in 1970 to close on 40 per cent by the early 1980s.

With a high DSR, the net real resource gain from further borrowing is reduced and the debtor country becomes particularly vulnerable to fluctuations in exports. In absolute terms debt-servicing commitments of non-oil developing countries on long-term debt rose from $15 billion in 1973 to close on $110 billion in 1982 and interest commitments from $4.6 billion to $41 billion.

These trends combined to produce potential (and in the event, actual) problems for both borrowers and the banks in the early 1980s. For the borrowing countries the volume of debt rose relative to exports and GDP. They became vulnerable to rises in (particularly dollar) interest rates and to other adverse movements in debt-servicing costs beyond their control, such as a deterioration in the terms of trade and recession in export markets. Each of these raised the real resource cost of debt servicing. Interest rates are clearly important when debt is priced on a floating rate basis: i.e., when long-term debt is incurred at short-term rates of interest. If the rate of interest rises above a debtor country's growth rate, to secure a net positive financial inflow the volume of new loans must exceed current debt-servicing commitments and this in turn implies a rise in the debt/GDP ratio. If at some point banks resist this (because of concern at their exposure and doubt about the debt-servicing capacity of borrowing countries) debt can be serviced only through a current account surplus which implies a net transfer of real resources by the debtor country.

The issue then arises as to the terms on which such a transfer can be made, even supposing a willingness on the part of the debtor country to make such an unaccustomed transfer. The terms become onerous if at the time export markets are weak and protectionist barriers are erected. Conditions are thereby created for a *transfer problem* of a kind not totally dissimilar to that of the 1930s. Following the first major oil price rise in 1973, industrial countries sought to minimize the potentially deflationary effect by an expansionary fiscal stance, offsetting the rise in the world savings ratio through a corresponding rise in domestic budget deficits. But the response was different following the oil price rise in 1979. Determined to avoid the potentially inflationary effect of the earlier response, fiscal and monetary policy became restrictive in many industrial countries. The average annual rise in total domestic demand in industrial countries in the period 1977–9 was 3.8 per cent but in the following three years it was reduced to 0.5 per cent. As a result, the volume of industrial countries' imports declined at an average rate of 1.3 per cent in the period (following an average rise of 6 per cent in the previous three years). In turn, the growth of real output of major developing country borrowers decelerated from 4.9 per cent in the period 1978–80 to 1.2 per cent in the following three years. This was the economic context of the debt difficulties that arose in the late 1970s and early 1980s. Some of the debt-servicing difficulties were associated with the policy stance in industrial countries.

For the banks in this period the problem arose of a potential non-servicing of loans, of being 'locked-in' to debtor countries and of an exposure which had become potentially serious in relation to the capital base. The ultimate danger was perceived to be that a default or series of defaults on external debt would induce a confidence problem for domestic banks which would have ramifications far wider than simply the financing of developing countries. This became a new potential confidence problem.

In the event, debt-servicing problems did surface in 1982 and 1983. The short-run conjuncture of higher nominal and real interest rates, weak export markets, more protectionist sentiment and adverse terms of trade movements, combined with the longer-run context of rising debt/GDP and debt/export ratios, produced debt-servicing problems for many developing countries, and most notably the heavily indebted Latin American countries.

Debt-servicing commitments are a claim on real resources (whether domestically produced or imported) which can be avoided only by further borrowing. In terms of national accounts identities:

$$Y = C + I + G + (X - M_p) \tag{1}$$
$$Y + M_p = C + I + G + X \tag{2}$$

where Y is real output, C is consumption, I is domestic investment, G is government expenditure and X and M_p are real exports and imports of goods and services. The availability of resources is given in identity (2). With debt-servicing commitments the identity becomes:

$$(Y - rD) + M_p = C + I + G + X \tag{3}$$

where r is the average rate of interest on external debt, D. The higher is r or D, the greater is the debt-servicing claim on real resources.

While these problems were surfacing, banks reduced the volume of new lending because of concern at their own portfolio and exposure positions, a desire for consolidation, capital constraints and the debt-servicing difficulties of borrowers. For the first time in over a decade, developing countries collectively, and some substantially, experienced a negative net financial inflow. With debt-servicing commitments exceeding the volume of new credit inflows, a net transfer of real resources was needed to meet current debt-service obligations. Between 1973 and 1981 21 developing countries had a net inflow of new funds that exceeded interest obligations by $2\frac{1}{2}$ per cent of GNP. In the late 1970s and early 1980s some countries, in order to maintain the flow of imports in a situation where interest obligations were rising faster than export receipts, had effectively been capitalizing interest obligations. The new position implied a substantial adjustment. The economic circumstances of the time made it difficult to service debt via exports and banks were reluctant to extend further loans.

Confidence problems

Following the rise in external indebtedness and the consequent exposure of banks, a certain parallel can be drawn between the position as it was beginning to be perceived in the early 1980s and the *confidence problem* as identified two decades earlier by Triffin.[4] The original confidence problem emerged with respect to a characteristic of the gold-exchange standard, in that the world's emerging liquidity needs could not be met by new gold supplies and hence there was a requirement for a US balance of payments deficit to make dollars available to central banks in surplus countries. While formally the US authorities maintained a fixed dollar price of gold, a confidence problem emerged when doubts were cast on the US government's ability to maintain convertibility of the dollar following years of steadily rising external liabilities in the context of a fixed gold stock.

The parallels between the two situations revolve around the magnitude of the debt and the balance of pressures that existed between balance of payments adjustment and financing. But there are a number of distinguishing characteristics between the problem that emerged in the early 1980s and that stated by Triffin. Firstly, unlike the situation in the 1960s when the problem was the dollar debt of the United States, the liabilities of the developing countries were in foreign currency. Secondly, the overwhelming proportion of the debt was owed to the private sector and not to central banks. Finally, instead of one country being the primary borrower the debt had become diffused, though still concentrated heavily on a few countries especially in Latin America.

The confidence problem identified by Triffin centred on the ability of one rich country (the United States) to meet its external obligations denominated in its own currency owed to central banks. The new confidence problem centred on the ability of several comparatively poorer countries to meet their foreign currency liabilities owed to private banks. A second parallel is that both arose through the failure to adjust balance of payments deficits. In the original case the US deficit provided international liquidity. Without it, and had the United States adjusted its deficit, a deflationary bias in the world economy could have emerged. Similarly, the external debt of developing countries resulted from a failure to adjust payments imbalances in the 1970s but this also avoided what would otherwise have been a stronger deflationary bias resulting from two major rises in the price of oil.

While the volume of external debt grew substantially over the 1970s, it was heavily concentrated on a few countries. Four countries (Brazil, Mexico, Korea and Argentina) accounted for half the aggregate developing country debt owed to banks. Debt problems emerged at various times during the 1960s and early 1970s but they were specific to particular countries and posed no serious confidence problem or difficulty for the international banking system. Hitherto in the postwar period there had not been generalized problems and this reduced the degree of vulnerability for banks with diversified portfolios. The real danger would arise if a situation developed where difficulties became generalized and several countries simultaneously were to encounter severe debt-servicing problems. This could arise because of a common cause (for example, world recession or protectionist moves), by countries following the example of a leader, or through internal political pressure on developing country governments. Alternatively, following Eaton and Gersovitz,[5] there are circumstances in which it might be rational for debtors to repudiate debt. At one point in 1983 there was discussion about the creation of a formalized 'debtors cartel' between Latin American countries, though this was not accepted by some of the largest debtors.

An official response

In the event, major dislocation was averted by a series of concerted operations involving the IMF, governments, central banks, private banks, and sometimes the BIS. The three common elements of the operations (which in 1982 and 1983 involved several debtor countries) were: (i) a restructuring of debt, (ii) banks' agreement to the provision of new funds and (iii) a requirement on the debtor countries to borrow from the IMF and to submit to IMF adjustment programmes. In one operation the BIS provided short-term 'bridging finance'.

This produced a *collective* banking operation (with funds being provided through collective agreement and past debt restructured on the same basis) in contrast to the highly competitive and individualistic ethos of international banking in the 1970s. The operations became collective in that banks developed combined operations between themselves but also involving official agencies. In the process, complex bargaining strategies evolved as banks sought to protect their balance sheet positions and cosmetically avoid reporting reduced profits. Debtor countries sought to renegotiate past loans and to maintain the flow of new loans.

The rescheduling operations were very substantial. In the period 1978–81 they involved about $1.5 billion of debt. In 1982 a total of $5 billion was involved, while in 1983 it amounted to $60 billion. External payments arrears amounted to over $50 billion at the end of 1982 against an annual average of $5–6 billion in the previous five years. There was an increase in the number, frequency and volume of reported arrears.

Reservations

While these *ad hoc* exercises alleviated immediate pressure, there were reservations over the method of balance of payments adjustment adopted, about the durability of the arrangements and an absence of consideration of longer-run mechanisms both to make the external debt position more secure and to ensure the financing of future current account deficits. The problems were handled on a piecemeal basis in that they were dealt with case by case. Waves of optimism and pessimism over the international debt issue and the banks' exposure were determined by whether banks were currently experiencing problems with particular countries. The danger was that the piecemeal approach forced attention away from the longer-run problems which would eventually surface. It also focused attention on mechanisms to deal with short-run difficulties as they arose, rather than devising more durable long-run solutions. In many ways, the 'solutions' simply passed the problem into the future. Short-term rescheduling operations created a potential bunching of maturities in 1986 and 1987, at which time the total level of debt would be yet higher. Unless in the meantime durable balance of payments adjustment was to be made, or financing mechanisms reinforced, such a bunching of maturities would be likely to cause similar problems to those experienced in 1982 and 1983.

A longer-term strategy, which would encompass the future role of international commercial banking, could usefully have been considered, though this was not accepted at the time by governments in industrial countries. The 1984 Western Summit in London reiterated the intention to adopt a case-by-case approach. External debt problems are long-term, however, and to the extent that only short-term adjustments were being made no permanent arrangements were instituted. A short-term response was made to longer-term issues. The inherent danger in these procedures was that at some point in a succession of short-term responses a crisis might not be contained. A more appropriate response in many cases would have been a major restructuring of debt, together with secure arrangements for future financing. The approaches of the early 1980s dealt predominantly with the immediately pressing current stock position of debt, while offering little in the way of consideration of future financing mechanisms.

Central to this is one of the major issues in the international monetary system, namely, the question of the appropriate balance between balance of payments adjustment and financing. The *costs* of adjustment are determined as much by creditor as by debtor countries through the economic environment they create. This can determine whether it is surplus or deficit countries that are forced to adjust, and the ease with which debtor countries are able to increase exports. The latter is determined largely by growth in their markets and the ease of access to these markets. The economic environment created by industrial countries determines the terms under which external debt is serviced. In particular, whether debt is serviced through a rise in exports at a high level of real income or by a fall in imports at a low level of income.

In the face of financing constraints, debtor countries in Latin America were forced to make substantial balance of payments adjustment. In 1983 the seven major Latin American debtors had a collective balance of trade surplus of $30 billion. Given the economic conjuncture of the time, this was secured predominantly through a cut in imports induced by expenditure-reducing policies. Debt was serviced through a lower level of real income. This raised the issue about the longer-run acceptability both of the implied net transfer of real resources (which arises however a trade surplus is created) and the method of creating the surplus at a comparatively low level of real income and output.

The problems of international banking and the debt position of developing countries are ultimately global economic issues and not exclusively banking problems. This is the perspective in any strategic planning on the role of all institutions (private and public) in the international financial system. While there is an obvious need for balance of payments adjustment by deficit countries, adjustment is usually secured at a higher level of world real income and output when surplus countries adjust. It is not self-evident that adjustment pressure should be directed predominantly at deficit rather than surplus countries.

The role of central banks

There is a further issue implicit in the *ad hoc* support operations of the early 1980s that warrants further investigation. This concerns the role of central banks and the IMF, and in particular their relationship with commercial banks. The Fund and central banks in countries whose banks had been involved in international lending on a large scale applied considerable pressure on them to maintain lending and to make new funds available to debtor countries in difficulty. This is perhaps understandable. Firstly, the IMF was anxious not to be regarded as a lender-of-last-resort to banks even if it is forced to be so for states. Hence, it moved to avoid the possibility of its resources being used simply to service and repay bank credit. Central banks would argue that commercial banks should remain committed simply to protect existing balance asset positions. Both would argue that, from a public policy standpoint, the flow of credit should be sustained.

Two problems immediately arose. Firstly, conflicting signals were being made as, on the one hand, banks were exhorted to be prudent but, on the other, were being encouraged to offer further support to indebted countries. The question arose as to what interpretation beleaguered banks were to put on this apparent conflict. Secondly, a new moral hazard was in danger of being created. If a central bank is involved in the commercial judgement of banks with respect to specific loans, it might subsequently be argued that, if the lending proves to have been imprudent, the central bank has a moral obligation to support the banks. The central bank might be viewed as implicated in 'imprudent lending'. It might be argued that the commercial banks were acting as the agents of the official sector, however much a central bank might counter that such action was originally taken in their interests. This argument might be difficult to sustain in a crisis. While the central bank might, for public policy reasons, be willing to act as a lender of last resort, the question arises as to whether it is appropriate for this action to be forced on it by virtue of authoritative 'guidance' having been given at some time in the past.

This new problem of central banking arises when central banks cease to operate at 'arms length' from the operations of their commercial banks. It is an issue that warrants further consideration and one that bristles with implications and moral hazard.

Debt and international monetary reform

A case can be made that in the early 1980s a longer-run approach to the international debt problem was required, and that it needed to be set in the context of global reform of the international monetary system. Ideally, such a reform programme would be devised so as to reduce the vulnerability to future debt crises and to maintain confidence in the system as well as ensuring the appropriate balance of pressures in the world economy as between balance of payments financing and adjustment. These pressures would relate to both surplus and deficit countries. Mechanisms to ensure the financing of the appropriate transfer of real resources in the world economy would also be incorporated.

Such a global strategy would address six key issues: (i) the current debt problem associated with a bunching of maturities and high interest rates; (ii) the management of banking problems that might emerge if a serious debt crisis emerged in the future; (iii) mechanisms for the future substantial and continuing financing requirement of developing countries; (iv) the future role of banks, governments and official agencies in this financing; (v) the establishment of a world economic environment conducive to a stable debt position; and (vi) the requirements to be made on debtor countries, particularly with respect to the conduct of economic policy. Such a programme would imply a multi-dimensional and multi-agency approach.

Addressing the first issue, consideration could be given to organizing a major restructuring of debt on a global basis through the aegis of the IMF. This would involve all major debtor countries in a concerted exercise, as an alternative to the piecemeal approach of the early 1980s. There would be no requirement for debt to be written off. On the contrary, a moral hazard would thereby be created that would prove to be difficult in the future. The precedent created would change the ground rules of the creditor/debtor relationship in a way that would induce future instability. But a concerted and global debt restructuring, which might involve taking debt off banks' balance sheets but at a cost to them, could be considered. Various detailed proposals were put forward in the early 1980s by various commentators. One mechanism might be through something analogous to the older idea of an IMF Substitution Account (considered in the early 1970s as a means of dealing with the then alleged dollar overhang) or through bond issues by the World Bank. The problems of organizing such a global restructuring would clearly be very great.

With respect to the second issue, international lender-of-last-resort facilities could be formalized in more precise arrangements as, for instance, discussed by Griffiths-Jones and Lipton.[6] There is considerable ambiguity about the lender-of-last-resort role at the international level.

An alternative approach to future financing arrangements could involve three structural changes as compared with the way the mechanisms evolved over the 1970s: (i) a greater pressure for balance of payments adjustment by both surplus and deficit countries; (ii) a shift at the margin in the provision of financing away from banks towards governments in industrial countries and official agencies such as the World Bank and IMF, with both institutions being substantially expanded; and (iii) a switch within the private sector from bank financing to bond markets, and other arrangements to shift financing from a floating rate basis and make servicing commitments less dependent upon American monetary policy.

Over the 1970s, bank borrowing tended to displace private direct investment in the financing of developing countries' current account deficits. As noted earlier, while their aggregate current account deficit rose from $11 billion in 1973 to a peak of $99 billion in 1981, net direct investment expanded from only $4.3 billion to $14 billion in 1982. The volume actually fell in the following two years. As a proportion of net private financing flows, foreign direct investment declined from over 60 per cent in the early 1960s to 50 per cent in the early 1970s and to around 30 per cent towards the end of the decade.

Direct investment financing has the advantage of not creating debt and of being 'serviced' when the use of funds is profitable, and it frequently includes a transfer of technology and skills. There would be advantage if the trend of direct investment in developing countries were to be increased, which as a minimum would require a hospitable climate in recipient countries. In practice, direct investment flows are likely to represent a larger proportion of current account financing in the future compared with the 1970s, as developing countries' current account deficits are expected to be smaller and banking flows less buoyant.

The climate for a 'grand design' type of approach to international finance issues was not propitious in the early 1980s. Nevertheless, in the series of *ad hoc* piecemeal responses implicit in the prevailing approach to debt problems, sight should not be lost of the longer-run issues. There is a case for these long-run issues, most especially the appropriate form of future financing, being brought into the domain of official consideration.

Parallel development

The financing requirement of developing countries is likely to remain substantial in a situation where banks feel increasingly constrained.

A programme of the type outlined implies increasing the resources of the IMF and the World Bank and other official agencies, with the World Bank's capital and borrowing capacity being increased substantially. It would also imply a correspondingly lesser role for commercial banks in pure balance of payments financing, designed to minimize the 'crisis problem' potential implicit in current arrangements.

Compared with the evolution of international banking and balance of payments financing over the 1970s, a more modest role could be envisaged for banks. Their involvement in strict balance of payments financing would be more circumscribed than in the past. This is both likely and desirable as the market, for all its imperfections, adjusts to the experience of the 1970s. But international banking developed during the decade in the context of a sharp rise in financial imbalances and a limited response from the official sector and the traditional means of balance of payments financing. While the absolute size of financial imbalances is likely to be smaller, financing requirements will remain substantial. If banks are to return to their more traditional role, alternative financing mechanisms need to be developed. In this sense, parallel development of the official and private sectors in international finance is warranted.

A wholesale withdrawal from the markets by banks would not be appropriate. Rather, a change in the balance between the roles of the official and private sectors in balance of payments financing is advocated.

Future roles of banks

The emergence of debt problems in the early 1980s raises the issue of whether, because there is an inherent tendency either for countries to 'over-borrow' or for banks to 'over-lend', the private banking system is the most appropriate mechanism for balance of payments financing. Perhaps, because of some market distortions, the market place might not produce an appropriate volume of such financing. The reform agenda outlined above indicates an enhanced role for the official sector based partly on reservations about the role of banks in balance of payments financing.

One problem is that, in practice, banks are not in a position to impose conditionality provisions to ensure that economic performance is such as to guarantee that debt is serviced. In a context where there are no clearly defined measures of 'creditworthiness' or of the borrowers' debt capacity, the absence of such provisions increases the banks vulnerability. Once a loan has been made, there is no control over the borrower's behaviour. Related to this is the consideration that, to the extent that claims are against a country rather than a project, there may be a tendency for banks to be less precise in their assessment and evaluation of projects. The problem arises because even though a project may be profitable, debt servicing may be impeded because of the country's external financial position. In this respect, loans are not based upon a precise calculation of the borrower's capacity to service the debt, which, because of the type of loan (for example, long-term maturity based upon a short-term interest rate), may deteriorate for reasons beyond the control of either the borrower or the country concerned.

In addition, banks have no control over the total volume of borrowing and hence the indebtedness of countries. In a highly competitive market, most especially if there is excess capacity, they have no influence over the behaviour of other banks. Individual banks may become vulnerable not so much because of their own actions, but because the total volume of indebtedness has expanded beyond the assumptions which they made. While the market mechanism might eventually respond to this, problems arise when the perceptions, interest and exposure of different banks vary markedly. Thus an 'over-borrowed' country may still be able to obtain funds from new banks which have a strategy to develop international business and are prepared to accept the known risk because their own planned exposure is small and controlled.

The number of banks active in the international lending market in general, and the syndicated Eurocredit market in particular, increased substantially over the 1970s. This was a factor behind the secular decline in lending margins, which suggests either a degree of market imperfection in the early 1970s, though it has since been competed away,[7] or a willingness on the part of new entrants to take a longer-term view of profitability. The increasing number and nationality of banks active in the market could impose a downward bias to margins to the extent that the terms are set by marginal banks. At any one time, banks in different countries have different interests in the market.

Changes in regulations can cause an upsurge in international lending by banks in a particular country. This stock-adjustment effect was powerful in the case of Japanese banks and also American banks after the abolition of capital controls in 1974. New entrants to a market (keen to develop new business) may take a longer-term view of profitability and may be prepared in the short run to write loans at unsustainable margins. Banks in different countries may face different risks on domestic business. They start with different portfolio mixes, and some may be prepared to develop international growth strategies rather than concentrate on immediate profitability. A Group of Thirty survey in 1981[8] noted that banks whose international assets had grown at a relative fast pace in the years up to 1978 (notably American banks) tended to expect a somewhat slower growth in subsequent years than those banks which had lagged at an earlier stage. It was judged that the era of rapid international expansion for large US banks had passed. In contrast, it was noted that bankers in Japan, whose proportion of international business was then relatively small, expected a large increase in their international business 'providing it is permitted by official guidance'.

A further factor to consider in any judgement about the role of banks is the *systemic* risk implications. The market mechanism has produced a degree of bank exposure substantially concentrated on four countries (Brazil, Mexico, Argentina, South Korea). In this sense the problem is systemic. While the underlying strength of these countries may be credible, and the four might be a diversified group, three have simultaneously encountered debt problems and banks' exposure is large relative to capital. The systemic risk also arises because of the public interest in the standing of what are ultimately national banks.

If the perception of banks is that there is a lender-of-last-resort to countries (either governments because of political considerations or official agencies such as the IMF), they might be induced to over-lend. The judgement would be based upon an implicit subsidy received by the banks through the existence of a LLR to some of their customers.

These issues, a detailed consideration of which would move beyond the scope of this chapter, raise the question of whether it is appropriate for banks to be the major mechanism for balance of payments financing. Nevertheless, it is not easy to specify control mechanisms in a highly competitive market environment.

The external financing requirements of developing countries are likely to remain substantial for the remainder of the decade. A major issue in the international monetary system centres on the appropriate role of the international banking sector in this financing. A combination of several factors are likely to make it more difficult for banks to meet this demand in the future. First, there is a potential capital constraint. In many countries whose banks have expanded their external assets sharply, capital ratios have deteriorated. At the end of 1980, for instance, the nine largest US banks had an exposure to Brazil equal to 43 per cent of capital, an exposure to Mexico of 38 per cent and Korea 19 per cent. The same banks had an exposure to developing countries in aggregate of 240 per cent of capital compared with 156 per cent three years earlier. The obvious solution is to raise more capital. But this might be difficult given the very exposure position under consideration and the pessimistic outlook for bank profits generally. In 1982 the nine largest US banks had their credit rating reduced by Moodys from Triple A, the principal concern being capital adequacy. Secondly, banks themselves might approach their own portfolio constraints in terms of the proportion of total assets and liabilities represented by foreign exposure in general. Thirdly, while a fungible concept, many banks have approached their limits as regards exposure to 'sovereign' borrowers. Finally, it is likely that the international banking environment will be more regulated than in the 1970s, which could also prove to be a constraint on further expansion.

For these reasons there is doubt about whether in the future banks will be able or willing to meet the financing requirement of developing countries on the same scale as during the 1970s. This raises the question of what alternatives would be available. One broad alternative is to increase non-debt financing options through official aid and long-term direct investment inflows. This would involve reversing the trend of the 1970s. The outlook for aid is not obviously optimistic. Nor can much be expected from long-term direct investment inflows, since these rose from $4.3 billion in 1973 to only $14.1 billion in 1982; in proportionate terms their contribution declined from 37 per cent in 1973 to 15 per cent in 1982.

This leaves alternative borrowing mechanisms in a situation where the traditional banking sector (that is, those banks active hitherto) either cannot or will not meet the financing requirement. The first option is to involve new banking institutions. It is clear that banks in different countries have different international exposures in general, and to developing countries in particular. Many banks have room in their exposure positions to increase their lending to developing countries. At various times in the 1970s new banks entered the market, and the share of loans to developing countries given by US banks declined. As US banks become less expansive, so European and Japanese banks increased their share, having at the time a smaller exposure. It is also clear that after 1979 OPEC institutions came into the market on a significant scale. But whether new groups will be as willing to move to the exposure levels of the US banks is an open question. It must be recognized that US banks originally entered the market in very different economic conditions and when developing country debt was considerably smaller and considered to be less risky.

A second borrowing option is to by-pass banks and financial intermediaries altogether. Surplus countries could lend directly to deficit countries. But this involves giving up the many and powerful advantages of indirect financial intermediation. A further option would be to ease developing countries' access to international bond markets. A third general option, and the one recommended earlier, is to shift at the margin the financing away from the private sector to official agencies, i.e. to the IMF, the World Bank and governments.

The final option is that *ex ante* deficits should not be financed, which implies increased pressure towards adjustment. This again highlights the fundamental issue with respect to international monetary arrangements, namely, the appropriate balance of pressures between balance of payments financing and adjustment, which shifted away from the latter during the 1970s probably to an excessive degree.

If, as in the early 1970s, attention were to be given to 'reform of the international monetary system' it is inconceivable that the debt position could be ignored. If another Committee of Twenty were to be established, its agenda would be significantly different because the issue of external indebtedness has become a central part of the system.

Concluding comment

International banking changed in the early 1980s as adjustments were made following the debt problems that emerged. It became a more cooperative, even collective, banking system compared with the aggressively competitive environment of the 1970s, as banks came to perceive a common interest. The nature of the industry changed. The issue remains as to whether this will prove to be a permanent feature of the market or only a temporary phase during a period of international debt difficulty. International banks developed a new partnership role with the official sector (particularly the IMF) as the Fund and central banks became involved in debt rescheduling operations and the parallel provision of more funds.

Above all, international banking became less expansive as more attention was paid to profitability, risk and exposure rather than to asset growth. This raises the issue of whether in the early 1980s a temporary consolidation was being made in the light of the problems being encountered at the time or whether the adjustment was more permanent. In the latter case, the growth of international bank lending would prove to be a temporary aberration of the 1970s (induced by the peculiar economic and financial circumstances of the decade) around a modest trend towards a steady inter-nationalization of banking. The international monetary system could then revert to a more traditional structure particularly with respect to the balance of roles of its *official* and *private* components.

Notes

1. B.J. Cohen, *Banks and the Balance of Payments*, London, Croom Helm, 1981.

2. David T. Llewellyn, 'Modelling International Banking Flows: An Analytical Framework', in J. Black (ed.), *Problems of International Finance*, London, Macmillan, 1984.

3. P. Stanyer and J. Whitley, 'Financing World Payments Imbalances', Bank of England *Quarterly Bulletin*, June 1981.

4. R. Triffin, *Gold and the Dollar Crisis*, New Haven, Yale University Press, 1960.

5. J. Eaton and M. Gersovitz, 'LDC Participation in International Financial Markets', *Journal of Development Economics*, Vol. 7, No. 1, March 1980, pp. 3–21.

6. S. Griffiths-Jones and M. Lipton, 'International Lenders of Last Resort: Are Changes Required?', Midland Bank International, *Occasional Papers on International Trade and Finance,* 1984.

7. K. Inoue, 'Determinants of Market Conditions in the Eurocurrency Market: Why a Borrowers' Market?', BIS, *Working Paper No. 1*, 1980.

8. M.C. Mendelsohn, *Outlook for International Bank Lending*, New York, Group of Thirty, 1981.

8
Balance of Payments Management: The IMF and the Third World
Graham Bird and Tony Killick*

Introduction

The period since the breakdown of the Bretton Woods system in 1971 and the first large increase in the price of oil in 1973 has not been a time of tranquillity. The changing world economic environment has created new challenges to which the international financial system has had to respond in order to avoid the collapse that has frequently been predicted as imminent. Problems associated with adjustment and financing which had existed before the early 1970s have been highlighted by events, and the ability of the system to cope has been under continual questioning. But whereas prior to 1971–3 the clear focus of attention had been on the balance of payments problems of industrial countries, there has subsequently been a considerable shift towards looking at those of developing countries, whether in the form of OPEC surpluses or the related non-oil developing countries' deficits. Interest in such problems has been further fostered by the whole North-South debate.

This chapter sets out first to examine how developing countries have fared within the international financial system in the period 1973–82 and second to look forward at ways in which their interests might be better served in future. It focuses especially on the facilities and policy conditions of the IMF and argues that there is a strong case for enhancing the Fund's contribution to adjustment and financing in the developing world. Although by no means without relevance to middle- and higher-income developing countries the Fund is potentially of great importance to the least developed, for whom

* Much of this chapter draws heavily upon a research project recently concluded at ODI with our collaborators Jennifer Sharpley and Mary Sutton, published in Tony Killick (ed.), *The Quest for Stabilization: the IMF and the Third World* and *The IMF and Stabilization: Developing Country Experiences*, London, ODI and Heinemann Educational Books, 1984.

commercial credit is neither available nor, perhaps, even desirable. It should be emphasized, then, that there is little point in treating developing countries as if they constitute a homogeneous group with similar payments problems which are susceptible to similar solutions. They do not. The chapter therefore suggests a less standardized approach to payments adjustment and urges the Fund to adopt a richer mix of policy measures.

The format of the chapter is as follows. The next section attempts to identify the size and nature of developing countries' payments difficulties. The following one shows how the international financial system has dealt with these difficulties through both the private and the official sectors and isolates a number of deficiencies associated with past arrangements. We then briefly examine the outlook for the global pattern of deficits and surpluses. Finally, we turn to the question of reform, taking up the particular case of the IMF and its conditionality. While brief mention is made of reforms which call for relatively substantial change, for instance, the introduction of a link between the creation of international liquidity and the provision of development finance, the low political feasibility of these leads us to concentrate on reforms which do not involve such major changes. However, the conclusion is reached that even modest alterations could still yield substantial benefits, by making the international financial system both more efficient and less inequitable.

The size and nature of non-oil developing country payment problems

The world economic environment in which non-oil developing countries operate has become more hostile since the beginning of the 1970s. A number of trends have contributed to this. First, there were the two oil shocks of 1973–4 and 1979–80 which exerted a direct adverse effect on their commodity terms of trade. Second, there was in the later 1970s and early 1980s a shrinkage in their export markets resulting from economic recession and growing protectionism in industrial countries. Among the effects of this was a fall in the relative and absolute prices of many primary product exports and this, too, exerted a strongly adverse influence on their commodity terms of trade. Third, there have been periods of high nominal interest rates and a general trend towards increasing real interest rates which, in association with a large volume of variable interest debt, have created problems of debt management for many of them.

Not all developing countries have suffered equivalently, however, with variations depending on factors such as the degree of reliance on imported oil and oil-related products, the commodity and geographical composition of trade, and the size and nature of external debt. This variety is aptly illustrated by Tables 7.1 and 7.2 in the previous chapter, which provide a statistical summary of the balance of payments problems of developing countries. Table 7.1 divides non-oil developing countries into sub-groups and shows their current account balance of payments for 1973–82.[1] While the balance of payments of industrial countries moved into surplus in 1978 as the surpluses of the oil-exporting countries declined, the non-oil developing countries have remained solidly in large and substantial deficit throughout the period, with the size of the deficit in relation to GDP being almost seven times greater than in industrial countries. Amongst them, the low-income countries have experienced the largest deficits relative to their exports. However, a considerable amount of care needs to be exercised in interpreting payments statistics. Not least, there is a problem in defining exactly what constitutes a payments problem. For example, while the current account may well be the best simple indicator of the long-term strength of the balance of payments, it is not an infallible guide. Countries with relatively large observed current account deficits need not necessarily be facing too many difficulties. There may be offsetting and sustainable capital inflows; or deficits may be temporary — self-correcting and self-financing in the longer term; or there may be adequate reserves or access to finance to get over short-term difficulties. At the same time, countries that do not appear to have so much of a balance of payments problem on the exclusive evidence of their external accounts may actually be in a grave situation simply because their deficits are not reversible and finance is not available.

Furthermore, it needs to be remembered that the balance of payments is ultimately a binding constraint. If only limited finance is available, the balance of payments *must* adjust in order to be consistent with whatever finance is available. At the extreme one could, in principle, envisage a developing country with zero access to finance having to manage its economy so that its imports were reduced to equality with its export earnings. Although the domestic implications of this might be that unemployment would rise and output, investment and living standards would fall, balance of payments statistics alone would fail to identify such a payments problem.

While recognizing the difficulties with the data, the information contained in Table 7.1 is consistent with the argument that non-oil developing countries have experienced severe balance of payments problems since 1973 absolutely, relative to other country groups, and relative to various other economic variables such as trade levels. Although a full analysis of the causes of these problems would require examination of both the domestic and external factors impinging on individual countries, some insight may be gleaned from an examination of the broader trends affecting them.

One well-known factor was the decline in their commodity terms of trade and the stagnation of export demand. Again, adverse movements were particularly marked for low-income countries. One element lying behind these figures was the changing relative prices of oil, non-oil primary commodities (in which many low-income countries have a high degree of export concentration), and manufactures. Indeed, in net oil-importing developing countries it was their deficit on the oil trade balance that accounted for the vast majority of their total trade deficit. These various factors strongly suggest that global developments, exogenous to individual countries, have had a great deal to do with the worsening in their balance of payments in recent years. While this is not to deny that internal mismanagement may still be serious, it does imply that this cause of deficits has been relatively less important in the period since 1973. This being so, it has a bearing on the design of adjustment policy and, by implication, on the provision of financing.

Adjustment and financing: past performance

The statistical pattern

Policy makers faced with balance of payments deficits may respond in a number of ways. The principles underlying their choice are reasonably straightforward. Initially, it is important to distinguish between those deficits which result from temporary phenomena, such as crop failures, and those of a more permanent nature, such as trend deteriorations in commodity terms of trade. Where deficits are temporary and self-correcting (and hence self-financing in the longer term), policy makers might be expected to favour financing, i.e. running down reserves or international borrowing. In these circumstances the underlying management of the economy need not be altered and there may be no 'adjustment' as such. However, this choice will not be open to countries with small reserves and little access to credit; in such cases the deficit will have to be corrected, no matter that it is temporary. The concept of a 'temporary' deficit has then to be evaluated in terms of the ability of the economy to finance it. In the absence of financing, short-term corrective measures will have to be undertaken even if the deficit is expected to correct itself after a while. Table 7.2 shows the extent to which financing has been used by non-oil developing countries since 1973, and gives the breakdown between reserve decumulation and borrowing. Only in 1975 did they actually decumulate reserves; during the remainder of the period reserves were accumulated, though the size of the accumulation varied considerably from year to year. However, the nominal overall values shown in Table 7.2 are somewhat misleading for two reasons. One is that, when broken down by sub-group, it transpires that reserve use has been a much more frequent occurrence, particularly for low-income countries and for other net oil importers. A second is that, when expressed in relation to imports, reserves have fallen quite dramatically for all groups.

Turning to the other means of financing, Table 7.2 again provides useful data. Borrowing from private sources features as the single largest source of funds. However, this is also rather misleading because, while major exporters of manufactures have indeed relied very heavily on private capital, low-income countries have borrowed little in this way and have instead depended on official credit and non-debt-creating flows. Furthermore, credit from the IMF in this period was heavily concentrated on low-income countries and other net oil importers. As of 1981, of a total outstanding use of Fund credit of $14.1 billion by all net oil-importing developing countries, $11.5 billion was used by low-income countries and other oil importers, with the major exporters of manufactures using only $2.7 billion.[2] The adequacy of the system in financing developing country payments deficits warrants closer examination, but it is first worth saying a little more about the nature of adjustment.

While the objective of any balance of payments adjustment strategy is to eliminate the unsustainable portion of any deficit, this may be achieved in a number of ways. From the alternatives available to them, policy makers will certainly favour those that bring about payments correction at the minimum cost in terms of other policy objectives, such as economic growth and employment. But where such corrective policies are long-term, they may not bring about the required adjustment rapidly enough. Other policies that exert a more rapid impact on the balance of payments will then have to be adopted, even though they involve higher welfare costs. Amongst the quicker-acting measures are import controls and demand deflation, both of which are designed to strengthen the balance of payments by reducing imports below what they would otherwise have been. Given recent shortages of finance, it is not surprising that low-income countries and other net oil importers have experienced periodic declines in import volumes during 1973–82, while the import volume of the major exporters of manufactures fell only once, in 1975. It is consequently not surprising to find that the World Bank's *World Development Report, 1982* shows that low-income countries experienced relatively slow economic growth, as compared with those developing countries where import volume expanded more rapidly. Nor, perhaps, is it coincidental that the lowest rates of growth for the major exporters of manufactures occurred in 1975, when import volume fell by 5.9 per cent, and in 1981, when import volume growth was at its lowest as compared with any other year in the period 1973–82.

Deficiencies of the system

Although the main focus of this chapter is on the IMF, it might be useful at this point to consider some of the deficiencies of 'the system' considered more broadly. For while the international financial system has been able to cope with the two oil shocks, the associated massive shifts in global payments imbalances, and the other major disturbances experienced by the world economy in the past decade, better than many feared and without any major banking collapse, a number of deficiencies have also been laid bare. There are questions of both efficiency and equity to consider here.

To take *efficiency* first. The system could be criticized on a number of interrelated grounds:

(i) It has given rise to an asymmetrical pattern of adjustment, with most of the burden falling upon the deficit countries (even though they cannot reduce their deficits without a corresponding reduction in the surpluses of the rest of the world). This pattern has fallen particularly acutely upon deficit countries (a) whose currencies are not reserve currencies and (b) which have low commercial bank credit ratings. The effect of this asymmetry is to impart a deflationary bias to the world economy and to prevent investible resources from being employed in the most productive uses.

(ii) An adequate flow of financing from surplus to deficit countries would have mitigated this asymmetry but (with the exception of a few relatively industrialized developing countries with large-scale access to international bank loans) many deficit countries have found it impossible to borrow as much as they need. This has forced many of them into demand repression and/or import quotas, thus giving a further deflationary twist to a world economy already in recession.

(iii) The condition just described has been aggravated by the tendency for commercial bank lending (and IMF policy conditionality in 1981–2) to be pro-cyclical.

(iv) This tendency, the heavy concentration of bank exposure in a small number of developing countries, the banks' apparent indifference during the phase of rapid credit expansion to the ways in which their credits were employed (which sometimes had little to do with achieving necessary re-structuring in the borrowing countries), and questions about the adequacy of official supervision of international banking, have resulted in a lower-than-desired degree of stability. This was powerfully illustrated by the alarms during 1982 (and since) about the possibility of defaults on bank loans by Mexico and, to a lesser extent, Brazil and Argentina.

The main question about the *equity* of the system has already been implied: that it has tended to operate in ways which place the greatest burdens upon precisely the poorer non-oil developing countries. These have little alternative but to borrow from the IMF, most of whose credits are short-term. Thus countries with already low living standards and a need for high rates of capital formation have had to restrain consumption and investment. Ironically, it is in just these countries that the costs of adjustment are likely to be largest, because of their poorly-developed economic infrastructure and public administrations, and relatively low factor mobilities.

Moreover, the ability of deficit non-oil developing countries to correct their balance of payments is itself contingent upon the policies simultaneously being pursued by the OECD group of countries. Contractionary policies in several of the most important of these, combined with somewhat protectionist trade policies, have strictly limited the capacity of non-oil developing countries to adjust through export expansion, as well as worsening their terms of trade. While the industrial countries comprehend this problem they do not see it as being in their own best interests to correct it. The lack of a truly effective mechanism for the coordination of national economic policies in a world of much increased interdependence certainly rates as a serious deficiency of the system, from both the efficiency and the equity points of view.

The IMF

As already shown by Table 7.2, the IMF has been of relatively little overall significance to non-oil developing countries as a direct source of finance, both by comparison with the size of their combined current account deficit and by comparison with the size of private capital flows. Indeed, in the three years following the peak year of 1976, when drawings from the Fund covered about 14 per cent of their deficit, they actually made net repayments to the Fund. Their use of Fund resources increased quite markedly during 1980–2, however, although by 1982 still only just over 6 per cent of the deficit was being covered. In quantitative terms, the Fund has played a small part in recycling international finance.

However, the importance of the IMF to non-oil developing countries should not be underestimated. First, the Fund has been a significant supplier of finance in particular years and in particular countries, sometimes covering as much as 40 per cent of the recorded deficit. As already mentioned, an increasing proportion of the Fund's business has been with low-income countries with little ability to borrow from the Eurocurrency market. As of end-1981, 66.7 per cent of outstanding IMF commitments were with countries with per capita GDPs of less than $700. Again, then, the overall figures for non-oil developing countries as a group may conceal more than they reveal. It should be added that a major change in the pattern of Fund lending occurred in early 1983, with large credits being approved for three of the richest developing countries — Mexico, Brazil and Argentina.

Second, for some middle- and higher-income non-oil developing countries the conditionality associated with Fund programmes may have some catalytic effect on commercial and other inflows of finance. Certainly debt rescheduling may be more willingly undertaken by the banks if agreement has already been reached between the debtor and the Fund on a programme of economic policies designed to strengthen the balance of payments. To the extent that a catalytic effect exists, the Fund is more significant than the size of its own credits would suggest. But it is difficult to say just how important the catalytic effect is. It has undeniably been a factor in particular cases and there is some evidence to suggest that there has been a positive correlation between IMF support and the inflow of Eurocurrency credit.[3] It was also a feature of the 1983 credits to Argentina, Mexico and Brazil that the Fund refused to approve these until the commercial banks had themselves agreed on reschedulings and new loans. But equally there are many examples of cases where the negotiation of an IMF loan has not resulted in private inflows (and more limited cases where Fund support has actually resulted in the banks pulling out), or where countries have been able to tap the Eurocurrency market even though they have decided not to borrow from the Fund.[4] Not infrequently the Fund actually places a ceiling on private borrowing. Furthermore, the apparently high failure rate of Fund programmes has led banks to place relatively less emphasis on these and more emphasis on their own assessment of the borrowing country's economic prospects.

Third, but leading on from the above discussion, the Fund not only provides finance but also has an important and potentially crucial influence over adjustment policy because the availability of a large proportion of Fund finance is conditional on agreement of a programme of economic policies and the attainment of certain specific targets.[5] To concentrate exclusively on its provision of finance is to neglect this very important component of the Fund's activities. Unlike the banks, the Fund cannot be criticized for paying insufficient attention to adjustment. However, it may be criticized for the particular approach to adjustment as reflected by the programmes it supports.

The conditionality attached to Fund credits comprises three chief components: preconditions, performance criteria and various other policy elements. Preconditions relate to policy actions which must be undertaken before an agreement is put up for approval by the Executive Board. Although commonly relating to measures such as devaluation and interest rate reform and included in a majority of credits, preconditions are not normally mentioned in the 'letters of intent' which formally set out the recipient government's intended programme, so there is a dearth of hard evidence on these.

In contrast, letters of intent do specify a wide range of measures relating to various aspects of fiscal and monetary, pricing, wages and trade policies. While failure to comply with such policies may damage a borrower's credibility with the Fund, it does not affect the flow of credit agreed under the programme, provided the performance criteria are met. For this reason this aspect of Fund programmes is less significant than the performance criteria, though the two components are related in the sense that the policy commitments undertaken should be consistent with the performance criteria to be achieved.

Performance criteria are policy targets or ceilings included in letters of intent in quantitative or objective terms. If these are breached, the government becomes ineligible for any outstanding instalments of the credit, unless the Fund agrees to a waiver or modification of the programme. Features of the variables chosen to act as performance criteria are that information on them should be available with only a short time-lag; they should give an accurate picture of economic performance; and should be within the control of the domestic authorities. Standard clauses relating to the avoidance of new multiple currency practices and payments restrictions are also usually appended to IMF agreements. Ceilings on credit to the government (or public sector) and on total domestic credit are by far the most common performance criteria used by the Fund, as confirmed by the Fund's own research.[6] However, the ceilings are usually on the rate of credit expansion and rarely call for absolute reductions in the total quantity of credit. Ceilings are often set on the acceptance of new external debts of certain maturities; sometimes a floor is placed on the minimum holding of international reserves.

The apparent preoccupation with credit ceilings might at first glance be interpreted as reflecting a fixed belief in the monetary approach to the balance payments. However, while Fund staff have indeed made major contributions to the development of the monetary approach, recent Fund research recognizes the complex and potentially adverse effects that credit control may have on output and employment, something which is inconsistent with the strict monetary approach.[7] Some of its publications also accept many of the criticisms that have been made of the monetarist model.[8] In addition, the Fund's advocacy of policies to alter relative prices is clearly at odds with the strict monetarist model, as is its interest in the composition of the balance of payments and the performance of the current account.

A quite different reason that has been given for the ubiquitous use of credit ceilings is that they possess the features required of a good performance criterion. But does credit control exhibit such features? Although data on credit creation are certainly relatively easily and quickly available, there is little point in concentrating on credit for this reason alone. Data shortage is an argument for collecting more data, not for using only the variables on which data are currently available. Furthermore, there must be considerable doubt whether one financial variable can accurately and fully summarize what is happening in the *real* economy. Emphasis on credit also reflects a view by the Fund that over-expansion of credit is the principal cause of payments deficits. But, as presented earlier, there is considerable evidence to the contrary. In circumstances where deficits have been caused by adverse movements in the terms of trade, the control of credit creation is likely to be a high-cost means of adjustment. Even if it does serve to reduce payments deficits, it may do little to encourage the underlying real adjustment that is required to strengthen the balance of payments, namely, shifting resources out of the non-traded-goods sector and into the traded-goods sector.

Financial restraint exerts its impact on the current account by deflating expenditure and the demand for imports. Any effects on structural adaptation are largely coincidental and may even be in the 'wrong' direction. With reduced aggregate demand and increased interest rates, it is likely that real output will fall. Furthermore, unless imports are exclusively consumption goods or 'inessentials', it is probable that development will become constrained by shortages of imported inputs and this will damage future investment and export performance. Working capital shortages resulting from credit restraints, and higher interest rates, may further aggravate the situation. Thus while the restriction of domestic credit may certainly strengthen the short-run balance of payments, it is likely to involve substantial economic costs and do little for the balance of payments in the long run. A final difficulty concerns the ability of the fiscal and monetary authorities to control precisely the rate of credit creation, given the numerous pressures which exert an impact on this variable, and the somewhat rudimentary domestic financial systems in many developing countries.

A devaluation is almost never a performance criterion, although it is more often a precondition. Currency depreciations seem to be associated with only between a third and a half of Fund programmes.[9]

Given the apparent narrowness of performance criteria, an important question relates to the scope for flexibility and adaptability. In principle, there is considerable scope. Credit ceilings may take on various forms and may involve various quantitative targets, more or less tight, and these variations may be used to reflect the characteristics of individual countries. Similarly the possibility of negotiating a waiver or a modification to the programme if initial targets are not realized provides further scope for flexibility. In addition, the existence of a range of facilities in the

Fund provides the possibility of tailoring the type of finance to the needs of individual countries. However, having said all this, evidence does suggest that there is a rather conventional type of Fund programme which, in terms of its most binding components, places heavy reliance on demand-side targets. Even in instances where the Fund does not identify over-expansionary demand policies as a principal cause of the deficit, there remains an apparent reluctance to break away from conventional performance criteria.[10] This is true even in the case of the extended facility (EFF). While supposed to deal specifically with longer-term structural problems, this is still essentially built around demand-side conditionality. In fact, the evidence suggests that credit ceilings under the EFF have been rather tighter than with conventional one-year stand-bys.

Concern of the type expressed above would, of course, carry little weight if Fund-supported programmes were generally successful. Unfortunately, there is accumulating evidence that Fund programmes are not achieving their objectives. On the basis of the results of internal Fund reviews and of independent analyses the evidence suggests that, in the general case, Fund programmes have limited effectiveness.[11] There is a tendency for them to move payments indicators in desired directions, and to affect other variables in certain ways, but these tendencies only occasionally pass standard tests of statistical significance. In terms of results which do pass such tests, the programmes appear to have a limited impact. More specifically, the evidence suggests that:

(a) programmes are associated with a modest short-term improvement in the current account but this is of low statistical significance;

(b) there appears to be a stronger tendency for the basic or overall balances to be improved, although the known statistical significance of the results is again low and the achievement often falls short of IMF programme targets, which are apt to be over-ambitious;

(c) there are indications that Fund programmes result in additional inflows of capital from other sources but the effect is that large and ambitious expectations are likely to be disappointed;

(d) there is no systematic association at all between Fund programmes and sustained liberalization;

(e) programmes have not generally had strong deflationary effects, but there are indications that negative growth effects were stronger in the most recent years;

(f) programmes probably result in a net short-run increase in the inflation rate, rather than the desired reduction, but significances are again low;

(g) both stand-bys and EFF programmes are subject to fairly frequent breakdowns.

It is necessary to add that the evidence surveyed is far from uniform, depending upon the period, variables and methodologies chosen. It is also important to bear in mind that there are large intrinsic difficulties in forming an assessment of the results of IMF programmes. On the other hand, the results summarized in no way depend upon some unique set of tests and the Fund's own assessments do not claim great success. To quote a recent internal staff review (of stand-bys in 1980 and Extended Facility credits in 1978–80): 'The Fund cannot be complacent about a situation in which almost half the cases have not shown any progress towards balance of payments viability. This may be no worse a record than in earlier years.'

In examining possible sources of this disappointing outcome, one possibility that comes obviously to mind is that it was due to poor programme implementation. There is a good deal of evidence that implementation leaves much to be desired. The IMF has experienced large difficulties in securing governmental compliance with a number of its key performance criteria, especially since 1973, with fiscal difficulties being a major source of non-compliance. Presumably as a consequence of this, programmes appear to have a meagre effect on the key policy variables to which they are directed. In particular, while they do tend to bring about a deceleration in domestic credit, this has slight claims to statistical significance. Even if we accept the basically monetarist premise underlying the Fund's emphasis on the control of domestic credit, it seems unlikely that strong balance of payments results could be expected from the limited deceleration they achieve in the expansion of domestic credit. What is even more damaging, however, is evidence indicating no more than a moderate connection between programme execution and the achievement of desired results. Thus the hypothesis that IMF programmes have little impact because of poor implementation receives only slight support from available evidence.

Probably the greatest reason for unsuccessful programmes in recent years has been the sheer strength of unanticipated shocks in the world economy, which have knocked off course the plans of most governments. A lack of political commitment to what are often seen as imposed programmes provides another explanation, to which we would add defects in the design of the programmes themselves.

Adjustment and financing: the outlook

The large sudden swings and jumps that have occurred in relative world prices in the past decade have made forecasting a more than normally hazardous business. It is, for example, particularly difficult to form a view of the likely future trend in real oil prices; and of the relative movements of the prices of manufactured goods and primary commodities. There is, none the less, some agreement among those who prepare global payments predictions that large non-oil developing country deficits are liable to remain a relatively constant factor in the global payments situation over the next few years. OPEC current account balances moved into deficit in 1983 but the counterpart improvements were largely concentrated in the balances of the industrialized OECD countries, other than the United States which was absorbing huge capital inflows.

In short, the problems of adjustment and financing that non-oil developing countries encountered in the decade from 1973 seem likely to persist at least into the medium term. A central question relates to how these problems will be handled and whether it is possible to improve on the way things have been done in the past. However, it is not legitimate to assume that the choice is simply between the old set of arrangements and some new improved set. It is unlikely that the recycling mechanisms that operated in the 1970s and early 1980s, with their great dependence on the private international banks, will be sustainable.

There are, of course, some reasons to believe that they could be. First, if banks are going to continue in the business of providing balance of payments finance, it is clearly the deficit countries that will remain the principal borrowers. In terms both of the demand for funds by deficit non-oil developing countries and the supply of deposits by surplus countries, it seems most probable that recycling by the banks will continue to be very significant. In any case the banks, taken together, are locked into lending to some non-oil developing countries. Although individual banks may have an incentive to withdraw from certain countries ahead of the rush, no bank seeks the international banking collapse that sudden variations in the pattern of lending might cause. Furthermore, in the past as some groups of banks have reduced their lending to non-oil developing countries so other groups have come in; the size of the industry has adjusted to maintain an inflow of private capital. This, however, is not the same thing as saying that the supply curve of individual banks is elastic, and the distinction between the two sorts of expansion (namely, more involvement by a given number of banks or by more banks) may have important implications should the size of the industry fail to expand further.[12] Yet optimists maintain, that with a few minor modifications and with the growing sophistication of their own risk analysis, and despite the alarms of 1982, the banks can continue to carry out the principal recycling role. They recognize, however, that bank lending will be unable to meet the financing needs of the least developed countries, which will have to be provided through bilateral and multilateral flows on concessional terms.

Pessimists, on the other hand, point to the banks' low capital ratios, the high exposures of certain banks in a small number of countries, the falling net transfer associated with any given financial inflow, falling spreads associated with lending to non-oil developing countries, and the vulnerability of the system to sudden strains caused by falling commodity prices and rising interest rates. They see a financial crisis involving developing country default as being far from impossible, and are sceptical of the attitude that says 'everything will turn out alright providing bankers keep their cool.'

Should the recycling mechanisms of the past prove unsustainable in the future the implications may be stated briefly, but they are fundamentally important. Failure to provide non-oil developing countries with the necessary amount of international finance will result in these countries having to undertake more adjustment, which will put their living standards at risk. The poorest countries are particularly vulnerable. But there are also global consequences. If developing countries adjust by reducing imports through deflation and controls it is not only their economic development that will suffer. The exports of industrial countries will fall, resulting in slower growth and higher unemployment for them as well. Although adjustment by non-oil developing countries by means of expanding exports would have fewer adverse consequences for world economic growth, this has in practice been resisted by industrial countries, via protectionism, for fear of the competition with domestic industries.

Given the costs of failing to provide adequate finance to non-oil developing countries, the unevenness of access to this finance, and the deficiencies of the existing arrangements for recyling and for encouraging appropriate forms of adjustment, there is considerable scope for improvement. In the final section below we take up the important example of possible reforms in the International Monetary Fund.

Reforming the IMF

It is the *costs of adjustment* which turn an unviable balance of payments into a problem. The task, therefore, is to minimize these costs, relative to the size of the needed adjustment. Implicit in many of the criticisms of past Fund policies is the view that it has paid insufficient attention to the cost-minimization task. The chief determinant of such costs is the extent to which adjustment is achieved through reductions in demand (and the associated losses of output and employment), as contrasted with an increased production of tradeable goods and services. Linked to this factor is the amount of financing that is available to support the adjustment programme and, therefore, the time available to achieve the necessary changes in output and demand.

What seems desirable, therefore, is for *Fund-supported stabilization programmes to be consciously set within a cost-minimizing framework.*[13] This would carry a number of important implications. First, it would involve placing greater weight on the 'primary' objectives of growth, employment and development specified in the Articles, and accepting them as constraining the design of stabilization programmes. The Fund already does this to some extent with respect to economic growth (and also price stability) but it has always declined to take explicit account of distributional consequences when designing its programmes. We suggest it should place greater weight on these considerations, which not only affect judgements about the desirability of specific measures but also greatly influence the likelihood that the programme will actually be carried out.

The greater attention to costs advocated here should be further extended to a more systematic and explicit consideration of the political consequences of stabilization programmes; indeed, one of the chief reasons for programme breakdowns is that governments often perceive the political costs of carrying through a programme to be greater than the payments crisis to which it is addressed. While the Fund does form political judgements, it is weak in this area. There are both ethical and efficiency grounds for urging the Fund to strengthen its capacity here. At the moral level, and to quote

Alejandro Foxley,[14] if one prefers an open, democratic society then policies 'that require a good deal of political repression to have a reasonable chance of success are certainly not a satisfactory solution'. At the efficiency level, programmes designed with sensitivity to the probable political consequences simply stand a better chance of being implemented.

Not the least of the advantages of the changes suggested above is that they would tend to narrow the differences between the objectives of the Fund and those of member governments. They open up the possibility that a higher proportion of programmes could be arrived at by consensus, thus increasing the probability of successful implementation. More extensive employment of resident Fund representatives would also facilitate the achievement of consensus, as would a cessation of the practice by which the Fund mission brings with it a draft of the letter of intent (admittedly open to negotiation) setting out what is represented as being the recipient government's programme.

Another consideration concerns the *degree of variety* in programme design. Although the Fund does seek to adapt programmes to specific country situations, it does so within narrow confines and, as we have shown, there is a rather well-defined 'conventional' IMF approach, based largely on demand management and exchange rate depreciations. It would be preferable to use a richer mix of policies and to accept the principle that programmes must be designed to address the causes of the problem in question. Demand-control programmes addressed to 'structural' problems are apt to be high-cost solutions; just as 'supply-oriented' programmes are, in the face of deficits resulting from excess money creation. In our view, country circumstances vary too much for any standard approach to be appropriate.

Next, we urge that the Fund should move away from its emphasis on quantified performance criteria and concentrate instead on achieving a consensus with member governments about the *policy measures* necessary to achieve the desired stabilization. The case for dispensing with quantified performance criteria in a wide range of circumstances relates to the attention biases they create; the large margins of error to which they are subject; the sometimes rather tenuous connection between them and the economic variables it is desired to influence; the barrier they may set up against a rounded judgement of the overall extent of programme execution. Instead, continuing access to Fund credit should depend upon an overall judgement about the extent of programme execution — what are known in Fund parlance as 'review clauses' — rather than upon observance of conventional performance criteria.

Under this approach programmes would still be monitored and tested, although failure to comply with policy conditions would initially trigger off consultation between the borrowing country and the Fund and a review of the programme, rather than immediately resulting in further finance being cut off. During the review the reasons for failure would be examined and a decision made with regard to future financial provision. A lenient attitude would be adopted in those cases where exogenous and unforeseen factors were responsible for the programme's failure and a new programme with new conditions would be negotiated.

For expositional purposes, it is convenient to identify two polar cases of countries facing a (non-temporary) balance of payments problem. First, there is what might be called a 'classic' IMF problem, of a persistent deficit attributable largely to excessively expansionary fiscal and monetary policies. At the other extreme, we may take the 'structural' case of a country confronted with an enormous increase in the unit cost of imports, a depressed foreign demand for its traditional exports and persistent, serious deterioration in the terms of trade, while it is pursuing responsible fiscal and monetary policies at home. These factors may be aggravated by structural weaknesses of a more domestic origin, or such weaknesses may themselves be the principal source of difficulty — lagging agriculture; high-cost industry; an inefficient marketing system.

As regards the 'structural' problems, the type of programme required is one that places primary emphasis on improved capacity utilization and on shifting the distribution of productive resources in favour of tradeable goods and services, plus supporting demand-management policies. Essentially, what is being urged is a redesign and reactivation of the EFF—something which, therefore, it should be possible to accommodate within the Fund's existing framework of activities. The precise nature of this type of programme can only be specified in a country context, and a specific illustration applied to the situation in Kenya as at mid-1982 has been published elsewhere.[15] The chief features of this are:

(a) It is set in a cost-minimizing, growth-oriented framework and is also designed to be consonant with the government objectives of poverty alleviation.
(b) It is a medium-term programme, designed to be executed over five years.

(c) The emphasis is upon a programme arrived at as a consensus, reflecting a genuine government commitment. We place some importance on the role of an IMF resident representative in this context, as also in monitoring the programme.

(d) A substantial number of measures to stimulate the production of exportable and import-substituting goods and services relative to non-tradeables are included, with at least the same status as other provisions of the programme.

(e) The inclusion, however, of supporting demand-management measures, including fiscal and monetary restraint, is recognition that the absence of such restraint could subvert the success of the measures directed at the productive system by preventing the necessary reduction in absorption (especially consumption) relative to output.

(f) Quantified performance criteria are replaced by a broader set of 'review indicators', although the necessity for careful and concrete monitoring of performance would still be fully recognized. Performance under these indicators would not govern eligibility for continued access to the credit, as in the case of existing performance criteria, but — like these criteria — it would trigger a review mission whose job it would be to form a rounded judgement of overall progress with the programme and to make recommendations about continued access on that basis. A review mission could be despatched at the initiative of either the government or the IMF.

(g) There would be an agreed timetable of execution of all, or a large proportion, of the programme elements and explicit provision for the ways in which progress is to be monitored.

(h) In addition to lending its own resources, the Fund would initiate actions to attract additional supporting finance from other multilateral, bilateral and, perhaps, commercial sources.

It is worth repeating that the type of programme just outlined is not presented as a new standard approach. The important principle is that programmes should be designed according to specific country circumstances. In practice, these are likely to include some combination of excess-demand and structural weaknesses, and will call for a blend of the Fund's traditional approach (subject to the various recommendations presented earlier) and of the type of measure just outlined.

Although the changes outlined above are relatively modest, they do have significant implications in a number of areas.

(i) For developing countries

If governments in developing countries refuse to accept the costs, in terms of domestic absorption, that balance of payments correction involves, and endeavour to avoid needed changes in the structure of the economy, then the outcome will almost certainly be that payments problems will become even more firmly embedded. The adjustment that will eventually be unavoidable is therefore likely to be much more costly for economic development. Similarly, developing countries need to be persuaded that a larger number of economic variables should come under discussion with the Fund than has conventionally been the case, if conditionality is to be made more appropriate. This requires a considerable shift in attitudes towards the Fund.

(ii) For the division of labour with the World Bank

In circumstances where the causes and cures of payments deficits may only be seen in a long-term structural context, the distinction between payments problems and development problems becomes largely artificial, as therefore does the traditional distinction between the Fund, as a payments institution, and the Bank, as a development one. Unavoidably, the division of labour between the two institutions becomes more blurred, especially as the Bank itself has moved into structural adjustment lending which in practice incorporates many of the features included in the proposals discussed above. However, a less well defined division of labour is not necessarily a bad thing. All that needs to be ensured, through cooperation, is that their activities are mutually reinforcing. With such cooperation, a consistent set of economic policies which assist the realization of both development and balance of payments objectives should be attainable. Under the above proposals the Fund retains the role of providing payments assistance linked to an adjustment programme in circumstances where deficits are non-temporary, and this does not constitute a break with its traditional role.

(iii) For relations with the private international banks

How might the private banks react to such changes in Fund

conditionality? Would the catalytic effect disappear? A number of points may be made. First, as noted earlier, the strength of the catalytic effect can be overstressed, especially where the Fund and the banks are involved in different countries. Second, even where the Fund and banks are both involved, particularly in certain middle-to-high-income developing countries, it is quite possible that the appropriate Fund programme will, in fact, look fairly conventional, since where excessive demand creation has caused the payments problems, emphasis on credit ceilings is quite reasonable. Third, the poor record of success of Fund programmes hardly encourages continuing confidence. This is much more likely to be provided by programmes that are successful, and the success rate may be raised by the Fund adopting a more flexible approach to conditionality, designed with the causes of the problem more directly in mind.

(iv) For the duration of lending and the resources of the Fund

An approach to conditionality that emphasizes real changes implies longer-term lending by the Fund than has so far been the case, since such changes are unlikely to be achieved within one or two years. Longer-term lending does, however, bring with it a fundamental difficulty: if the Fund is to extend its lending in this way it will initially require increased resources. A need for more resources also arises from the strong case for the IMF to take on a larger share of the task of recycling international finance in order to assist world payments stability, economic development and the security of the international banking system. From where are the additional resources to come? Broadly speaking, there are five options: (a) increased IMF quotas; (b) *ad hoc* borrowing; (c) borrowing from private capital markets; (d) gold sales; and (e) a form of SDR link.

(*a*) *Increased IMF quotas.* In many ways this is the most straightforward alternative. It is undeniable that the ratio between quotas and world imports has fallen dramatically since the 1960s, over a period when the size of problems with which the Fund might in principle have been expected to deal has been increasing — a situation which will not have been adequately redressed by the $47\frac{1}{2}$ per cent quota increase agreed for 1983–4. Furthermore, using increased quotas to raise resources would permit the Fund to expand that part of its lending that is at sub-market interest rates. However, increasing quotas does have other implications. One is that the availability of both low- and high-conditionality finance will be increased. Indeed, given that an increase in quotas may be used to replace policies on 'enlarged access', the availability of low-conditionality finance will increase proportionately to high-conditionality finance. A second is that increased quotas lead not only to an increase in the supply of Fund resources but also to an increase in the demand for them. Since the proposals regarding Fund conditionality must be expected to increase the demand for resources without affecting supply, an increase in quotas may fail to compensate for the effect of the modifications. Other means of expanding the Fund's resources may therefore still be required.

(b) *Ad hoc borrowing*. This means of raising resources has been used in the past. Although offering a useful and often expedient way of meeting potential shortages of liquidity, it does not offer a satisfactory long-term solution to inadequate resources. It does not provide a reliable source of finance, witness the fact that, political considerations apart, the scope for future borrowing from Saudi Arabia hinges crucially on the price of oil and the Saudi balance of payments situation.

(c) *Borrowing from the private sector*. Direct borrowing by the Fund from private capital markets raises a number of questions. Would private banks lend to the Fund in circumstances where they are not prepared to lend to developing countries directly? Would the Fund lend on commercial terms similar to those under which it borrowed or would it attempt to transform the maturity and terms of the loans? If it were to lend on softer terms than those on which it was borrowing, where would the finance for such subsidization come from? Would all developing countries benefit from such arrangements or would there be distributional variations particularly between the more and less creditworthy developing countries?

The incentive for private banks to lend would have to arise from the rate of return offered to them by the Fund and their own assessment of the risk involved, which could be influenced by the ways in which the Fund used the extra resources. The banks would presumably assess the risks associated with lending to the IMF as being less than those involved in lending directly to developing countries, and would thus presumably accept a lower rate of return. In terms of widening their portfolio of assets, the prospect of lending to the Fund could be quite attractive since it would enable the banks to combine relatively high-return, high-risk lending direct to developing countries with relatively low-return, low-risk lending to the IMF. However, it could actually encourage them to pull out of direct balance of payments financing, an area in which the Fund has the traditional expertise. Furthermore, IMF lending financed by commercial borrowing might be expected to possess a somewhat skewed distribution unless some form of interest rate subsidization for ultimate borrowers could be devised.[16] It could discriminate against low-income countries. At the same time, it might also be unpopular with middle-income countries, who might see IMF borrowing as crowding out their own direct borrowing. Countries previously enjoying access to the Eurocurrency market might be compelled to turn to the Fund and become subject to the discipline of conditionality.

(*d*) *Gold sales.* This is not a new idea, since the Fund has already used the partial sale of its gold holdings to finance the operations of the Trust Fund and thereby to provide assistance, at low conditionality, essentially to the least developed countries. The Fund has thus, in effect, accepted that this constitutes an appropriate use of its gold. The pros and cons of using gold in this way have been thoroughly investigated elsewhere.[17] What emerges is that there is a strong case on grounds of equity for such sales and no legitimate argument against them on grounds of efficiency.[18]

The principal problems with gold sales arise, first, from variations in the market price of gold and therefore fluctuations in the receipts from selling any given quantity; second, from the fact that the major beneficiaries may turn out to be the purchasers of gold, mostly industrial countries, rather than developing countries; third, from what happens when all the gold has been sold; and finally from the way in which the finance is to be used once acquired.

The first problem simply makes the exercise of maximizing receipts that much more complicated, with further complications resulting from the fact that developing countries will have their own time preference rate for resources. However, this has not prevented the auctioning of gold in the past. The second problem could, in principle, be dealt with by introducing some form of international gold capital gains tax. In practice, it seems highly unlikely that such a tax would be acceptable. The only practical solution would be to use IMF gold as collateral for raising private loans rather than selling it, but in this case the finance made available would not be concessionary. The third problem may be resolved by using only the interest from the investment of receipts from gold sales (possibly in World Bank projects) rather than the full capital value; although this would imply a continuing flow of finance, it would, of course, also mean that much less finance would be available initially. Finally, the revenue raised through gold sales could be used to help finance existing IMF activities modified as suggested earlier. Alternatively, it could finance subsidies on Fund finance.

(*e*) *An SDR link.* Most proposals with regard to the establishment of an SDR link keep the creation of SDRs separate from the activities of the General Account. In principle, however, the link could be organized so as to provide extra resources for the General Account. In effect, SDRs would be used to augment other Fund resources. Although the mechanics by which this could be achieved are various, one important implication of this type of link is that the SDRs thus created would be allocated to borrowing countries on a conditional and quite possibly repayable basis, and would thus lose many of their previously distinctive features. Under this form of link the appropriateness of IMF conditionality would again be a crucial issue. Of course, a number of the powerful industrial countries remain opposed not only to any form of SDR link but even to a further conventional allocation of SDRs. There is nevertheless a most powerful case to be made for such an allocation, as recently argued by Williamson.[19]

Concluding comment

It is, of course, arbitrary to single out the IMF in this discussion of reform. What the Fund can and ought to do can only be decided in a more general context, which includes other aspects of payments financing, international trading policies, the roles of the commercial banks and other financial institutions, and the economic policies of the major industrial countries. Just as the ability of the deficit non-oil developing countries to achieve balance of payments adjustment is contingent upon the actions of the rest of the world, so the preferred policies and resources of the Fund can only be finally settled in the context of an overall view of the total flow of resources to deficit countries and the terms upon which these are made available.

Thus, while limitations of space have prevented us from giving much attention to the future access of non-oil developing countries to private capital markets, this is certainly a major topic. Similarly, the future volume and distribution of concessional development assistance are of critical importance to the poorer developing countries whose needs tend at present to fall in the gaps left by existing institutions. Nevertheless, the IMF has a central role to play and should, therefore, be strengthened.

Notes

1. For most of this chapter the classification of countries is the one used by the IMF. Developing countries are divided into two groups — 'oil-exporting countries' and 'non-oil developing countries'. The countries in the former category are: Algeria, Indonesia, Iran, Iraq, Kuwait, Libya, Nigeria, Oman, Qatar, Saudi Arabia, United Arab Emirates and Venezuela. Non-oil developing countries are sometimes broken down into sub-groups. There are the 'net oil exporters', those developing countries which, while not having significant oil production or exports, export more oil than they import. They are: Bahrain, Bolivia, Congo, Ecuador, Egypt, Gabon, Malaysia, Mexico, Peru, Syrian Arab Republic, Trinidad and Tobago, and Tunisia. From amongst the 'net importers of oil' there are, first, the 'major exporters of manufactures', namely: Argentina, Brazil, Greece, Hong Kong, Israel, Korea, Portugal, Singapore, South Africa and Yugoslavia. Next there are the 'low-income countries' whose per capita GDP, as estimated by the World Bank, was no greater than $350 in 1978. These are: Afghanistan, Bangladesh, Benin, Burma, Burundi, Cape Verde, Central African Republic, Chad, China, Comoros, Ethiopia, The Gambia, Guinea, Guinea-Bissau, Haiti, India, Democratic Kampuchea, Kenya, Lao, Lesotho, Madagascar, Malawi, Maldives, Mali, Mauritania, Nepal, Niger, Pakistan, Rwanda, Senegal, Sierra Leone, Somalia, Sri Lanka, Sudan, Tanzania, Togo, Uganda, Upper Volta, Vietnam and Zaire. Finally, 'other net oil importers' include the developing countries excluded from the above categories. Occasionally other classifications are used, such as 'middle-income developing countries', but these are reasonably self-explanatory.

2. See International Monetary Fund, *World Economic Outlook*, Washington DC, 1982, Table 29.

3. See Graham Bird and Timothy Orme, 'An Analysis of Drawings on the International Monetary Fund by Developing Countries', *World Development*, June 1981.

4. Graham Bird, 'Financing Balance of Payments Deficits in Developing Countries: The Role of Official and Private Sectors and the Scope for Cooperation between Them', *Third World Quarterly*, July 1981.

5. The *World Economic Outlook*, 1982, reports that 'by far the greater share of Fund financing since 1979 has been provided on terms involving upper credit tranche (or high) conditionality. More than three-quarters of the Fund's financial commitments during 1980 and 1981 were made in support of programmes involving rigorous adjustment efforts. By contrast, in the period following the oil price increases of 1973–4, approximately two thirds of the resources provided by the Fund to member countries were made available on terms involving a low degree of conditionality.'

6. T.M. Reichmann and R. Stillson, 'Experience with Programmes of Balance of Payments Adjustment: Standby Arrangement in the Higher Credit Tranches', *IMF Staff Papers*, June 1978; and T.M. Reichmann, 'The Fund's Conditional Assistance and the Problems of Adjustment', *Finance and Development*, December 1978.

7. Mohsin S. Khan and Malcolm D. Knight, 'Stabilization in Developing Countries: A Formal Framework', *IMF Staff Papers*, March 1981.

8. Carl P. Blackwell, 'Monetary Approach to Balance of Payments Needs Blending with Other Lines of Analysis', *IMF Survey*, 20 February and 6 March 1978.

9. See T. Killick et al., *The Quest for Stabilization: the IMF and the Third World*,

London, ODI and Heinemann Educational Books, 1984, chap. 6.

10. Out of a sample of thirty IMF programmes, there were ten cases where over-expansionary demand was not mentioned as a principal cause of payments problems, and in six of these cases it was not even regarded as a secondary cause. However, there did not appear to be any reduced tendency to set credit ceilings in these cases; the ceilings may, of course, have been less tight, but the evidence did not permit a test of this hypothesis. Looking more closely at the three programmes in 1974–9 where excess demand was not seen as either a principal or secondary cause of payments deficits, in only one case did the programme deviate from the conventional demand-side type. This illustrates that, while it is unusual for the Fund to support a supply-side programme, it is not unheard of. For further details see Killick et al., op. cit., chap. 6.

11. For published evidence see W.A. Beveridge and M.R. Kelly, 'Fiscal Content of Financial Programs Supported by Stand-by Arrangements in the Upper-credit Tranches, 1969–78', *IMF Staff Papers* (2), June 1980; T.A. Connors, 'The Apparent Effects of Recent IMF Stabilization Programmes', Federal Reserve System International Finance Discussion Paper No. 135, April 1979; Donal. J. Donovan, 'Macroeconomic Performance and Adjustment under Fund-supported Programmes: the Experience of the Seventies', *IMF Staff Papers*, 29 (2), June 1982; G.C. Johnson and T.M. Reichmann, 'Experience with Stabilization Programmes Supported by Stand-by Arrangements in the Upper-credit Tranches, 1973–75', IMF, unpublished paper, February 1978; T.M. Reichmann, 'The Fund's Conditional Assistance', op. cit., and Reichmann and Stillson, 'Experience with Programmes', op. cit. Chapter 7 of Killick et al. also makes extensive use of unpublished Fund staff assessments, as well as drawing attention to the conceptual and practical difficulties of arriving at a definitive judgement.

12. For a detailed discussion of international banking flows to non-oil developing countries see Morgan Guaranty, *World Financial Markets*, June 1983.

13. The term 'cost minimization' is admittedly being used loosely here, to describe a conceptual framework rather than any precise quantification. We do not intend to imply that all adjustment costs are capable of being measured in value terms.

14. Alejandro Foxley, 'Stabilization policies and their effects on employment and income distribution: a Latin American Perspective', in William R. Cline and Sidney Weintraub (eds), *Economic Stabilization in Developing Countries*, Washington DC, The Brookings Institution, 1981, p. 225.

15. Cf. Killick et al., op. cit.

16. Private banks' assessment of the creditworthiness of the Fund would also depend on their estimation of the Fund's usable resources, its holdings of gold, SDRs and currencies, and the degree of international support for its activities. Certain technical problems would be associated with direct borrowing by the Fund. For instance, its holdings of particular currencies, which could be affected by borrowing, in turn affects countries' access to Fund finance (Morgan Guaranty Trust, 'The Limited Role of the IMF', *World Financial Markets*, April 1982). See Graham Bird, 'Interest Subsidies on International Finance as a Means of Assisting Low-income Countries', paper presented to the Annual Conference of the Development Studies Association, Dublin, 1982, and *World Development*, June 1983, for a discussion of interest rate subsidies.

17. See David A. Brodsky and Gary P. Sampson, 'Gold, Special Drawing Rights and Developing Countries', *Trade and Development*, No. 2, Autumn 1980, and 'Implications of the Effective Revaluation of Reserve Asset Gold: the Case for a Gold Account for Development', *World Development*, July 1981.

18. That gold sales are not neutral with respect to resource flows is insufficient argument when it is recalled that the existing system is not distributionally neutral.

19. See John Williamson, *A New SDR Allocation?*, Washington DC, Institute for International Economics, 1984.

9
Rules and Institutions in the Management of Multi-Country Economies

Tommaso Padoa-Schioppa*

Introduction

Multi-country economies at the crossroads

If we abstract from the presence of actual governments and states, and define an economy as 'a set of economic agents who are engaged in various forms of exchange and interdependencies among themselves, and share a certain number of common interests', it is clear that many economies are 'multi-country', in the sense that their geographic area falls under the jurisdiction of more than one sovereign state.[1] The rules, arrangements, and institutions for multi-country economic cooperation that were created in the 1940s and 1950s at both the world and regional levels have developed the cross-border movement of raw materials, manufactured goods, capital and labour to a degree never reached before, thus enormously contributing to the increase in welfare and the preservation of peace in the past few decades. They have brought the process of integration to such an advanced stage that in our day not only economic well-being, but also economic disturbances and potential crises, are often international by nature.

In the 1930s, the system of fixed exchange rates also acted as a powerful transmission mechanism of crisis from one country to another. When it collapsed, competitive devaluations and trade restrictions aggravated the world depression. The fundamental problem, however, was one of domestic economic management, while international economic integration was still virtually negligible. In contrast, in the 1970s and 1980s, an important part of

* F. Saccomanni, A. Steinherr and L. Tsoukalis have contributed with helpful comments. The views expressed are the sole responsibility of the author.

the problem is not just reflected in the international economy, it is indeed rooted in it. This is the case as regards natural resources, borrowing and lending, exchange rates, trade and even unemployment.

This evolution has profound consequences for the conduct of economic policy. As long as the policy maker concentrates on the national economy, a growing proportion of his problems appear to escape his control because they are determined by exogenous events: changes in oil prices, world interest rates, imported inflation, payments crises, etc. However, what is given at the national level becomes a variable in the wider context, and if the focus shifts all the way to the world economy, then very little is exogenous.

In a rational decision-making process, the international repercussions of national decisions should not be neglected, and for several reasons. First, the instrument-target approach of Meade and Tinbergen shows that it is necessary to have at least as many independent instruments as policy targets in order to ensure that the latter are met. Since, however, what appears to be an independent instrument in a national setting may cease to be so in an international context, coordination is necessary. Second, the impact of a national instrument may in some cases be stronger on a partner country than on the domestic economy. The only way to match domestic instruments with foreign objectives is again via cooperation. Third, as was shown by Cooper,[2] uncoordinated policies, even when eventually capable of achieving their targets, may entail longer adjustments and sometimes oscillatory paths. Coordination can help in shortening the adjustment period and can dampen down oscillations. In short, a multi-country economy can hardly operate efficiently if the range of policy actions does not encompass all the sovereign nations of which such an economy is made up. In fact, no government can keep the economic promises for which it has been elected in the absence of a favourable international environment, i.e. unless compatible and, if possible, complementary promises have been made by other governments in other countries, and there is willingness to play the game cooperatively.

The trouble is that international economic cooperation is not only more necessary today, it is also more difficult to achieve because, with growing interdependence, the existing 'instruments' have become increasingly inadequate to avoid or solve international conflicts. In the monetary field, there was in the past universal acceptance of fixed rates and of the dollar as the international currency; both have been abandoned, and nothing has really taken their place. In the commercial field, the geographical area which is significant for GATT has grown wider than that institution's geographical sphere of influence; in addition, it is almost powerless to deal with a number of trade conflicts. In the area of macro-policies, even the weak infrastructure represented by the common acceptance of the Keynesian paradigm as a basis for cooperative efforts has been lost and not replaced, so that today not only policy objectives, but also doctrines and ideologies, tend to conflict. In a fourth important area, that of capital movements, a fully fledged, largely uncontrolled, international financial system has superseded segmented national markets.

Multi-country economies have thus reached a state of contradiction: on the one side, national sovereignty is formally indisputable and undisputed, and is even 'aggravated' by the deeper involvement of both governments and public opinion in economic matters; on the other side, national sovereignty is increasingly eroded by growing economic interdependence. Such a contradiction cannot, and will not, last for very long. Either the necessary improvements and adjustments will be made in the system of international economic cooperation, or there will be a severe deterioration of commercial and financial relations. Of course, neither the strengthening nor the disintegration of the existing system of multi-country cooperation need occur in a dramatic way. Historic dates such as 9 May 1950 or 15 August 1971 are rather the exception than the rule.

The search for paths along which international economic relationships could evolve towards a better order usually takes one of two approaches. Either specific problems, such as sovereign debt or exchange rates, are singled out in order to identify technical solutions. Or an effort is made to devise comprehensive new arrangements (a 'new Bretton Woods', global negotiations etc.). Neither of these approaches is followed here. Instead, we shall analyse the methods of international cooperation and focus attention on two limited but general issues that are rarely discussed explicitly, and that are nevertheless at the heart of the problem of international cooperation both in the partial and in the systematic approach: the role to be played by *rules*, and the importance to be attached to the evolution of *institutions*. The experience of the present writer is that, more often than is said or even thought, failures in international cooperation depend not so much on conflicts of interests as on conceptions and misconceptions concerning the two key policy 'ingredients' of rules and institutions.

Rules

Opposite trends nationally and internationally

It may be useful to start by commenting briefly on the concepts of rules and discretion.

In a fundamental sense, whenever a choice has to be made between conflicting objectives, judgment and discretion are necessary. From this point of view, all policies are discretionary, and what is called a preference for rules simply reflects a belief that conflicts between objectives are apparent but not real (for example, that there is no trade-off between inflation and unemployment) and that, even when such conflicts do exist, frequent twists in preferences have greater costs, in terms of uncertainty and the risk of mistakes, than benefits in terms of the achievement of final objectives. In a more practical sense, a rules-approach is one in which the responsible agency (the central bank, the budgetary authority, etc.) acts to stay on a predetermined path of so-called intermediate targets, giving to these a kind of priority over final policy objectives.

In no way can it be said that a rule has a stronger legal basis than discretion. For not only are rules often self-imposed but, more importantly, discretion exercised within the law is as lawful as the mere execution of a stringent norm. On the other hand, it is obvious that a rules-approach is only meaningful if the interpretation of the rule is straightforward, since the grey area where interpretation is needed is in practice left to discretion.

In the last fifteen years the place of rules in economic policy has undergone an evolution which seems at first sight surprising. In *domestic* policies the view has gained ground that the area of discretion had grown too wide and that more rules were needed. In monetary matters, this change has taken the form of at least partial abandonment of fine-tuning and adoption of commitments to quantitative targets. An example was the creation in 1981 of the Gold Commission in the United States, with the purpose of examining the possibility of reintroducing a gold standard to stabilize inflation and exchange rates. In budgetary matters, the drift away from discretion has emerged in a revival, as a constitutional requirement, of the classic prescription of balancing the budget. Legislation along such lines has been proposed, for example in the United States and Italy. In both these areas of policy, replacement of discretionary power by rules is deemed necessary to limit both actual and potential mismanagement by the executive power.

In the *international* sphere both opinions and actions have, on the contrary, moved from rules to discretion. This is one of the most significant aspects of the abandonment of fixed exchange rates in 1973. In the early 1970s, under the joint influence of theoretical thinking and difficulties in macroeconomic management, policy makers came to see flexible exchange rates as a way to free domestic choices from international constraints. Since it was recognized from the start that pure floating was an academic abstraction and that some management would always be necessary, a cooperative effort was undertaken to establish the rules of a new international monetary system. In the Committee of Twenty, however, it soon became apparent that no simple set of rules could be defined for a system somewhere in between the extremes of freely flexible and fixed exchange rates. Eventually, the only feasible solution was to forego the establishment of rules and to ask the IMF to carry out surveillance of each country's policies and their impact on exchange markets. Earlier attempts at defining statistical indicators and precise rules to govern intervention in exchange markets had to be abandoned. As stated in the 1980 *Annual Report* of the IMF: 'Surveillance must be judgmental'.

Several explanations can be suggested for the paradox of these opposite trends in the 'rules versus discretion' issue. First, while in the national sphere the need may be felt to protect policy decisions from the pressures of political constituencies, and a reduction in discretion can be seen as a means to this end, in the international sphere such a need does not arise or at least is not apparent. Thus, it could be argued that the reduced involvement of national interest groups in the international sphere is both an advantage and a disadvantage: it facilitates efficient and rational decision-making in the pursuit of global welfare, but it may be seen as an element of weakness in the process of democratic control.

Second, in the early 1970s, the situations in the domestic and in the international spheres were almost exactly opposite: considerable discretion in the former, many rules in the latter. It was natural, and perhaps appropriate, to interpret the increasing problems of the time as the joint result of misuse of domestic discretion and excessive rigidity of international rules.

Finally, the complexity reached in the international economy and the decline of a dominant power, accompanied by a much increased number of actors and a fully integrated international capital market, all contributed to the demise of the fixed parity system. These same factors also made it exceedingly difficult, both technically and

politically, to formulate a new alternative rule. *Ad hoc* arrangements
and largely discretionary interpretation of loose policy prescriptions
came to be regarded as the road to wisdom.

Beyond these special circumstances, there is also the more general
fact that the government function is perceived in very different ways
in a national and in an international framework. In the former, a shift
from discretion to rule appears to be a way to less government; in the
latter, a way to more of it.

Why more discretion is needed

Various arguments suggest that nowadays the management of multi-
country economies requires a widening of the scope for discretionary
decisions and a more efficient method of taking such decisions, in
some instances replacing rules, but more generally as a complement
to them.

The first consideration refers to the crucial area of exchange rates.
It is widely agreed that neither fixed nor perfectly floating rates are
viable solutions for the future. Unfortunately these two regimes
happen to be the only simple and unambiguous rules that can be
devised. What lies between them is an interplay between private,
profit-oriented agents and public, policy-oriented institutions, with
discretionary management as the critical factor. The essential point
is that, in an interdependent world, floating must be managed *jointly*
and discretion has therefore to be *joint* discretion. There is no
practical possibility of framing and disciplining managed floating in
such a way that, by complying with a certain number of simple rules,
careful and judgmental consideration of the interest of the partners
on a case-by-case basis becomes unnecessary.

A second, related point concerns the coordination of
macroeconomic policies. In its heyday, the rule of fixed rates was
largely sufficient, with the help of a stable, dominant and scarcely
open US economy, to enforce an acceptable degree of *de facto* policy
coordination. In a polycentric world of managed floating, the
process is much more complex and requires the discussion of a wide
range of instruments and policies, including the balance of
payments, interest rates, and budgetary and incomes policies. Each
of these variables has a place in the deliberations of national policy
makers; each has direct or indirect influence on other countries. In a
multi-country economy they form a matrix which is much too
complex to be governed by a simple rule. Setting priorities, weighing
the relative importance of different variables, making intertemporal

choices, and deciding which countries should act, are problems that only judgment can solve.

The increased probability of unforeseen events and disturbances of worldwide magnitude requiring a prompt policy reaction is a third reason. Here economic actions are often foreign policy instruments, when they are not substitutes for military intervention: oil embargoes, freezings of assets, economic sanctions, etc. In a world that is more divided politically and strategically than it is economically, this is perhaps inevitable. And since the opposing camps are themselves conglomerates of sovereign countries, often without clearly established internal leadership (the Arab League, the NATO countries, the non-aligned countries, etc.), the possibility of taking discretionary decisions at a national level does not automatically produce consistent action by any group of countries.

A fourth and final consideration is that in certain areas an integral part of a policy may consist in leaving economic agents in uncertainty as to whether public authorities will intervene or not. A major example, one that international conditions today and in the foreseeable future make particularly important, concerns the function of lender of last resort. There must be one, but its interventions should not be taken for granted; that is, they must be discretionary.

To sum up, a movement from rules to discretion in the management of multi-country economies is in many ways necessary, because it corresponds to the nature of the problems which have to be dealt with in the present situation. Seen from this point of view, developments that have taken place in more recent years point in the right direction. But greater reliance on discretion does not mean that the management function in a multi-country economy has to be weakened or softened. On the contrary, it means that it has to be made stronger, more effective and more adaptable to complex and unforeseen situations. In this sense, there are good reasons to question whether the evolution that we have witnessed has really entailed a sharpening of multi-country management actions or, on the contrary, a loosening of the already too loose arrangements we used to have. This leads us to the problem of institutions.

Institutions

Institutions and cooperation

The *Concise Oxford Dictionary* defines an institution as follows: 'established law, custom, or practice; organization for promotion of some public object; buildings used by this'. This suggests the possibility of a great variety of organizational forms, with the solemnity of a comprehensive and written constitution not being absolutely essential. To be sure, the 'promotion of a public object' can occur in an efficient and systematic way through uncodified cooperation, and this 'practice' may become sufficiently 'established' to deserve the name of institution. In the international sphere, such an informal approach was the pre-1914 gold standard; an example of a formal institution, based on an international treaty, is the Bretton Woods system. It is the difference between these two approaches to monetary organization that Keynes was implicitly stressing at the end of the Bretton Woods conference, in his wry remarks about the American habit of always negotiating with the help of an army of lawyers.

True, institutions are instruments of organized cooperation; and well-established cooperation can be seen as a kind of institution. However, such common elements should not generate misunderstandings. Indeed, it is essential to be fully aware of the sharp borderline between an 'institutional' and an *ad hoc* approach to cooperation.

Ad hoc cooperation is a method by which partners meet, discuss, and, *if* they agree, act together. If they do not agree, they will skilfully draft a press communiqué to present to the public the sense of a joint commitment to general values and goals, and then return to their respective capitals to conduct, within the limits of their national autonomy and strength, mutually inconsistent and possibly conflicting policies. The history of the last ten years provides numerous examples of both these possible outcomes, perhaps more of the latter than of the former.[3]

Institutionalized cooperation starts where the *ad hoc* approach ends. It ensures that decisions and actions will be taken *at the system level* even if the parties fail to agree. In other words, it guarantees not that the right *decisions* will be taken, but that decisions will be taken at the right *level*: in our case, this means the level of the multi-country economy, as defined above, whose contribution to the 'public good' is sought.

The distinction between institutionalized and *ad hoc* cooperation is particularly important in the international sphere, where failure to agree on a common course of action means unilateral, uncoordinated, and probably conflicting actions by the individual parties. The danger of confusion is specially great today, now that the practice of international consultations (in Committees, Councils,

Conferences, Summits, etc.) has been largely 'institutionalized', giving the public the impression that a form of international management does exist.

It is worth noting that the institutional approach is superior not only to unsuccessful but also to successful *ad hoc* cooperation, because it is more permanent and more certain in character. The institutional approach is defined by the rules on which it is based, for example allowing decisions to be taken by majority voting rather than by the unanimity which so often hampers the effectiveness of cooperation. With cooperation, the existence of a public good has to be acknowledged anew every time, so that its realization is difficult. With an institution this existence is assumed.

To be effective, an international institution requires the transfer of some power from the national to the international level. This, however, does not mean that nations have to *surrender* control of the area of competence concerned. They will continue to exercise this control at a different level, that is, within the multi-country institutions. It does not imply either that control is a zero-sum game, so that what is gained at one level is lost at another. On the contrary, if the principle of establishing management at the lowest possible level is observed, the very purpose of an international institution is to *regain* control over phenomena which, due to increasing interdependence, would otherwise escape what is deemed to be a necessary management function.

Why institutions should be strengthened

The simple reason why, at the present stage of the evolution of multi-country economies, a satisfactory performance of the minimum functions of management requires a strengthening of institutions, is that the alternative method, namely, *ad hoc* cooperation, is bound to fail in too high a proportion of cases. This is due to many causes.

In the first place, as has been argued above, the areas involving a genuine common interest of the multi-country economy which require *discretionary acts of policy* rather than the mechanical application of rules, have become wider. Even at their best, cooperative methods are in general too slow to produce the necessary decisions at the right time. Notwithstanding the good intentions of the partners, the process of defining a course of collective action rarely meets the deadlines set by the pace of economic reality. As a consequence, action is taken at the lower, suboptimal level of the nation state, thus creating welfare losses and unnecessary frictions. Cooperation fails because the machinery of high-level diplomacy between nation states is congested.

Furthermore, *cooperative methods rarely operate at their best.* Their performance lies in the hands of two professions, officials and politicians, who are subjected to the severe constraints of local constituencies, even when they personally have a truly cosmopolitan outlook and a genuine willingness to cooperate. The electorate, particularly in periods of recession, is generally more in favour of selfish inward-looking measures than either ministers or officials. Top officials are usually engaged on the domestic front, and sometimes regard activity on the international side as a waste of time and those in charge of it as too prone to compromise and to grant concessions.

The *process of educating officials* involved in international negotiation takes time. Indeed, the success of a cooperative approach very much depends on the personal relationships between those involved in the process and on their familiarity with the values and traditions of this particular 'branch of government'. Today, however, political instability has so accelerated the turnover of governments and high-ranking officials, that the training process often fails even to maintain the existing degree of know-how and willingness to cooperate. The result is an erosion of the capital of international goodwill that is necessary for efficient *ad hoc* cooperation.

Compromises in the *ad hoc* cooperative framework are also becoming more difficult because the number of *negotiating parties* grows with the number of nation states and the wider participation in international bodies. It has been said that the Bretton Woods conference was a meeting of 'one and a half' countries; the IMF now gathers together close on 150 nations. The difficulty of large group negotiation is compounded by the increasing spread of interest positions among countries, particularly during periods of economic recession. Economic summit meetings between the heads of governments of the seven major Western countries illustrate the difficulty of reaching decisions even among a small number of countries. When these decisions are announced, their interpretation immediately becomes controversial and their acceptance by those excluded remains a problem.

Also, the *information base* for decision-making is becoming so complex and controversial that cooperation is increasingly suffering from a well-known dilemma: those who have the authority and vision to judge and decide do not sufficiently master the details of the problem, while those who have 'studied the dossier' often have too weak and narrow a perception of the need and urgency to reach agreement. This is particularly so when economic problems are strongly interconnected. Recent years show examples both of how it is virtually impossible to arrive at a synthesis of issues in meetings where specialists assemble and of Summits where heads of state willing to compromise get lost in the details.

Finally, what policy makers increasingly have to face are international *problems at the intersection of different areas* rather than problems pertaining to one area alone: trade and exchange rates, exchange rates and financing, financing and aid, etc. Yet both *ad hoc* cooperation and the existing system of international institutions are highly specialized and offer very few possibilities of negotiating 'packages' involving different areas. The Summits of the seven Western industrial countries are a notable exception, with the promotion of interdepartmental cooperation nationally as well as internationally. Unfortunately, however, they suffer from other drawbacks: congestion of problems relative to the time available for dealing with them, lack of a 'central' independent body entitled to speak for the common interest, absence of essential partners such as developing countries or OPEC, preference for publicity rather than substance.

Even if the above seem quite compelling arguments, it is nevertheless worth considering the popular objections to the main contention that international institutions should be strengthened. Though phrased in many different ways, they all boil down to questioning either the need for or the possibility of building stronger institutions.

As to *need*, the argument is usually formulated by saying that if every country keeps its own house in order, international order will automatically follow. In a weaker form, the priority of domestic order is advocated. In either form, these objections ignore not only interdependence, but also the fact that 'order', far from being a single valued variable, is the very object of political choice in a democratic society. The flaw in the 'own house in order' argument is that it presents a necessary condition as a sufficient one. In practice, its strength lies in the fact that it is generally used by large strong economies to justify a certain disregard for the consequences that their policies may have on other countries.

As to *possibility*, it is of course an open question whether it is realistic to pursue the objective of strengthening international institutions at a time when so many wise men have relegated supranationalism to the attic of post-war dreams. One should not forget, however, that institutions also change without requiring dramatic moves or even new legislation. In many instances institutions are simply reshaped by the changing nature of the problems confronting them. Some claim that a recent example of such a change is the new role played by the BIS in arranging bridging operations for debtor countries in liquidity difficulties. Since such systemic changes can take place independently of each nation's will, it would certainly be preferable to control them rationally rather than to accept the force of events. Nor should it be feared that changing an institution takes too much time. Even if that were the case, it would be better to advance late than never. But, more importantly, this is *not* the case. What takes time is the negotiation on details. Historical experience shows that systemic changes are negotiated quickly because what makes them possible are special political, or crisis, circumstances which usually do not obtain for very long. The Bretton Woods conference lasted a few weeks. The EMS was set up in about six months. In contrast, an EC negotiation to harmonize technical norms on rear reflectors of automobiles may take years.

One final word is perhaps in order to counter a common criticism raised as regards the performance of existing international institutions, namely, that they are not, after all, so much better nor so much more efficient than the gatherings of national leaders practising *ad hoc* cooperation. The answer to that criticism is simply to admit that it is true. Indeed, present-day institutions, inasmuch as they are not really given the charters, the powers and the instruments to follow a genuinely institutional approach, are bound to fall back into the *ad hoc* pattern and to act as an additional partner in the exercise of *ad hoc* cooperation. Thus, the ultimate sense of the prescription to strengthen international institutions is that of setting in motion a process whereby they are given the means to play their proper institutional role.

Examples in international money and finance

The questions examined above are particularly relevant in the field of international money and finance, and for several reasons. Monetary and financial intermediation are areas where governments and public authorities have always played an important role, and interdependence, particularly in exchange rates, is there by definition. Also, in the last two decades the process of internationalization has been particularly rapid in financial matters. Moreover, the evolution of financial markets, institutions, and instruments has been extremely rapid and has posed new problems for the role of governments. Finally, the dissociation between savings and investments has come so much to involve countries as well as individual economic agents that the process of financial intermediation has become genuinely international.

Exchange rates among large currencies

Exchange rate relationships between major currencies are perhaps the outstanding example in the last twenty years of the difficult search for the right balance between rules and discretion, on the one hand, and between the cooperative and the institutional approach, on the other.

In the pre-1971 system, the borderline between rules and discretion was drawn in such a way as to leave a large role to the rule of fixed rates and a small one to the discretion of changes in parities, a discretion that tended to be exercised at the national rather than the international level. The consequence was that rules tended first to be too rigidly followed and then to be broken. Under that regime real exchange rates moved a long way from plausible equilibrium levels because of insufficient, rather than excessive, mobility of nominal exchange rates. When par values were changed, as happened with the pound sterling, the Deutschmark, and the French franc, they tended to move too late. More importantly, those changes were essentially the result of unilateral decisions taken by the countries concerned, with the IMF providing little more than a formal ratification.

The Bretton Woods system would have functioned more efficiently, and perhaps would have not collapsed, if parity changes had been more timely and multilateral in nature. Ideally, multilateralism and the central institutions should have exerted greater pressure to enforce changes in parity, and in the price of gold, on countries which were reluctant to undertake them. But the system had been created out of the experience of the 1930s, in which exchange rate mobility had been abused, and it had an implicit bias in favour of fixed rates. The area of discretion was embodied in the rather loose concept of 'fundamental disequilibrium'. Thus, the combination of a weak institutional framework and the stigma associated with the condition of fundamental disequilibrium, particularly for deficit, high-inflation countries, produced the excessive rigidity that eventually led to the breakdown of the system.

August 1971 was followed by the attempt to establish new parities and to reform the international monetary system. Both failed on the critical front on which the pre-1971 system had also failed, namely, the establishment of an efficient mix of rules and discretion on the one hand, and of *ad hoc* and institutional cooperation on the other. As regards the Smithsonian parities, they came under increasing pressure, and when the pressure became unbearable the outcome was a regime of floating rates rather than a realignment.

As to the reform of the international monetary system, the long and difficult work of the Committee of Twenty produced a regime which can be seen as the 'negative' of the pre-1971 situation: discretion and rule have, so to speak, exchanged roles. In the post-1973 situation the variability of exchange rates has become the multilateral rule, while 'discipline' has become the object of unilateral discretion. In other words, the lesson drawn from the period up to 1973 has been that the multi-country economy should not aim at any form of declared, negotiated, and defended parities. Rather, it had to accept 'realistically' the impossibility of returning to a par value system and try to avoid exchange rate manipulation for trade purposes by the members of the system. The avoidance of such dangers was entrusted formally to IMF surveillance, and in practice to what came to be called the Library Group and later the Group of Five.

Ten years of experience with these arrangements have convinced both economists and policy makers that the new 'order' is not satisfactory. Inflation, protectionist pressures, uncertainties and inefficiencies in the allocative process are among the consequences of the long and profound cycles in real exchange rates that have been experienced. Between minimum and maximum levels real exchange rates have moved by 60 per cent for the British pound, 40 per cent for the dollar and the yen, and 20 per cent for the Deutschmark. One could almost say that the pre-1971 and the post-1973 systems have paradoxically produced the same result of protracted misalignments of real exchange rates. This paradox ceases to exist if it is recognized that, seen from the points of view of the 'rules versus discretion' and of the 'institutional versus *ad hoc* cooperation' approaches, they largely belong to the same category. They both fail to offer a satisfactory solution to the problem of multilateral discretionality.

One could almost go so far as to say that if this central problem had been fully resolved, the functioning of the two systems would have produced essentially the same results. In one case, discretion would have been used to reduce exchange rate rigidities associated with a fixed parity system; in the other, it would have been used to reduce excessive movements associated with a floating system.

Historical events can be read in several ways, which are not necessarily mutually exclusive. The interpretation suggested here for the experience of the last decade and a half of monetary cooperation is not that the Bretton Woods rule at some point became inappropriate and that the Committee of Twenty later failed to invent a new, more appropriate one. The movement from rule to discretion was unavoidable, and it could have taken place even under the old Articles of Agreement of the IMF. Similarly, the new, looser rule incorporated in the amended Articles of Agreement was, again, probably appropriate insofar as it recognized, at the normative level, the need for greater discretion. In both cases what was missing was the exercise of the required discretion, and this was due, in both cases, to a fundamental weakness of the institution which should have practised this discretionality. This does not mean that the decisions taken would always have been the right ones, just as policy decisions taken at the national level are not always the right ones. Nor does it mean that the institution had necessarily to be a formal one, working on the basis of formal legislation.

The outcome of the 1973–6 reform negotiations is not the technical failure of the Committee of Twenty to devise a new rule. It is the political failure of the major countries to devise efficient institutions. The talents and powers of the great men of the 1970s were deployed to manage an unviable system skilfully rather than to create a better one. And one cannot help feeling a sense of lost opportunities both in seeing the state of cooperation among the major world currencies today and in reading the reassessment of the past and the proposals for the future that are now offered by those same men. The wisdom of the saying 'do not bequeath ideals, bequeath institutions' has been lost at a crucial time.

European monetary cooperation

The evolution of European monetary cooperation over the same period has followed a somewhat different pattern and is, on the whole, more of a success story.

Compared to the world system, the European system perhaps

presents more differences than analogies. Most of these differences turned out to have a favourable influence on the process of monetary cooperation. Firstly, the Community institutions are equipped to take decisions, and to introduce important institutional innovations, by means of procedures which are much simpler than those required at the world level. For example, the 'snake', the European Monetary Cooperation Fund, and the EMS were all created by a decision taken at the level of Ministers and Central Bank Governors, without any process of parliamentary ratification. This is due to the considerable powers that the Treaty of Rome grants to the Community institutions, and to the Council of Ministers in particular. Moreover, no country in the Community has a parliament which limits the negotiating ability of the executive so much as the Congress does with the Administration in the United States.

Secondly, economic integration between Community countries is both wider and deeper than economic integration worldwide. The interdependence between monetary, trade, financial and macroeconomic cooperation is much more evident. Policy conflicts and inconsistencies emerge and develop their negative consequences faster in the tight Community system than in the rather loose international context. Thus, the Community perceived the dangers that its trade relationships were running because of the lack of a commonly agreed monetary order some years before this same danger became evident at the world level.

Thirdly, the problem of leadership manifests itself in rather different terms at the Community and the world levels. At the latter, after a long period of almost unquestioned domination, the United States has reached a position in which it does not have the power to impose its solutions to problems, but it does have enough power to prevent solutions which it dislikes. In Europe there is greater balance, so that the need for compromise is fully recognized.

If these three elements tend to give the Community a certain advantage over the world system, a fourth one, more specific to the monetary field, tends to be a source of complication. This is the fact that European monetary integration around one of the member currencies is far more difficult than an equivalent aggregation around the dollar. The Deutschmark, which could be regarded as the natural candidate, dominates the European monetary scene much less than the dollar does in the world context. Moreover, the German authorities have long been reluctant to let their currency play a major international role. And other large European countries would be unwilling to accept a DM-based system.

For Europe, as for the world, the problem of monetary cooperation is essentially one involving the leading currencies of the area. Small countries, which are in general relatively more open, tend to peg to leading currencies anyway. Indeed, more than fifty countries are currently pegging their currencies formally to a major currency; two-thirds of them are pegged to the dollar.

In the period up to 1978 the West European countries, taken as a group, pursued two inconsistent paths: full independence in macroeconomic policies, and the creation of a system of stable intra-Community exchange rates. The first path prevailed over the second. While Germany and some small countries like Austria, the Netherlands, Belgium, and Switzerland, were successful in keeping inflation under control, France, the United Kingdom and Italy experienced long periods of double-digit inflation (reaching for the last two countries levels of more than 20 per cent), made periodic attempts to stabilize prices, and never succeeded in participating in an exchange rate system for more than relatively short periods. Moreover, the exchange rate 'system' was probably conceived too much in a 'Bretton Woods way' to be realistic. The idea of a rigid rule was implicitly dominant. That of an institution capable of discretionary decisions did not emerge.

From March 1976 to March 1979 the snake became a system of small currencies pegged to the Deutschmark. It had thus failed to link together the major European currencies, but it played an essential role in preparing for the EMS. Not only did it show that a regional system of declared and defended parities could function even in the post-Bretton Woods era, but, more importantly, it provided a first test of the special blend of rules and multilateral discretion that was later, and in more difficult circumstances, going to characterize the EMS.

The EMS is too recent to require more than a brief mention. The analogy of its provisions with the Bretton Woods arrangements, and the wide divergence of inflation rates in Europe, explain the scepticism with which it was hailed in some quarters. And had it been known in 1978 that the following years were going to be troubled by a second oil shock, a dollar shock, the longest recession of the postwar period, continuous trade frictions and a debt crisis, not only would the scepticism have been much greater, but perhaps the founding fathers would not have had the courage to undertake what was considered a bold initiative even with the expectation of a more stable environment.

The EMS has succeeded in supporting intra-Community trade

with a sufficient degree of monetary order, in reducing exchange rate variability, and in exerting a reasonable, though not decisive, pressure on national governments to orient macro-policies towards monetary stability and coordination. In all the EMS countries growth rates in monetary aggregates were lower in 1978–82 than in 1974–8. Moreover, since the inception of the EMS there has been a significant increase in the correlation between the interest rate movements of the participating countries. Central rate decisions have become truly collective decisions, rather than multilateral ratifications of unilateral decisions: the system has achieved here something that Bretton Woods probably never achieved. Moreover, it has become increasingly the case that parity changes are accompanied by important changes in other aspects of economic policy. Realignments have not been unduly delayed, and when they were delayed, this was basically justified by the need to reach the point in which a country's domestic situation made it politically possible to accompany a realignment with a meaningful policy change.

The EMS has obtained these results by combining rules and discretion, by distributing decision-making powers between the national and the supranational level, and by linking trade, macro-economic and monetary considerations in a way that can be, *ex post*, recognized as more balanced and more efficient than perhaps any of the other experiences in multi-country economies over the last fifteen years. Of course, the fundamental incompatibility between unrestrained national sovereignty in fiscal and monetary policy and *de facto* capital mobility and supranationalism in trade and exchange rates remains. From this point of view the EMS has not fundamentally corrected the precarious nature of the management of a multi-country economy. This also suggests that it is not realistic to blame the EMS for the still insufficient degree of economic convergence among Community countries. But the fact remains that the EMS has been quite successful in linking discretion with institutionalized cooperation in a world in which discretion tends to go with uni-lateralism and cooperation tends to be sought by way of rules.

Conclusion

For more than twenty years multi-country economies, as measured by world trade and international financial intermediation, have grown at about twice the speed of national economies, as measured by GDP and 'domestic' financial assets. This extraordinary dynamism has enabled them to evolve out of the systemic problems arising from the coexistence of sovereign powers. It has reduced conflicts. It has enlarged vested interest in the maintenance of open trade. It has fully developed not only the potential of the arrangements and institutions created in the 1940s and in the 1950s, but also the opportunities offered by a certain lack of arrangements and institutions. It has concealed the shortcomings and the lacunae of the instruments available for the management of multi-country economies.

The wide divergence between these two speeds of growth cannot fail to be a transitory phenomenon, one that lasts the time needed to fill the gaps due to pre-existing trade and financial barriers. As long as it is under way, the process of removing these barriers which was initiated at some point in the past continues to play the role of an act of government, replacing in some way active management of the multi-country economy. When this function is exhausted and the multi-country economy's growth rate tends to slow down to that of national economies, it will become clear that, while national economies often have an excess of government, multi-country economies have too little of it.

In difficult times, when risks, uncertainties, and conflicts are experienced in trade and financial relationships, the same economic agents which benefited so much from the removal of barriers and from international economic integration, themselves turn to 'governmental' powers for support and protection. Today, governmental powers are only national. With the exception of the European Communities, there is no multi-country economic power to which an individual economic agent can address itself directly. The almost inevitable consequence is that government interventions in support of the economy tend to have a protectionist character and to erode the capital of international cooperation and goodwill. Here is where the process of multi-country economic integration could easily go into reverse: in the 1930s it took only four years for world trade to shrink from three to one million gold dollars.

This chapter suggests that an important condition for avoiding the danger of disintegration is to accept the movement from rules to discretion that has characterized the evolution of international economic relationships in the last decade, but also firmly to establish the exercise of discretion at the level of the multi-country economy concerned, rather than letting it fall to the level of national economies. As an official, the present writer is acutely aware of the enormous, almost insurmountable difficulty of progressing in the direction suggested. Caution, realism, awareness of the narrow limits of what is concretely possible, are indispensable instruments of any successful action. However, they do not replace the sense of what is the necessary direction and this has been the concern of this chapter.

Notes

1. The world itself is a multi-country economy, as common interests are embodied in the existence of world trade and of worldwide financial relationships. 'Tighter' multi-country economies can be identified at lower levels, by considering dimensions of common interest such as geographical proximity, similarity of political and economic institutions, complementarity in natural endowments, common history etc. Canada and the United States, Luxemburg and Belgium, OPEC, Scandinavia are thus more integrated multi-country economies than the world, or the American or the European continent. Largely non-integrated areas may gradually give rise to an 'economy' following political and institutional events, as happened for Sicily and Piedmont after the unification of Italy. Alternatively, an economy may exist and function, albeit in a precarious way, without the benefit of political institutions, as happened for Alsace–Lorraine–Saar–Luxemburg–Wallonia. Indeed, the relationship between economic and political-institutional integration is a two-way relationship. International arrangements and rules (IMF, GATT, etc.) may initially only reflect the existence of multi-country economies, but they help in providing additional coherence, integration and common interests. The example of a multi-country economy which has developed its organization almost to the point of giving rise to a fully-fledged institutional system is the European Community.

2. Richard N. Cooper, 'Macroeconomic Policy Adjustment in Interdependent Economies', *The Quarterly Journal of Economics*, February 1969.

3. See Kenneth W. Dam, 'The Role of Rules in the International Monetary System', Miami, Law and Economics Center Monograph, 1976. Dam argued strongly in favour of what he calls the cooperative approach based on an analysis of the reform of the international monetary system after the disintegration of the Bretton Woods system. He points out that the divergence of interests and of views between the United States and the major European countries was too pronounced for agreement on a new set of rules of general and durable applicability. He argues that, in addition, the complexity of the negotiation was such that the constitution-drafting approach would have taken much too long. In his view 'cooperation' was not simply the only feasible approach but also one with a degree of flexibility absent from the constitution-drafting approach. Dam concludes by theorizing about 'Group of Five' type of meetings as the appropriate post-Bretton Woods 'system'. To clarify the terminology: Dam's 'cooperation' is our '*ad hoc* cooperation'; and his 'constitution-drafting approach' is our 'rule'. 'Discretion plus institutions' is not considered. For the depth and quality of his analysis Dam is the outstanding example of the common failure to distinguish

between the two issues of 'rules versus discretion' and '*ad hoc* versus institutionalized cooperation'. The result is that a single line of reasoning is used to reach what seems to us a desirable conclusion on the first issue and an undesirable conclusion on the second.

10
The New International Monetary 'System' and Prospects for Reform
Loukas Tsoukalis

The Bretton Woods conference of 1944 produced a set of basic rules intended to provide the framework within which monetary relations among sovereign countries would take place. They were a form of written constitution, and the International Monetary Fund was designed to ensure its everyday application. The Bretton Woods system was an integral and indeed absolutely crucial part of the postwar effort, led by the United States, to liberalize international economic relations on a multilateral basis. Yet it was also built on a clear assumption that, as regards monetary affairs, the invisible hand of the market had to be firmly guided by national public authorities and international institutions. Monetary systems in the past had developed in a more spontaneous and gradual way; Bretton Woods, on the contrary, signified a conscious attempt to design a new international system which would remain under collective management.

The common rules agreed were neither comprehensive nor inflexible. As with any written constitution, their interpretation and application were to a large extent a function of the objective needs and the prevailing balance of power in the system itself. The rules regarding the creation of liquidity were highly inadequate; thus, the provision of international liquidity through the monetization of US balance of payments deficits was not the result of a conscious design. Similarly, the asymmetry which appeared in terms of balance of payments adjustment between surplus and deficit countries was not the inevitable outcome of jointly agreed rules. It was more a reflection of the practical difficulties encountered in applying the rules which had been intended to ensure such symmetry.

The post-war international monetary system lasted for about two and a half decades. It coincided with an unprecedented period of growth and stability in the world economy, and both came to an end at about the same time. It is impossible to separate clearly cause from effect. However, in the view of the majority of economists, and despite the recent rewriting of history by the radical right, the Bretton Woods system has contributed significantly to the post-war economic boom and the liberalization of international economic relations.

The emerging new 'system'

The international monetary system was radically transformed during the 1970s. The first important turning-point came in August 1971 when the US Administration unilaterally decided to end the convertibility of the US dollar into gold, which had been one of the main pillars of the post-war system. This convertibility had, in fact, for some years before 1971 been a myth; it was able to survive only so long as the main holders of dollar assets refrained from exercising their formal right to demand convertibility into gold. In August 1971 the Nixon Administration decided to remove the sword of Damocles hanging over the Federal Reserve. The official end of dollar convertibility was also the first step in a US campaign to demonetize gold completely.

Gold became the subject of a long and often acrimonious debate, with the Americans and the French playing the role of protagonists. It seemed like a continuation of the 1960s debate, but the issues involved and the policies pursued by the interested parties were very different. In a period characterized by large balance of payments disequilibria, resulting from the oil price increase of 1973, the main issue concerned the role which gold reserves would play in financing the payments deficits of the industrialized countries. The compromise which was finally reached formed part of the Jamaica agreement of 1976 and the subsequent Second Amendment of the IMF Articles of Agreement. The official price of gold was abolished and with it all its monetary uses by the Fund. One-sixth of the gold holdings of the IMF were to be returned to member countries and another one-sixth to be auctioned, with the profits going to a Trust Fund for developing countries. Finally, central banks were allowed to buy and sell gold to each other at mutually acceptable prices.

For the Americans, the agreement was supposed to lead to the demonetization of gold, while for the French 'l'or s'est banalisé'. The meaning of the two interpretations was substantially different, and so were the expectations held by the two sides. Gold has remained stored in the vaults of central banks which have been extremely reluctant to use it, except *in extremis* as collateral, for balance of payments financing. In some respects, it can be regarded as an asset of last resort. It has so far played a marginal and passive role, but it can certainly not be ignored. Gold reserves of central banks valued at market prices account for more than half their official reserves. Moreover, demand for gold very much depends on current inflation and interest rates as well as on expectations about the future. More generally, it depends on the degree of confidence in the stability of the international financial system. Thus, it may well be too early to relegate gold to the relics of monetary history.

The suspension of dollar-gold convertibility led to the *de facto* establishment of a dollar standard. Despite long periods of weakness of the US currency and the high degree of instability in exchange markets, there has been remarkably little shift to other national currencies or composite units in terms of invoicing practices in international trade and the asset composition of commercial and central banks. Some diversification away from the dollar did take place, and this led to the emergence of a multiple currency standard as described by Thygesen in Chapter 5. However, this diversification has been rather limited, and the dollar still remains by far the most important international unit of account, means of payment and store of value. The process of diversification has in fact been reversed during the recent period of strength of the US currency, associated at least partly with high nominal and real interest rates. But a new period of dollar weakness could well be accompanied again by a frantic search for alternative means of payment and stores of value. It is in such times that the inherent instability of a multiple currency standard becomes pronounced.

Fixed exchange rates, the other main pillar of the Bretton Woods edifice, were abandoned in March 1973, when most of the major currencies were floated against each other. This was presented at the time as a temporary expedient, with governments giving in temporarily to market pressures. The objective, shared by the large majority of both officials and academics and reiterated in the Committee of Twenty reform negotiations, remained the establishment of fixed but adjustable exchange rates, although differences still persisted as to how 'fixed' and how 'adjustable' those rates should be. Virtually everybody seemed to agree that the pre-1971 system had been too rigid and that more flexibility was desirable. However, the form and degree of flexibility still remained to be settled.

With the benefit of hindsight, the discussions and sometimes the haggling over exchange rates, which characterized the early 1970s, have proved to be largely irrelevant. The temporary expedient was finally legalized in Jamaica in 1976 and was later incorporated in the IMF Articles of Agreement. Floating was now legal; in fact any exchange rate system that a member country cared to choose. The legalization of floating was, however, accompanied by recognition of the need for some degree of management of exchange rates and for joint supervision of the policies pursued by member countries which might directly or indirectly influence exchange rates. Hence, the surveillance function entrusted to the Fund. But the rules governing surveillance inevitably remained vague and non-operational. Officials of the IMF have often insisted that surveillance needs to be exercised with discretion and it may, therefore, be underestimated by outside observers. Nevertheless, developments in exchange markets in recent years have raised serious doubts about the ability of the Fund to exercise real influence over the exchange rate policies of countries which are not dependent on it for conditional finance.

Floating has been neither clean nor universal. Very few governments have been prepared to allow the market free rein over the external value of their currency, and most have adopted over the period some form of exchange rate target. Therefore, floating became 'dirty' or 'managed', but without any jointly accepted rules of conduct. On the other hand, many countries have decided to peg or loosely link their currency to another (such as the US dollar or the French franc), while others have formed regional exchange rate arrangements of which the European Monetary System is by far the most important.

Another important qualitative change which took place in the 1970s but which, unlike the other two mentioned above, did not necessitate any re-writing of rules, is the partial privatization of the creation of international liquidity. This happened through the large-scale financing of balance of payments deficits which followed the 1973 oil price increase. The growth of international credit and capital markets, which developed outside the control of national authorities, had started much earlier. But 1973 was a turning-point into a new era marked by exponential growth. This has had a dramatic effect on international monetary and also trade relations. The role of international banking has drastically changed the trade-off between adjustment and financing of payments deficits. It has also contributed, although this is still debatable, to the explosion of international liquidity during the 1970s and its subsequent contraction, as well as to world inflation. It has turned international liquidity into a more endogenous or demand-determined variable. And up to 1980, it also helped to marginalize the IMF in its role as a provider of short-term balance of payments finance and thus indirectly in its influence over the adjustment process.

Since 1980, and as a result of a combination of events ranging from high interest rates to economic recession and protectionism, the world has been reaping the fruits of the seeds which had been very profitably sown by international banks, with a great deal of official encouragement, back in the 1970s. The development of the international debt crisis has raised serious questions about the stability of the Western financial system. Old problems have also resurfaced, such as the regulation of international credit and capital markets and the issue of the lender of last resort. On the other hand, the attempt to manage the crisis has produced a new kind of 'cooperative' relationship among commercial banks as well as between central banks, commercial banks and international organizations such as the IMF and the BIS.

Although the international monetary system went through a radical transformation in the 1970s, some observers would still refuse to talk in terms of a collapse of the post-war order, because of the survival of some important elements that constituted the original Bretton Woods system. Market convertibility remained; in fact, in the case of many industrialized countries it was extended in recent years to capital transactions. On the other hand, some form of multilateral management of the system was preserved, although the role played by the IMF, and international cooperation in general, were inevitably affected by the change of the exchange rate regime and developments in international banking.

With the abandonment of fixed exchange rates and the lack of any clear rules governing the floating system, the Fund lost an important function. With very limited resources to deal with the recycling problem of oil surpluses, which was mainly taken care of by the commercial banks, the IMF was allowed to play only a marginal role in the mid- and late 1970s. Unconditional financing of balance of payments deficits through the creation of new facilities and quota increases accounted for only a small percentage of the total deficit financing requirements of oil-importing countries. The IMF's role was to a large extent restricted to helping some poor countries with no access to international credit and capital markets. In recent years, however, as the international debt crisis developed and private bankers began to get cold feet, the situation has changed dramatically. More and more countries have been forced to resort to IMF conditional finance and thus to subject themselves to IMF scrutiny of their domestic economies and also their exchange rate policies. Agreement with the IMF came to be seen increasingly as a pre-condition for further bank loans to countries trying to cope with the servicing of their external debt. The Fund also played a crucial role in complex debt re-scheduling negotiations which involved the governments of debtor and indirectly also of creditor countries and the central banks from both sides, as well as a host of international banks. Here, the Fund was treading on new and highly dangerous ground.

The question as to whether an international organization such as the IMF can be anything more than the sum of its parts (or in other words what can be its margin of manoeuvre vis-à-vis its political masters, some of whom are clearly more equal than others) is both longstanding and probably still unresolved. IMF policies, as well as changes in the rules of the game and their interpretation, have essentially been a reflection of the perceived interests and attitudes of a small group of industrialized countries, with the United States still occupying a dominant position. Some of the important decisions regarding the revision of the Articles of Agreement and the management of international monetary relations were in fact taken at summit meetings of the heads of government of the five, and later seven, leading industrialized countries of the West, or by the Group of Ten. This was no different from the pattern established in the 1960s. What is interesting, although with the benefit of hindsight, not very surprising is how little effect the accumulation of large oil surpluses has had on the relative influence of the new creditors in the management of the system. Making Saudi Arabia a permanent member of the Executive Board of the IMF was hardly commensurate with the financial power, albeit circumscribed by other economic and political factors, of the new creditors.

Under the Bretton Woods system coordination of national macroeconomic policies was ensured through fixed exchange rates. This worked quite effectively as long as the main reserve currency country, namely the United States, pursued non-inflationary policies. Floating exchange rates were sold as part of a package which would restore the autonomy of national monetary policies and also insulate countries from external shocks. Thus, international economic policy coordination lost its *raison d'être*. As most countries gradually discovered that floating rates could not deliver everything that had been promised, interest in international cooperation resurfaced in many quarters. Yet, publicly declared good intentions proved to be extremely difficult to translate into concrete action. More than ten years after the advent of floating rates policy makers still found themselves in the elementary class of international economic cooperation.

The emerging new international monetary 'system' (which some prefer to call a 'non-system' because of the conspicuous lack of jointly accepted rules about exchange rates and the process of adjustment, the creation of international liquidity and reserve assets) signifies a clear shift to the market. It constitutes, therefore, a conscious, or unconscious, negation of the idea of a collectively managed system with a tight official control over markets, which had been the central idea in both the American and the British plans submitted at the Bretton Woods conference in 1944. Moreover, unlike the original Bretton Woods system, its successor has not been the product of an international negotiation. In fact, the difference between the emerging new 'system' and what was originally envisaged in the reform negotiations of 1972–4 is truly remarkable. It is therefore legitimate to ask: has the market given birth to a new system, and was it a natural birth?

Factors of change

The obvious place to start is with Robert Triffin who was first to point to an inherent contradiction in the gold-dollar standard. Continuous deficits in the US balance of payments, which, short of gold revaluations and the creation of a truly international reserve asset, were the only means of adding significantly to international liquidity, did in the end undermine confidence in the US currency. What is surprising is that the system survived as long as it did, which was mainly due to the various palliatives used by the US and other governments during the 1960s. The official suspension of dollar-gold convertibility in 1971 removed the external constraint on US domestic economic policies without at the same time displacing the dollar from its status as an international currency. This was probably not clearly perceived by all parties concerned at the time.

The system of fixed exchange rates was based, among other things, on the assumption of limited capital mobility. This was clearly Keynes's intention at the Bretton Woods conference. But with the introduction of the external convertibility of the major European currencies and the yen in 1958, the rapid internationalization of production and trade and also technological developments in communications and banking, the international mobility of capital grew very fast indeed. This development, combined with the constant deficits in the US balance of payments and the rapid accumulation of dollar assets by non-residents, undermined the Bretton Woods system, and fixed exchange rates in particular.

The acceleration of inflationary pressures in the mid- and late 1960s was another important factor. They partly emanated from policies pursued in the United States and then transmitted to other countries. They also arose from the gradual breakdown of the postwar social consensus on which non-inflationary growth had been based in many Western industrialized countries. In fact, it was the combination of growing inflation and the divergence of policies and perceived interests among the major participants which finally led to the abandonment of fixed exchange rates. While for the Americans floating was the means of restoring the international competitiveness of US products and also removing the balance of payments constraint, for the Germans floating meant insulation from imported inflation. All this was accompanied by the growth of economic nationalism which was clearly manifested in the 1971 negotiations over exchange rates, which had a distinct neo-mercantilist flavour.

International monetary relations in the 1970s have usually been closely associated with the oil crisis and the economic recession, with the implicit assumption that monetary developments had to respond to events in the real economy. But the two important turning-points in terms of the Bretton Woods system, namely, the suspension of dollar-gold convertibility and the advent of floating rates, occurred before the first big increase in oil prices and the onset of the world recession. The argument has often been put forward that the first oil shock and the subsequent need for the recycling of large amounts of petrodollars made both the return of fixed exchange rates impossible and the partial privatization of the creation of international liquidity inevitable. But even this argument takes a number of political choices for granted. It was certainly not inevitable that recycling would take place mainly through the private banking sector. There were alternative schemes put forward at the time which laid much greater emphasis on intergovernmental arrangements involving both oil-producing and oil-consuming countries, or on international organizations such as the IMF. But those alternatives presupposed certain political choices and agreements among Western countries which proved impossible. Moreover, the role that international banks came to play in recycling was not as 'spontaneous' as it sometimes appears. 'Official guidance', as Llewellyn argues in Chapter 7, did seem to play a considerable role. Economists sometimes talk of the high liquidity preference of OPEC investors, which is then supposed to explain at least half the story of the role played by the international banks. But one may be permitted to think that high liquidity preference is not something inherited by descent or conditioned by long exposure to the desert heat. Surely, this preference for liquid assets must also be related to the international political and economic environment prevailing at the time, which was man-made and therefore not to be treated as a purely exogenous variable in policy analyses.

On the other hand, given the way in which recycling finally did take place and given also the divergence of policies and interests among the major industrialized countries, it is probably true that a return to fixed exchange rates was impossible. But this was the outcome of a number of conscious or unconscious political decisions.

Political explanations of the changes that took place in the international monetary system during the past decade usually stress the shift in the balance of power away from the United States and towards Western Europe and Japan in the 1960s, and then subsequently the emergence of oil power. The argument is sometimes put forward that, short of a truly supranational authority, an international monetary system requires a leader, preferably of the benevolent dictator kind, who will ensure the application of the rules of the game. The United States, so the argument goes, used to play this role in the early stages of the Bretton Woods system but gradually lost its predominant position.

Power is a difficult concept to use, and the economics profession has little familiarity with it. It is undoubtedly true that if economic power is measured in terms of world GDP, industrial production, exports or foreign reserves, there has been a dramatic decline in the US position vis-à-vis the rest of the world since the end of World War II. However, unlike international trade where the stage is dominated by three major actors — the USA, the European Community and Japan — of fairly comparable weight, in international monetary relations the large asymmetry between the United States and the rest of the industrialized world, not to mention the developing countries, still remains. This is clearly manifested in the predominant position of the US dollar as an international currency and the decisive influence which US domestic economic policies continue to have on international liquidity and interest rates. The events of the early 1980s speak for themselves. Moreover, it is extremely difficult to identify one important decision or development in the international monetary system during the last decade or so which does not bear the stamp of American influence. This is certainly true with respect to gold exchange rates and the role of international banks. The argument certainly does not imply omnipotence; it does, however, imply a certain degree of power to influence events which is still significantly larger than that enjoyed by any other member of the system. Instead, therefore, of attributing the transformation of the Bretton Woods system to the alleged decline in American power, I think it is more useful to try to explain why the United States decided that it was no longer in its interest to preserve the old system.

Bretton Woods was also based on an ideological consensus among the major industrialized countries about the role of government economic policies. This consensus relied on the wide acceptance of the Keynesian paradigm, which also began to disappear in the early 1970s. Keynesianism is probably the victim of its own success, having laid the foundations for a long period of high economic growth, full employment and the rise of the welfare state. This seems to be particularly true of the Western European experience, where the growing openness of national economies has been an additional factor undermining the effectiveness of Keynesian economic policies.

The demise of the Keynesian paradigm has not been followed until now by any other generally accepted theory in the economics profession. Different competing theories and general confusion may be the inevitable characteristic of the interregnum. But this confusion has had direct implications for policy decisions. The frequent and abrupt policy reversals that have characterized the 1970s and 1980s cannot be totally unrelated to short-lived fashions in economic theory.

Monetarism has provided the biggest challenge to the old Keynesian orthodoxy, without, however, succeeding in replacing it as the new generally accepted paradigm. Its influence on economic thinking and government policy has been considerable. Monetarism, especially of the closed-economy brand associated with Friedman, with its emphasis on mechanical rules for the control of the money supply, its advocacy of floating exchange rates and its neglect of global economic interdependence, was totally incompatible with some of the main principles of the Bretton Woods system.

At the same time, the monetarist ascendancy reflects to a large extent a general ideological shift to the right, manifested *inter alia* by the rediscovery of 'the magic of the market place' and the mistrust of the economic role of governments and international institutions. The relation between ideas and the real world is a difficult one to determine. Were policy makers of the 1970s and also possibly of today again the victims of academic scribblers a few years back? Or is Strange perhaps right when she says in Chapter 1 that economic theories are like detergents on a supermarket shelf, from which politicians choose the one which will legitimize their predetermined course of action?

Was the Bretton Woods system transformed under the pressure of real economic forces or was it abandoned by governments? This is not a pedantic question, and the answer, not surprisingly, lies somewhere between the two. Large amounts of highly mobile speculative capital, combined with growing inflation and divergent economic policies, made the system of fixed exchange rates untenable. On the other hand, the attraction of floating had already been sensed by some of the leading participants who thought they would gain from the new system. Similarly, the role which private banks came to play in balance of payments financing was partly the result of a long-term trend of internationalization of credit and capital markets and the specific needs arising from the big oil price increase of 1973. But it was also strongly influenced and indirectly determined by more general political decisions.

The shift to the market which the new 'system' represented may be seen to a large extent as an inevitable outcome of the increasing complexity of international monetary relations, growing liberalization and the gradual loss by governments of their control over financial markets and, more generally, their ability to fine-tune the domestic economy. However, it also reflected the inability of the major countries to agree among themselves about new forms of collective management which would take the above changes into account. The new 'system' therefore came about largely by default.

A wide divergence of interests among the major participants was a characteristic of the reform negotiations which took place in the context of the Committee of Twenty between 1972 and 1974. It was certainly a highly ambitious (and probably unrealistic) exercise to try to draft detailed rules for the management of a monetary system which was infinitely more complex than the one which White and Keynes had had to deal with three decades before. Countries were unwilling to abandon their monetary sovereignty and this constituted a major obstacle to designing new rules of collective management. But probably even more important was the divergence of perceived interests and the policies pursued by the major countries. When the 'oil shock' sounded the death knell of the reform exercise undertaken by the Committee of Twenty, there seemed little prospect of overall agreement. Moreover, the most powerful country, the United States, gradually lost interest in international monetary reform and saw instead many benefits for itself in the way in which the system was developing 'spontaneously'.

The 1970s saw the end of an era, and not only in international monetary relations. The divergence of interests which became manifest in the early 1970s was followed by a decade characterized by growing nationalism and little international economic cooperation. The intellectual justification for this development was very conveniently provided by the economics profession.

The best of all possible worlds

The emergence of the new international monetary 'system' has coincided with a turbulent and highly unfavourable world economic environment. The 1970s marked the end of the post-war 'economic miracle': growth decelerated rapidly, together with investment ratios and productivity rates, mass unemployment raised its ugly head again and inflation galloped. The era of cheap energy also came to an end, and a very abrupt end indeed as manifested by the first and then the second 'oil shock'. Meanwhile, tension and open conflict in international economic relations escalated while the importance attached to cooperative solutions drastically diminished.

The question of cause and effect immediately springs to mind, but the answer is far from obvious. Theoretical work on the subject is scarce and our sophisticated models are still highly inadequate to provide a clear answer. Were the changes that took place in the international monetary system an important contributory factor to the economic recession of the past decade, or is money just an epiphenomenon? Were those changes the best that could be achieved under the political and economic circumstances, and what were the theoretical or feasible alternatives? The debate around these questions continues; in fact, there still seems to be too little of it, given the importance of the subject.

Floating exchange rates were presented as the inevitable outcome of growing inflation and the divergence of economic policies among the main partners. The big balance of payments disequilibria which followed the first 'oil shock', and the need to recycle large amounts of petrodollars, were seen as adding considerably to the inevitability of floating. Under those circumstances, any attempt to stick to the previous system would have created chaos in exchange markets and serious tension between countries, with long periods of misalignment of exchange rates and pressures for trade protectionism following as a result. Thus, floating rates could be seen as a kind of damage-limitation exercise, with government policies and the international political and economic environment taken as given. Such a minimalist approach would probably command wide support among policy makers and professional economists.

The 'inevitability' or 'the best of all possible worlds' argument was not the only one on which floating exchange rates were sold. The prospectus that accompanied them was itself a good example of an aggressive and efficient market strategy, which should, after all, be expected from exponents of the return to the market theory. The evidence so far suggests that this prospectus was, to say the least, misleading. In contrast to sales advertisements, floating exchange rates have proved to be highly volatile, and 'overshooting' has been a regular phenomenon. It may be little comfort to policy makers and traders to know that we now have elaborate models to explain both the volatility and the 'overshooting' of exchange rates. Moreover, the period of floating has been characterized by strong and persistent misalignment between the major currencies, although the concept of misalignment is itself anathema to a pure floater.

Even if most economists may agree with the above few observations about the performance of floating rates, they will certainly disagree among themselves about the causes of volatility and even more so about the effects or the possible alternatives to the present system.

Although markets have provided traders with some means of dealing with the uncertainty arising from exchange rate volatility, as pointed out by de Lattre in Chapter 3 of this book, those means are both inadequate and costly. Forward exchange markets, for example, cannot eliminate the price uncertainty for a company engaged in a series of foreign trade transactions, for the simple reason that the forward rate fluctuates at least as much as the spot rate. The increased uncertainty is likely to have had a negative effect on international trade, and there is now some evidence supporting this argument. Increased uncertainty, combined with persistent misalignment of exchange rates, can also have a negative effect on productive investment and the international allocation of resources. It can strengthen protectionist pressures in countries with overvalued currencies, as was clearly the case with the United States in 1983–4. On the other hand, a long-term effect of exchange rate volatility may be the reduced importance of the price factor in international trade and the further strengthening of the process of economic concentration, given the cost of insuring against the resulting uncertainty.

In practice, floating exchange rates have not provided governments with an all-powerful and painless medicine for balance of payments adjustment. This is amply demonstrated by Wegner in Chapter 4. The J-curve effect, low elasticities, labour market rigidities and floating itself have turned the exchange rate into a less effective instrument of adjustment than had been generally expected. Nor have floating rates eliminated or even seriously reduced the need to hold foreign reserves. On the other hand, in a world of high capital mobility and continuous shifts in currency portfolios, national money supply targets lose their meaning.

Many governments soon abandoned the idea of an independent monetary policy and adopted some form of exchange rate target. But perceptions still differ considerably, as witnessed by the persistent large divergence in attitudes over exchange rates and monetary policy between the Americans on the one hand and the countries of the EMS on the other. These differences are not only the result of ideological factors or different perceptions of the same objective reality. For the Europeans, the openness of their economies and the rigidity of their labour markets considerably reduce the attraction of floating rates. For the Americans, on the other hand, the international role of the dollar reduces the cost of exchange rate volatility.

Up to the end of the 1970s, the role played by international banks in the first round of petrodollar recycling was hailed by most people as a big success and another example of the efficiency and flexibility of the market. Intergovernmental cooperation, it was argued, could not have been relied upon to effect such a massive transfer of funds across frontiers so smoothly. And so efficiently, one might add. There may have been some doubts about the equity of the operation, but that is not a problem that markets need to bother about, and in any case the voice of those poor countries with no access to bank finance was not very strong.

Attitudes have changed rapidly since then, as the international debt crisis has begun to loom heavily over world economic recovery and the Western financial system. Economists and politicians have rediscovered the problem of confidence in financial markets and the crucial role of the lender of last resort. People have also realized that banks collectively can make very serious mistakes, especially under 'official guidance' and in the belief that 'countries do not go bankrupt', which was itself based on a shocking ignorance of history. In recent years some people have also learned from bitter experience that the market on its own can not take care of the problem of international debt, if only because of the very high economic cost for society as a whole.

The international debt crisis has been unnecessarily prolonged because of the refusal of the main Western governments to accept real responsibility and the need for long-term solutions to the problem. They preferred instead a short-term piecemeal approach, in the vague hope that the problem would sort itself out if the right economic conditions prevailed. The result was a high economic cost borne by the indebted countries, which were forced to adopt strong deflationary and import-restricting measures, as well as by the rest of the world through the reduction of international trade and the increasing uncertainty arising from fears about the stability of the international financial system.

Although there is clear evidence of irresponsible lending by banks, the size and timing of the international debt crisis of the early 1980s is closely related to the macroeconomic and trade policies pursued by the major industrialized countries, among which US policies have pride of place. High interest rates and the slow growth of international trade cannot be considered as exogenous economic variables in the context of a highly interdependent world economy. The fallacy of the 'own house in order' argument and the real cost to the world economy of the lack of any effective coordination of national marcoeconomic policies became increasingly evident in 1982–4 because of the international repercussions of the US policy-mix. US policies are singled out for no other reason than their disproportionate influence on the rest of the world. Asymmetries did not disappear under the new 'system'. On the contrary, they were accentuated.

There is probably a strong element of truth in the argument that the main changes that took place in the international monetary system in the 1970s were inevitable, given the prevailing economic and political environment. The reform exercise undertaken by the Committee of Twenty lacked the main preconditions for its success. One could have wished for different policies and more foresight on the part of governments, but this is only a theoretical issue. One could go even further and argue that some changes, such as the

advent of floating exchange rates, may have given the world
economy the flexibility to cope with abrupt changes and growing
economic nationalism at a relatively low cost.

But, as time passed, the costs and deficiencies of the 'non-system'
grew, or at least they became more apparent. People now have some
real experience of floating exchange rates and the results fall far
short of expectations. The role of private banks in balance of
payments financing has not proved to be an unmitigated success, and
the stakes are very high indeed. Crude monetarism and mechanical
rules failed to deliver the goods promised in societies with mixed
economies and highly complex structures; and the 'chacun pour soi'
principle, translated into national economic policy, was in open
contradiction with the degree of international economic
interdependence already reached. The result has been a growing
readiness among economists and politicians to look to the new
international monetary 'system' for some of the factors behind the
failures of the last decade.

The meaning and feasibility of reform

Dissatisfaction with the new 'system' has eventually led to calls for
international monetary reform. References have been made to a
new Bretton Woods conference and the subject has appeared on the
agenda of the regular summits of the leading Western industrialized
countries.

Any reform would inevitably involve an attempt to restore some
form of collective management and official control. It would thus
imply at least a partial reversal of the shift to the market evidenced in
the 1970s and also reflected in the Second Amendment of the IMF
Articles of Agreement.

Calls for reform have come from those who believe, as Aglietta
does (Chapter 6), that money cannot manage itself or, to follow
Williamson in Chapter 2, that markets cannot reconcile that which is
not deliberately coordinated. This is probably the lowest common
denominator for all the contributors to this volume. Differences of
opinion, however, can and do arise regarding the specific nature of
the reform and the areas to be covered as well as the optimum mix of
rules and discretion, the distribution of power between the private
and the official sector, and the respective roles of national and
international institutions.

In the present economic and political context, any attempt to draft a new monetary constitution, following the example of the Bretton Woods conference, is probably neither feasible nor desirable. The Bretton Woods conference has been described as a meeting of 'one and a half' countries. Power is now much more dispersed. Although large asymmetries still exist, there are quite a few countries or groups of countries with strong views on particular issues and ready to exercise their veto power. Despite growing dissatisfaction with the *status quo*, large differences of attitudes and perceived interests still exist. Short of a major breakdown or a dramatic change in the international environment, it is extremely difficult to envisage a new monetary constitution, with fairly detailed and comprehensive rules, based on a broad consensus reached in an international negotiation. The experience of the Committee of Twenty is hardly encouraging, and it may be quite a few years before a new attempt is made in this direction.

Power is not only more dispersed among countries; private institutions have also become important actors in their own right as is certainly the case with the international banks. National and international official institutions have gradually lost their tight control over financial markets. Thus, international monetary relations may no longer be amenable to simple or rigid rules.

The argument put forward by Padoa-Schioppa in Chapter 9 in favour of international cooperation based on more discretion and stronger central institutions has a great deal of appeal in a highly complex multi-country economy. In this perspective, monetary reform would not be the product of a particular international negotiation leading to the adoption of a new set of rules. On the contrary, it could be a gradual process based on developing patterns of cooperation which would in turn rely on a shared perception of a common interest in collective management.

There are, however, also risks inherent in this approach. Where the rules are vague and collective management relies essentially on joint discretion, then concrete decisions may be difficult to take and even more difficult to implement. This is where the role of central institutions becomes crucial in order to avoid inaction, which is a characteristic of *ad hoc* intergovernmental cooperation. On the other hand, rules are usually a guarantee for the weak against the abuse of power by the strong. Can collective management based on discretion rather than rules be anything more than a euphemism for one-way coordination or for the domination of one or more countries? An indirect and also incomplete answer to this question may be that any attempt to devise rules which do not reflect the balance of power in the system will be doomed to failure.

In view of the low probability of a comprehensive international monetary reform in the foreseeable future, most proposals have concentrated on specific areas. Exchange rates undoubtedly provide the main focus of attention. In an attempt to reduce the excessive volatility and misalignment which have characterized the period of floating, proposals have been put forward for the setting up of 'target zones' for the exchange rates of the major currencies. The emphasis is, however, on wide bands of fluctuation and flexibility, at least in the initial experimental stages.

In practice, any international exchange rate arrangement would require the participation of the United States, the EMS countries as a bloc, and Japan. It would therefore be strictly an affair of a small group of big industrialized countries. This should, *ceteris paribus*, increase the chances of agreement and effective cooperation in a context in which specific rules can only be of limited use. Such an arrangement would require that all the parties concerned adopt exchange rate targets. And this should be translated into a responsibility to intervene in exchange markets in order to smooth out short-term fluctuations and, even more important, to coordinate their monetary and, for the non-monetarists, fiscal policies as well.

The close coordination of national macroeconomic policies, implied in such an exchange rate arrangement, would mark a radical departure from the pattern established during the last decade. The crucial question is, therefore, whether such a coordination could work in practice and whether the countries concerned would be prepared to accept the responsibilities and the constraints involved. The joint management of exchange rates would necessitate a shift in American attitudes which would be much more dramatic than anything required from the Europeans or the Japanese. The United States has never really accepted an external constraint on the conduct of its economic policies nor has it taken the international implications of such policies much into account. The 'own house in order' argument and the advocacy of floating rates as a means of restoring the independence of national monetary policies have, not surprisingly, found much support in the United States. Basic economic asymmetries explain to a large extent the difference of attitudes between the Americans on the one hand and the Europeans on the other, with the Japanese still keeping a low profile on international monetary issues.

The growing openness of the US economy, probably coupled with a renewed weakness of the dollar, may eventually bring about a change in US attitudes which will be a precondition for any form of international exchange rate arrangement. With no international currency of their own and with more open and highly interdependent economies, the Western Europeans have more quickly, although reluctantly, accepted the constraints on national autonomy. This has been the foundation stone of the EMS which is sometimes presented as a model for an international exchange rate arrangement, although the latter would need to be much more flexible than the European system.

The issue of the control of international liquidity is even more controversial and, therefore, the chances of any meaningful agreement appear to be very small indeed. In view of the recent international debt crisis and the deep concern expressed by private bankers, some shift back to official rather than private sources of international liquidity is very likely. The exponential growth of international banking in the 1970s may indeed prove to have been a historical aberration, with the signs of a return to a much slower long-term trend becoming increasingly evident. This raises two issues of immediate concern, namely, the need for a long-term solution to the accumulated international debt and the provision of additional liquidity from official sources in order to compensate for the expected partial withdrawal of commercial banks in the financing of future balance of payments deficits.

The need for some form of long-term rescheduling of the international debt is becoming increasingly evident to Western policy makers as the limits of tinkering with the problems are gradually reached. The first hesitant steps have already been taken in this direction. Any long-term solution is likely to strengthen the new cooperative relationship between the private and the official banking sectors which has been developing in recent years and in which the IMF has sometimes played the role of a catalyst. Official control over the international activities of the commercial banks and the question of the lender of last resort are likely to be major issues in the next few years. Some degree of official regulation of Euro-currency markets may be the price that private banks will have to pay for the bailing-out operation, arising from accumulated bad debts, and for the provision of a safety net by the central banks.

The gradual shift back to more traditional forms of balance of payments financing and the expectation of large disequilibria in the foreseeable future raise the question of the adequacy of official sources of finance. The choice between adjustment and financing of balance of payments deficits can never be a purely technical question nor can there be any specific rules designed to deal with the problem. The choice will continue to be a political one, and therefore political decisions will need to be taken mainly about the size and form of IMF liquidity as well as the conditions applying to its use. The developments of the 1970s and early 1980s have accentuated the asymmetry in the relation between the Fund and its member countries. While the influence exercised by the IMF over the economic policies of many developing countries has considerably increased, its influence over the policies of most industrialized countries has virtually disappeared. Access to bank finance is the crucial factor, and it is likely to remain so in the near future.

The IMF and its political masters will need to take decisions regarding the size of Fund-related assets and conditionality which will have important repercussions for those countries seeking access to IMF finance, and for the world economy in general. A very restrictive approach to IMF liquidity, coupled with a more limited role in payments financing by the private banks, will have strong deflationary consequences for the world economy. This obviously implies that international liquidity is not entirely demand-determined, and will be even less so in the foreseeable future. Moreover, as Bird and Killick remind us in Chapter 8, the effectiveness of IMF programmes in the past leaves much to be desired. In what is bound to be a very delicate relationship with many developing countries, the Fund officials and the executive directors will need to think hard about the flexibility of the IMF in its approach to different countries as well as its political sensitivity.

Proposals for an effective control of official international liquidity have always been associated with the introduction of an SDR standard or a standard based on some other internationally created reserve asset. The development of a *de facto* dollar standard in the 1970s, coupled with the timid appearance of a few other national currencies as international reserve assets, was contrary to the opinion expressed by a large majority both of professional economists and of policy-makers in the context of the Committee of Twenty in favour of moving gradually to a system based on the SDR.

Thousands of pages have been written about the inefficacy and the arbitrariness of the dollar standard or any other monetary system based on one national currency. The fledgling multiple currency standard which emerged during the 1970s may have provided an answer, albeit a highly inadequate one, to the problem of asymmetry arising from the right of seigniorage, by extending this 'exorbitant privilege' of the reserve-currency country to a few others besides the

United States. Meanwhile, however, this development has added a new source of instability to the system, which is likely to increase during a new period of dollar weakness as holders of the US currency try to diversify their portfolios. Such a development may then lead to a revival of the Substitution Account. It is probably indicative of official shortsightedness that the Substitution Account is revived with each major crisis of the US currency, and is subsequently dropped.

Official opinion seems to be increasingly reconciled to the multiple currency standard as the one likely to prevail in the foreseeable future. This reconciliation (maybe resignation) to a system which is generally considered to be inherently unstable is closely associated with the belief about the political infeasibility of an SDR standard. Such a standard would entail, among other things, turning the IMF into a world central bank. We are clearly very far from such supranational solutions; a shift to an SDR standard, if it ever materializes, is bound to be a very slow and gradual process.

It may indeed be true that a comprehensive reform of the international monetary system would be counterproductive in the present economic and political context. However, a number of problem areas will remain and important decisions will need to be taken. Even refusal to take action is a decision in itself. Success in restoring some form of collective management of international monetary relations will first of all depend on the degree of convergence of attitudes and policies among the major countries. This may take a long time, unless it is precipitated by big crises which are usually the most effective means of concentrating the minds of busy politicians.

It will also depend on the willingness of major countries to give up or merge some part of their national sovereignty in terms of economic policy. Here, the European Community experience may be of some relevance. The EMS has often been presented as an example of successful cooperation among sovereign countries intended to ensure some degree of exchange rate stability. However, despite its undeniable success, the EMS and the history of European monetary cooperation in general also show the enormous difficulties that exist in establishing an effective system of international collective management. After all, the EC countries have very similar political and economic structures, a high degree of economic interdependence, a long history of close cooperation and common institutions. The EMS, as it stands at present, falls far short of the degree of cooperation assumed in some of the reform proposals referring to the international monetary system. If the Europeans are so reluctant to develop the ECU into a real international currency, why should we be more optimistic about the SDR? If the European Monetary Fund still remains a plate on a door in Luxembourg, why should the IMF be expected to assume some of the functions of a world central bank? Last but not least, if convergence of economic policies is such a slow and arduous process inside the EC, why should the Europeans expect the world's dominant and relatively insular economy to accept any external constraints in the conduct of its economic policies?

In fact, a further pre-condition for closer and more effective cooperation among the Americans, the Europeans and the Japanese with respect to exchange rates and monetary policies may be the establishment of greater symmetry among the partners. This would come about through the further opening of the US economy and also the strengthening of the international role of the ECU and the yen. Thus, the creation of a real multiple currency standard may act as a catalyst in this respect. Greater symmetry would make international economic policy coordination more attractive to the Americans and less onesided for the others.

In some respects, the gradual process of reform referred to above is a search for a form of collective management that best corresponds to the degree of international financial interdependence already reached. The main developments in the international monetary system during the 1970s were a negation of this link between collective management and international interdependence. More recently, the pendulum has started moving in the opposite direction. If the movement is not fast enough, the economic costs will be considerable and so will the forces of nationalism and disintegration.

Index